CREATIVE (AND CULTURAL) INDUSTRY ENTREPRENEURSHIP IN THE 21ST CENTURY

CONTEMPORARY ISSUES IN ENTREPRENEURSHIP RESEARCH

Series Editor, Volumes 1–6: Gerard McElwee

Volume 7 onward: Paul Jones

Volume 1: Innovating Women: Contributions to Technological Advancement Edited by *Pooran Wynarczyk and Susan Marlow*
Volume 2: Social and Sustainable Enterprise: Changing the Nature of Business Edited by *Sarah Underwood, Richard Blundel, Fergus Lyon and Anja Schaefer*
Volume 3: Enterprising Places: Leadership and Governance Edited by *Lee Pugalis and Joyce Liddle*
Volume 4: Exploring Rural Enterprise: New Perspectives on Research, Policy and Practice Edited by *Colette Henry and Gerard McElwee*
Volume 5: Exploring Criminal and Illegal Enterprise: New Perspectives on Research, Policy and Practice Edited by *Gerard McElwee and Robert Smith*
Volume 6: New Perspectives on Research, Policy and Practice in Public Entrepreneurship Edited by *Joyce Liddle*
Volume 7: New Perspectives on Entrepreneurship Education Edited by *Paul Jones, Gideon Maas and Luke Pittaway*
Volume 8: Entrepreneurship and the Sustainable Development Goals Edited by *Nikolaos Apostolpoulos, Haya Al-Dajani, Diane Holt, Paul Jones and Robert Newbery*
Volume 9A: Creating Entrepreneurial Space: Talking Through Multi-Voices, Reflections on Emerging Debates Edited by *David Higgins, Paul Jones and Pauric McGowan*
Volume 9B: Creating Entrepreneurial Space: Talking Through Multi-Voices, Reflections on Emerging Debates Edited by *David Higgins, Paul Jones and Pauric McGowan*
Volume 10: International Entrepreneurship in Emerging Markets: Nature, Drivers, Barriers and Determinants Edited by *Mohamed Yacine Haddoud, Paul Jones and Adah-Kole Emmanuel Onjewu*
Volume 11: Universities and Entrepreneurship: Meeting the Educational and Social Challenges Edited by *Paul Jones, Nikolaos Apostolopoulos, Alexandros Kakouris, Christopher Moon, Vanessa Ratten and Andreas Walmsley*
Volume 12: Entrepreneurship in Policing and Criminal Contexts Edited by *Robert Smith*
Volume 13: Global Migration, Entrepreneurship and Society Edited by *Natalia Vershinina, Peter Rodgers, Mirela Xheneti, Jan Brzozowski and Paul Lasalle*
Volume 14: Disadvantaged Entrepreneurship and the Entrepreneurial Ecosystem Edited by *David Grant Pickernell, Martina Battisti, Zoe Dann and Carol Ekinsmyth*
Volume 15: Entrepreneurial Place Leadership: Negotiating the Entrepreneurial Landscape Edited by *Robert Newbery, Yevhen Baranchenko and Colin Bell*
Volume 16: Bleeding-Edge Entrepreneurship: Digitalization, Blockchains, Space, the Ocean, and Artificial Intelligence Edited by *João J. Ferreira and Patrick J. Murphy*
Volume 17: Nurturing Modalities of Inquiry in Entrepreneurship Research: Seeing the World Through the Eyes of Those Who Research Edited by *David Higgins, Catherine Brentnall, Paul Jones and Pauric McGowan*
Volume 18A: Creative (and Cultural) Industry Entrepreneurship in the 21st Century Edited by *Inge Hill, Sara R. S. T. A. Elias, Stephen Dobson and Paul Jones*
Volume 19: Extracurricular Enterprise and Entrepreneurship Activity: A Global and Holistic Perspective Edited by *Sarah Preedy and Emily Beaumont*

CONTEMPORARY ISSUES IN ENTREPRENEURSHIP RESEARCH   VOLUME 18B

CREATIVE (AND CULTURAL) INDUSTRY ENTREPRENEURSHIP IN THE 21ST CENTURY: POLICY CHALLENGES FOR AND BY POLICYMAKERS

EDITED BY

INGE HILL
The Open University, UK

SARA R. S. T. A. ELIAS
University of Victoria, Canada

PAUL JONES
Swansea University, UK

AND

STEPHEN DOBSON
University of Leeds, UK

United Kingdom – North America – Japan
India – Malaysia – China

Emerald Publishing Limited
Emerald Publishing, Floor 5, Northspring, 21-23 Wellington Street, Leeds LS1 4DL.

First edition 2025

Editorial matter and selection © 2025 Inge Hill, Sara R. S. T. A. Elias, Paul Jones, and Stephen Dobson.
Individual chapters © 2025 The authors.
Published under exclusive licence by Emerald Publishing Limited.

Reprints and permissions service
Contact: www.copyright.com

No part of this book may be reproduced, stored in a retrieval system, transmitted in any form or by any means electronic, mechanical, photocopying, recording or otherwise without either the prior written permission of the publisher or a licence permitting restricted copying issued in the UK by The Copyright Licensing Agency and in the USA by The Copyright Clearance Center. Any opinions expressed in the chapters are those of the authors. Whilst Emerald makes every effort to ensure the quality and accuracy of its content, Emerald makes no representation implied or otherwise, as to the chapters' suitability and application and disclaims any warranties, express or implied, to their use.

British Library Cataloguing in Publication Data
A catalogue record for this book is available from the British Library

ISBN: 978-1-80455-907-9 (Print)
ISBN: 978-1-80455-906-2 (Online)
ISBN: 978-1-80455-908-6 (Epub)

ISSN: 2040-7246 (Series)

INVESTOR IN PEOPLE

CONTENTS

About the Editors vii

About the Contributors ix

Chapter 1 Creative and Cultural Industry Entrepreneurship in the 21st Century: Challenges by and for Policymakers
Inge Hill, Sara R. S. T. A. Elias, Stephen Dobson and Paul Jones   1

Unusual and Temporary Places for CCI Entrepreneurship

Chapter 2 Temporary Art Spaces: A Conceptual Framework
Hayley Reid, Andreana Drencheva and Malcolm Patterson   23

Chapter 3 Cultural Entrepreneurship at the Aardklop Arts Festival: An Ecosystem Perspective
Saskia de Klerk and Nada Endrissat   35

Chapter 4 Out of the Studio and into the Street: A Case Study of Street Art Opportunities During COVID-19
Leigh Morland and Ekaterina Sheath   49

Economic Perspectives on CCI Entrepreneurship

Chapter 5 Essential Puzzle Piece for CCI Entrepreneurship: CCI Managers' Mental Models Concerning Collaborative Processes with nonCCI
Kristiina Urb   65

Chapter 6 Entrepreneurial Performance and Competition Within the Creative and Cultural Industries: Challenges for Cultural Entrepreneurs in a Developing Country
Tafadzwa Masiye, Alison Lawson and Kuldeep Banwait   81

Chapter 7 Make it Work: Strategies of Creative Entrepreneurs for Coping with the Tension from Artistic and Economic Logics
Nanne Migchels and Milou van der Linden   93

Organising Clustering of CCI Entrepreneur

Chapter 8 Play, Experimentation, and Proximity in the Creative Industries
Stephen Dobson, Lorena Raquel Serrano Tamayo and Sue Hayton — 109

Chapter 9 Building Online Communities to Support Women Creative Entrepreneurs During Lockdown
Beki Gowing — 123

Chapter 10 The 'Creative Village': A Creative Entrepreneurship Framework for Catalysing Africa's Creative and Cultural Industries
Adeyinka Adewale, Jean-Pierre Choulet, Chike Maduegbuna, Barry Van Zyl and Stephen Budd — 137

Cognitive Aspects of Doing CCI Entrepreneurship

Chapter 11 Exploration of Entrepreneurship Education and Innovative Talent Training Model: New Normal Perspective
Lei Jian Qiang, Oo Yu Hock and Osaro Aigbogun — 157

Chapter 12 Neuroentrepreneurship: Pierce the Veil of Creativity in Workplaces
Rajat Sharma and Rita Devi — 171

Social Spaces and Placemaking for CCI Entrepreneurs

Chapter 13 Community and Creative Entrepreneurship: The Dynamic Relationship between Social Workspaces and Creative Entrepreneurs
Annette Naudin — 185

Chapter 14 Creative Placemaking in the Scottish Rurality: Comparing Two Small Towns
David Rae — 199

Chapter 15 Heritage Craft Entrepreneuring in 'The Wild': The Role of Entrepreneurial Placemaking for Rural Development
Birgit Helene Jevnaker and Inge Hill — 213

Index — 227

ABOUT THE EDITORS

Inge Hill, PhD, FRSA, is a former award-winning microentrepreneur, and a Lecturer in Entrepreneurship at the Open University, UK. Her research investigates micro-exchange processes for SMEs and is rooted in process and practice theories. She investigates creative entrepreneurship, business support and economic development policy in urban and rural contexts, applies entrepreneurship-as-practice theory, and publishes on qualitative methodologies. She is an Associate Fellow of the Research England funded National Innovation Centre for Rural Enterprise, for which she co-leads the research stream on rural creative enterprises. She founded and directs the Open University research cluster Rural Economy. She has published widely, including with *Local Economy, Entrepreneurship Regional Development* and the *International Journal of Entrepreneurial Behaviour and Research*, and is on the Editorial Review Board. She regularly reviews AHRC/ESRC funding applications and for *Cultural Trends, Industry and European Journal of Management*. She serves on the Council of the British Academy of Management and is the lead editor of this edited book.

Sara R. S. T. A. Elias, PhD, is an Associate Professor at the University of Victoria's Peter B. Gustavson School of Business and a Research Associate of the Center for Psychosocial Organization Studies. Her research interests include creative entrepreneurial processes, entrepreneurial imagining, arts entrepreneurship, aesthetics in organisations and entrepreneurship, entrepreneurship as practice and qualitative methodologies. These research interests stem from her background in business, engineering and music, as well as from her experience as an arts entrepreneur, music manager, performing artist and Managing Director of *Associação CICO*, an international centre for promoting the performing arts, headquartered in Portugal. She is Associate Editor of the *Scandinavian Journal of Management* and is a member of the editorial boards of *Art, Culture & Entrepreneurship* and *Organizações & Sociedade*. She has published in *Organization Studies, Organization Theory, Organization, Journal of Management Inquiry, International Journal of Entrepreneurial Behavior & Research* and *Organizational Research Methods*, among others.

Paul Jones, PhD, Professor, Professor of Entrepreneurship and Innovation at the School of Management, Swansea University. He is Editor-in-Chief in the *International Journal of Entrepreneurial Behaviour and Research*. He is also an Associate Editor with the *International Journal of Management Education* and a Senior Editor on *Information Technology and People*. He is also a Series Editor of the Contemporary Issues in Entrepreneurship Research book series published by Emerald Publishing. His research explores entrepreneurial behaviour and small business management.

Stephen Dobson, PhD, is an Associate Professor in Creativity and Enterprise at the School of Performance and Cultural Industries, University of Leeds. His research interests span several areas related to cultural and creative industries and entrepreneurship including: entrepreneurial identity and creative enterprise, the creative workplace and leadership for fostering innovation and creativity, critical management, cross-disciplinary creativity, cultural and creative industries policy and digital enterprise. He is the Director of International Activities for the School of Performance and Cultural Industries.

ABOUT THE CONTRIBUTORS

Adeyinka Adewale, PhD, is an Associate Professor of Leadership Ethics and Entrepreneurship and the Deputy Director of Studies in the Department of Leadership Organisations and Behaviour at the Henley Business School. He regularly gives keynote addresses and facilitates workshops with private and public sector audiences on themes around leadership, entrepreneurship and ethics in Europe, Africa, Asia and the United States. His work in recent years has involved working with creative and tech entrepreneurs around Africa in building sustainable businesses for the future. He is a published author and reviewer for top management journals and leading textbook publishers. He serves on the board of exciting start-ups and charities in Africa through which he affirms his dedication to contributing his expertise to Africa's development.

Osaro Aigbogun, PhD, is a management specialist and certified management consultant with a background in the pharmaceutical industry, academia and management consulting. He has taught students from over 75 different countries and led programmes at the tertiary level for about a decade. He currently directs several research projects and sits on the examination board for doctoral candidates. He has spoken at several international conferences and delivered training and workshops on a wide range of subjects, including global issues in entrepreneurship, crisis management, critical thinking, management of innovation, corporate strategy and supply chain resilience. His current research focusses on developing innovative models and analytical methods for supporting the operation of the global pharmaceutical supply chain. He is a Fellow of the Institute of Management Consultants, a Fellow of the Higher Education Academy in the United Kingdom, and a member of the British Academy of Management.

Kuldeep Banwait is a Principal Lecturer in Marketing at Oxford Brookes University where he is responsible for talent management and development of the marketing subject group. Before joining Oxford Brookes, he spent several years at the University of Derby, where he was a Senior Lecturer and Course Director across both undergraduate and postgraduate courses.

Prior to joining academia, he worked in the Events and Hospitality sector, which defined his philosophy as a marketer that brands should visualise the world from the eyes of the customer and be open to the idea of co-creation in order to turn their pains into gains. His doctorate and subsequent journal publication studied the increase in marketisation in the English higher sector and its impact on universities. His main research interests are university branding and co-creation, corporate social responsibility and brand heritage.

ABOUT THE CONTRIBUTORS

Stephen Budd is a British music Industry Executive and artist Manager based in London. He is a Director of the Artist and Producer of management company Stephen Budd Music Ltd, the OneFest Festival, of Damon Albarn's Africa Express project and is the Co-founder of the NH7 Weekender festivals in India and helped create the DMZ Peace Train Festival in Korea. He is a recognised TV commentator on music industry issues that regularly appears on a variety of British TV news shows. He has created charity projects including co-producing Amnesty International and Sofar Sounds' 'Give A Home' global concert series for refugees and War Child's 'Passport Back To The Bars' concert series. And in 2022, The Music Venues Trust 'Passport Back To Our Roots' concert series to raise money for COVID-19 endangered live music venues. He served a three-year term as Co-chairman of the Music Managers Forum, the trade body for artist managers.

Jean-Pierre Choulet is Vice Dean Africa, Henley Business School. He is also Director of Development and Alumni, Henley Business School, and Executive Director of the Reading Real Estate Foundation. He has over 25 years of international experience at the executive level in Higher Education. He is also a Non-executive Director of Audencia Business School. He is passionate about how talent and leadership are critical assets for generating an impact from digital transformation. For the past 15 years, he has been delivering programmes to mentoring and coaching entrepreneurs, including leading them successfully to the pitching level to trigger the investment they need to move to the next step. Since 2017, he has been leading Henley Business School's development in West Africa, with a focus on Nigeria, Ghana, Togo and Benin.

Rita Devi is a Faculty member at the School of Commerce and Management Studies, Central University of Himachal Pradesh, India. She has eight years of postgraduate teaching and research experience and her areas of specialisation are human resource management and organisational behaviour. She has been meritorious throughout her studies and was awarded a JRF scholarship for pursuing her PhD. She has contributed to the academic field as a dedicated academician. She has published more than 15 research papers and book chapters in reputed journals. She has presented in multiple national and international conferences/seminars. She has also attended and organised numerous faculty development programmes and workshops. Her research interests include: emotional intelligence, leadership, entrepreneurship, cross-cultural management, sustainability and organisational development.

Andreana Drencheva, PhD, is a Senior Lecturer (Associate Professor) in Entrepreneurship at King's Business School. She received her PhD in Work Psychology in 2016 from the Institute of Work Psychology at the University of Sheffield. Her research investigates why and how individuals and communities engage in (social) entrepreneurship and with what the intended and unintended impact.

Nada Endrissat is a Professor at the New Work Institute at Bern Business School, Switzerland and has held visiting positions at the University of California, Irvine,

About the Contributors

United States, Université du Québec à Montréal, Canada and the University of the Sunshine Coast, Australia. Her current research interests include the transformation of work and new forms of organising with a particular focus on creative and cultural industries. Her research has been published in academic journals such as *Human Relations*, *Organisation Studies* and *Information & Organisation*.

Beki Gowing is a Senior Lecturer in Fashion Enterprise at London College of Fashion where she leads the enterprise pathways for the Fashion Business School and Communications Programme. After starting her career in buying, she launched the textile design studio Print & Press London which designed and manufactured fabrics for the fashion and homeware industry. She has a Master's degree in Creative and Cultural Entrepreneurship and a PG Cert in Acceptance and Commitment Therapy informed coaching, both from Goldsmiths College, University of London. She is a Coach and Creative Business Consultant for start-ups and SMEs at Enterprise Nation and Hatch Enterprise. Her research interests include peer coaching, enterprise communities, empathy and collaboration.

OO Yu Hock, PhD, Professor, a Ministry of Education-Malayan Teachers College trained teacher-cum-Associate Professor at the University of Malaya (UM) Kuala Lumpur, secured his PhD, MPA and MS Ed from the University of Southern California, Los Angeles, United States, under a Ford Foundation Fellowship. Five years later, awarded a Fulbright Scholarship under the American Council of Learned Society, he was a Visiting Scholar at the Hubert Humphrey Institute of Public Affairs and University of Minnesota, Minneapolis-St. Paul, United States, with research support from the Asia Foundation and Toyota Foundation. A continually active government-retiree advocate-writer of 'life-long learning' and 'knowledge-share consultancy exchanges', he has lectured, supervised and examined a spectrum-topic mix-list of local and foreign Masters and Doctoral graduates. Currently, a Visiting Professor in Bangladesh and Africa, he is an active Governing Board Member of Global Academicians Research Academy and its Malaysia Chapter President, engaged in e-conferences with subsequent Scopus-indexed publications in Research Gate.

Sue Hayton is a creative industry professional with a career that spans visual and performing arts, publishing and heritage. She has been influential in the generation of ideas and creativity in cross disciplinary and cross domain relationships. Expanding this interest, she developed Leeds Creative Labs as a tool for collaboration between academic researchers and creative practitioners. Her research interests include creative research methods and creative knowledge exchange, exploring the role of artist as researcher and as catalyst for innovation. She is a consultant to the Centre for Cultural Value at the University of Leeds.

Birgit Helene Jevnaker, PhD, is Professor (em.) of Innovation and Economic Organisation at BI Norwegian Business School, Department of Leadership and Organisational Behaviour, Oslo. She has published extensively on creative design and collaboration, innovation and entrepreneurship, knowledge and management learning, arts and leadership and sustainable organisation (shorturl.at/djmI4). She was awarded the BI's Development Prize for her executive leadership programme. Her recent coauthored book *Reimagining Sustainable Organization* won the European Academy of Management 2023 best book award.

Saskia de Klerk, PhD, is the Discipline Lead for Marketing, International Business and Tourism at the University of the Sunshine Coast. She holds an adjunct position as an Associate Professor at North-West University, South Africa, and a Senior Lecturer Research position at the University of New South Wales, Australia. She is serving as a topic editor and reviewer for several international reputed journals. She teaches international business, cross-cultural management, venture growth and innovation. Her research interests include networking, entrepreneurship and regional entrepreneurial ecosystem development. She is interested in supporting the development of an entrepreneurial mindset and articulating pathways to transition into entrepreneurship and sustainable practices in regional ecosystems through a circular economy, and bricolage strategies. Her research can be viewed via Google Scholar, LinkedIn and ResearcherID.

Alison Lawson is Head of the Discipline of Marketing and Operations at Derby Business School, University of Derby. She has worked in higher education for 14 years, and prior to this, she worked in book publishing, both in commercial and not-for-profit organisations. Her main research interests are in social marketing for positive behaviour change, marketing for social goods, arts/heritage marketing and consumers' emotional attachment to products and services. She is also a methodology geek and writes a blog called Musings on Methodology.

Milou van der Linden is the founder of Like Lightning, a company that creates business illustrations as a visual tool to support business processes or implement change. Milou van der Linden herself is a creative entrepreneur with the ability to bring together business, innovation and the creation process. She graduated as a Master of Business Administration from Radboud University, Nijmegen.

Chike Maduegbuna is an entrepreneur, founder, CEO of Afrinolly Nigeria Limited. Afrinolly Nigeria Limited is a Creative Hub in Lagos built to address inadequate Audio and Video Post-Production facilities in Nigeria. Afrinolly's App won Google's Android Developers Challenge for Sub-Saharan Africa in September 2011 and since 2012, Afrinolly has embarked on various activities that aim to promote Movie Production and Distribution in Nigeria. He is on the Steering Committee of Nigeria Economic Summit Group. He is on the Technical Working Group for Creative Industry for National Development Plan for Nigeria. Also, he is currently on the board of LEAP Africa. He trained as an Accountant with PriceWaterhouseCoopers and obtained BSc Economics from the University of Nigeria, Nsukka and MSc Development Management from the UK Open University.

Tafadzwa Masiye MA (HONS), MBA, is a College Director in an embedded pathway college. He is a current PhD student at the University of Derby attached to the Market Sensing Group at the College of Business Law and Social Science. His area of research is creative entrepreneurship with a particular interest in co-creation as a market development strategy for entrepreneurial artists in Malawi, Zambia and Zimbabwe. This research is inspired by lived experiences of working in that region and encountering artists who often struggle to sustain their livelihoods from their artistic work. The research will hopefully find sustainable strategies for developing access to international markets.

Nanne Migchels is an Assistant Professor at Radboud University, Nijmegen. He teaches marketing and entrepreneurship. His research interests focus on creative industries and the management of entrepreneurial ecosystems. He studied Agricultural Economics at Wageningen University and holds a PhD in Technology Management from Eindhoven University of Technology.

Leigh Morland, PhD, is a Freelance Academic and Associate Faculty at the School of Performance and Creative Industries, University of Leeds. Previously, she held the positions of Head of Student Enterprise Development, University of Huddersfield and Subject Group Leader for Entrepreneurship and Sustainability, The Business School, University of Huddersfield. She has over 25 years of experience in teaching at Universities and is an advocate of Action Learning and teaching case studies. Her research interests include the role of space and place in business start-up, lone behaviour in coffee shops, speciality coffee, and cultural regeneration in towns.

Annette Naudin, PhD, is an Associate Professor with responsibility for Learning and Teaching at the College of English and Media at BCU, where she is a member of the Birmingham Centre for Media and Cultural Research. Prior to working in academia, she set up and ran a creative enterprise for 10 years and developed programmes to support entrepreneurship in the creative and cultural industries. She completed a PhD (2015) at the University of Warwick, exploring cultural workers' experience with entrepreneurship. Since then, her research has been concerned with inequalities and the challenges faced by creative and cultural entrepreneurs, the relationship to cultural policy, to place and to higher education provision.

Malcolm Patterson, PhD, is a Senior Research Fellow at Sheffield University Management School, The University of Sheffield. His research interests include organisational culture and climate, cross-cultural behaviour, human resource management and performance and the relationships between work conditions, employee affect and behaviour.

Lei Jian Qiang, PhD, is an innovation and entrepreneurship training expert with a background in the business incubation industry, academia and management consulting fields. Currently, he is the Director of the Science and Technology Park Training Center of Guangxi University, China. He is also President of the China Chapter of the Global Academic Research Academy. He is also a Start Your Business Entrepreneurship Trainer approved by the International Labour

Organisation. He has taught tens of thousands of college students at various levels and has led higher education courses for over a decade. He has published dozens of journal articles and spoken at several international conferences on related subjects of innovative talent cultivation models. His research mainly explores entrepreneurship education and the development of innovative talent ability.

David Rae, PhD, is a Professor of Enterprise at Leicester Castle Business School, De Montfort University, Leicester, United Kingdom. His mission is to maximise the value created for all, by connecting research, enterprise, innovation and learning between universities, businesses and society. Since 1996, he has held senior academic roles at six universities. He has been deeply involved in research, development and teaching on entrepreneurial learning, development and enterprise education for over 20 years, gaining his PhD in Entrepreneurial Learning in 2003. His work was recognised as the European Entrepreneurship Education Award Winner 2020. This award cited his contribution at the national, European and international levels as the 'boundary spanner between entrepreneurial learning and enterprise education'. He has contributed to entrepreneurship research, education, policy and regional development, within Europe, North America, Africa, and South Asia. He continues to research intercultural, minority and sustainable entrepreneurship, creative industries and entrepreneurial collective intelligence.

Hayley Reid is a PhD researcher and artist at Sheffield University Management School, The University of Sheffield. Her research explores the influence of temporary art spaces on artists' wellbeing through a collaborative doctoral partnership with a Leeds-based arts organisation, East Street Arts. Her art practice takes a mixed-media approach, combining fiction and poetry writing with textile and video work.

Rajat Sharma is a Faculty member at the School of Commerce and Management Studies, at Career Point University, Hamirpur, Himachal Pradesh. He has more than one year of experience in teaching especially in the field of human resource management and organisational behaviour. He has participated and presented research papers in more than 10 national and international conferences and seminars and has produced numerous publications on the UGC Care List and in peer-reviewed journals. He has attended and organised various faculty development programmes and workshops.

Ekaterina Sheath is a freelance illustrator based in Leeds. Through community engagement, on-location drawing and research, she shares hidden stories and transforms local spaces into cultural assets. A core value is representation: celebrating diversity and equality. Working with social organisations she brings engaging and educational illustrations to communities. Examples of her clients include: Leeds City Council, Leeds BID, Victoria Quarter, Trinity Leeds Shopping Centre, Canal & River Trust and Kiezfonds Lichtenberg (Berlin). She has been short-listed for the World Illustration Awards 2022 and chosen as 'Twenty of the Most Exciting Illustrators to Follow in 2022' by Creative Boom.

About the Contributors

Lorena Raquel Serrano Tamayo is a cultural researcher exploring music policy as a tool for social development while managing projects within the European and US markets. Also, working on the first fan-driven platform for the live touring industry. She has over seven years of experience in marketing communications and PR for the creative industries and has worked for the US, CA, EU and UK markets. Thus, she is interested in cross-cultural communication. Her main interest and passion are to understand and research creativity and innovation to improve businesses in creative industries.

Kristiina Urb has been involved in the CCI for over 15 years in different managerial, consulting and expert roles locally and internationally. She was a co-founder and manager of a graphic design agency and a company combining new technologies and audio-visual solutions. She used her experience and knowledge to research CCI and consult creative and cultural organisations and companies in different expert roles. She leads the Creative Industries and Smart Cities research group at Estonian Business School. She has recently published, among others, in the *European Journal of Cultural Management and Policy* and in the book *Management, Participation, and Entrepreneurship in the Cultural and Creative Sector* by Springer International Publishing AG. Her research interests are mainly focussed on creative industries and informal institutions.

Barry van Zyl is a world-renowned musician with over 30 years of experience in the creative sector, from performance and production to education, strategy and business development. Having toured the world for 21 years with South Africa's most famous export, Johnny Clegg, and while working with artists like Annie Lennox, Ladysmith Black Mambazo, Peter Gabriel and Die Antwoord, he completed an MBA at the Henley Business School and is now focussed on executive education in the areas of personal development, entrepreneurship and innovation. Since 2018, he has been a growing new business for Henley Business School, starting in Nigeria and then in other areas of west and east Africa, with the aim of 'building the people, that build the businesses that build Africa'. He is a tutor on the MBA programme internationally and is the chair of Henley's pan-African Alumni community.

CHAPTER 1

CREATIVE AND CULTURAL INDUSTRY ENTREPRENEURSHIP IN THE 21ST CENTURY: CHALLENGES BY AND FOR POLICYMAKERS

Inge Hill[a], Sara R. S. T. A. Elias[b], Stephen Dobson[c] and Paul Jones[d]

[a]*The Open University, UK*
[b]*University of Victoria, Canada*
[c]*University of Leeds, UK*
[d]*Swansea University, UK*

ABSTRACT

Our chapter focuses on the disconnect between economic and cultural policies and the needs of individual firms and creative industry professionals, all of which affect creative and cultural industry (CCI) entrepreneurship in the 21st century. After a review of selected policy trends and the overlooked role of creative industries in developing more sustainable liveable communities worldwide, we discuss recommendations by chapter authors in volumes 18A and 18B for useful policy actions, not only in and for their respective countries of study but also for other geographical contexts. Our particular focus is on how the CCIs have contributed to developing sustainable societies and meeting many targets of the Sustainable Development Goals. Thereafter, we provide an overview of the fifteen chapters distributed over five sections: 'unusual and temporary places for CCI entrepreneurship', 'economic perspectives on CCI entrepreneurship', 'organising clustering of CCI entrepreneurs', 'cognitive aspects of doing CCI entrepreneurship', and 'social spaces and placemaking for CCI entrepreneurs'. Topics discussed include CCI entrepreneurship in rural areas (heritage entrepreneuring, book festivals), social work spaces, creativity and neuroentrepreneurship, strategic networking management for creatives, tensions from economic and artistic logics, collaboration challenges, street art and arts festivals. Countries considered include Estonia, Nigeria, Norway, South Africa, the United Kingdom, and Zimbabwe. We conclude the chapter with a selection of policy implications of chapters in both volumes 18A and 18B, and a research programme and manifesto for researchers to develop novel insights for policymakers, aimed at strengthening the important role of the CCIs in creating more liveable sustainable communities and economies.

Keywords: Creative and cultural industry entrepreneurship; sustainable development goals; policies for creative industries; policymaking; research impact; actionable research findings; cultural policies

RECENT TRENDS THAT DEMONSTRATE THE VALUE OF CREATIVE INDUSTRIES AND POLICY CHALLENGES

While the cultural and creative industries (CCIs) are well established as generally thriving and have shown significant growth rates, pre- and post-COVID-19, policymakers in most countries find it difficult to identify their wider value for societies (and economies) (Hill et al., 2023). Recent research has stressed the importance of entrepreneurial context and regions benefiting from increased identity (Jones et al., 2018). Most strategies for the CCIs tend to focus on digital businesses, and possibly web(site) services and gaming industry sub-sectors, yet are silent on the needs and significance of crafts and the performing and visual arts, to name a few of the nine industry sectors subsumed under the CCIs in the United Kingdom's (UK) definition (DCMS, 2023).

While definitions of CCIs vary, we refer in this chapter to the UNESCO definition that CCIs are industries with the 'principal purpose of production or reproduction, promotion, distribution, or commercialisation of goods, services, and activities of a cultural, artistic, or heritage value' (UNESCO and World Bank, 2021, p. 8). As the industries subsumed under this label are vastly diverse (e.g., advertising, web design, architecture, crafts, visual arts, and performing arts), attributing impact on economic development to convince policymakers to invest more into supporting the creative industries is difficult, mostly, because specific evidence is often missing.

To highlight examples of national and subnational policies aiming to support a wide selection of creative industry sectors, we selected the United Kingdom and Canada as illustrations of how policymakers have developed solutions, partially fit-for-purpose, but with the insight that 'something' has to be done. The editors and many of the authors are based in these countries; hence, the lived experience of these interventions' outcomes has influenced the choice of geographic focus.

In 2023, the Department for Culture Media and Sport (DCMS) data for the UK (DCMS, 2023a) showed that there were almost 265K businesses in 2023 in the United Kingdom, which represented 9.7% of all UK businesses. The 2023 data also illustrate a positive post-COVID-19 picture for the sector with the number of businesses gradually increasing from March 2019 to March 2023 by 6,680 (9.1%). The CCIs, however, have generally followed the trends of businesses in the United Kingdom with a slight growth post-COVID-19 to March 2022, followed by a decline in 2022–2023.

As a response to the somewhat challenging economic environment that the creative industries have faced in rebuilding, restructuring, and refinding the market after the pandemic, the UK government published 'Creative Industries Sector Vision' in 2023 (DCMS, 2023b) to set out its strategy for increasing growth in the CCIs. Developed in partnership with the Creative Industries Council, the sector body in the United Kingdom, the strategy sets out ambitions for the UK CCI sector, aiming, by 2030, to:

- grow creative industries in creative clusters by an extra £50 billion;
- build a pipeline of talent into the sector;
- support a million extra jobs; and
- develop stronger connections between the creative industries and place.

Place is an important dimension of the UK Sector Vision strategy and is specifically related in that manuscript to wellbeing, the environment, and soft power through international relations. In Scotland, the strategy points to the 'Creative Placemaking' methodology to support community-led change through the development of creative hubs, as well as increased high street ownership for communities (DCMS, 2023b). The links between CCI enterprises and places are an important thread in this UK strategy.

A case study of a 'devolved nation' is Wales, in the United Kingdom—comparable to yet different from a federal country. This sub-national example demonstrates how regional units can make a difference for their creative economies alongside and in addition to national policies. For example, the CCIs are extremely important to the economy in Wales, contributing more than 5% of Welsh gross domestic product (Fodor et al., 2023). Evidence suggests that the creative industry sector employs over 35K people in over 3,400 businesses, generating £1.7 billion for the Welsh economy. The Welsh government has effectively supported the CCI with several additional policies, including a New Creative Skills Action plan (2022–2025). This plan includes a £1 million fund to support the creative sector, including the television, film, music, and digital content industries (Welsh Government, 2022).

The action plan seeks to support individual talent within the creative industries by finding, supporting and nurturing Welsh creative talent, and encouraging individuals to consider the sector as a viable career choice, mirroring the UK strategy with a location focus on Wales. The creative industry sector is now integrated into the education sector within Wales to ensure a pipeline of suitably qualified talent. The plan was designed to ensure the creation of opportunities to support the CCI sector, to create a workforce that reflects all the communities within Wales, and to address the disconnect between people leaving the education sector and industry employment needs (Fodor et al., 2023). The £1 million creative skills fund has been created to support skills and training projects in the sector with between £15K and £200K available for individual successful projects (Welsh Government, 2022). Further research is required in due course to assess the effectiveness of this project.

In Canada, the Department of Canadian Heritage (2017) developed the 2017 Creative Canada policy framework, which aimed to support Canadian cultural offerings and encourage diversification and innovation in the Canadian economy (Kim, 2021). As detailed by the Department of Canadian Heritage (2017), this framework entailed a C$1.9 billion investment in the cultural industries and the development of new programmes aimed at promoting the exportation of Canadian content. It sought to preserve cultural diversity by 'supporting the cultural activities of cultural minorities, Indigenous creators, and female producers' (Kim, 2021, p. 430). This framework came in the sequence of various creative economy projects, including the creation of several agencies in the 1980s by Canadian provincial governments that promoted the cities of Montréal, Toronto, and Vancouver as key creative clusters (Kim, 2021). The 2017 Creative Canada policy framework not only re-emphasised projects by the various Canadian provinces but also amplified them into the federal echelon with the overall goal of improving the economy at the national level and of 'positioning Canada as a world leader in putting its creative industries at the centre of its future economy' while creating jobs and fostering growth (Department of Canadian Heritage, 2017, p. 5).

Despite these aims, the Creative Canada policy framework has also faced some backlash. For example, because private capital was encouraged to commercialise cultural goods and make Canadian content more visible, the domestic market had to be deregulated and private investors (including those accused of cultural invasion) were given benefits, resulting in the understanding that the framework was driven by a market rather than an artistic logic (Kim, 2021). This insight illustrates the incessant and ongoing tension between artistic and economic logic in the creation of craft, cultural, and artistic offerings (Becker, 1978; Eikhof & Haunschild, 2007; Elias et al., 2024). Furthermore, Indigenous communities and Francophones were disappointed and sceptical about the framework because it did not seem to focus on producing or promoting their cultural offerings (Marsh, 2017). Overall, what this backlash demonstrates is that any policy and its outcomes are always complex, and that in a Canadian context, non-commercial logics and cultural values play an important role in national cultural politics (Kim, 2021).

While these economic development trends of the CCI sectors are well demonstrated, how to support creative firms and individuals at the local level, so that precarious livelihoods (e.g., fluctuating income levels, portfolio income including part-time jobs, and creative businesses) can be turned into more stable livelihoods, is for many policymakers a 'black box'. Anecdotally, we know how many struggle to understand why someone would not take a job or start a business that simply 'makes more money from the start'.

Challenges for policymakers at all levels (local, regional, and international) include the limited understanding of the key features of 'doing business differently' to other industry sectors. Hence, the sometimes-negative connotation attributed to 'life-style' businesses, as being run part-time by the retired and 'women next to childcare', is still more prevalent than data and academic research findings demonstrate. While the societal impact of audience participation on mental health and overall well-being is academically demonstrated as positive (Putland, 2008; Stickley et al., 2015), such findings rarely reach policymakers in a way that they positively affect spending in these industry sectors.

Lastly, policymakers have, to date, received limited insights from existing research on *how* creative firms operate outside of creative hubs or craft centres (Velez-Ospina et al., 2022). They also require a greater understanding on the kinds of business support that creative firms require that fit with their socio-economic goals and enable them to manage tensions arising from community, social, creative, and economic goals (see Hill, 2021, for craft businesses, and Watson, 2023 for music businesses).

Our mission with these two volumes, 18A and 18B, is to make the societal contribution of the CCIs to national economies more visible. At the end of this chapter, we conclude with a manifesto for more policy research so that the operations of creative firms are understood in greater detail, which hopefully will lead to more policy investments for the benefit of sustainable societies and socio-economically thriving local communities and economies.

THE CONTRIBUTION OF THE CREATIVE AND CULTURAL INDUSTRIES TO SUSTAINABILITY

While it has been acknowledged that CCIs have a positive impact on society (e.g., well-being, community cohesion, and potential local economic development), how this impact is achieved is currently under-researched. In addition, the significant role of CCIs for achieving the Sustainable Development Goals (SDGs) (UN, 2015) seems to only be a whisper amongst experts (Apostolopoulos et al., 2018; Klein et al., 2021). To address this lack of clarity, this section outlines what we know and, subsequently, what further research we need.

In 2021, the United Nations emphasised the important link between CCIs and sustainability when announcing 2021 as the International Year of Creative Economy for Sustainable Development:

> [c]ultural and creative industries, which include arts and crafts, advertising, design, entertainment, architecture, books, media and software, have become a vital force in accelerating human development. They empower people to take ownership of their own development and stimulate the innovation that can drive inclusive sustainable growth. (Palaniverl, 2019, para 1)

However, what is the role of the CCIs for sustainable development and how can it be strengthened? Moreover, why should policymakers be interested? First, some authors highlight the fostering of creativity more generally as an outcome of CCI's activities that support more sustainable economic activities (Burford et al., 2013). Others highlight the economic aspects of CCIs in providing employment opportunities in their supply chains in other sectors (retail, tourism), particularly for marginalised society groups and regions (Dobson et al., 2020; Li et al., 2021; Pagan, 2020). A third group of authors focuses on relational aspects, highlighting how CCIs teach humans to live in better balance with nature and foster intergenerational relationships, important for social cohesion (e.g., Cattaneo et al., 2020). Regarding the second question above, *policymakers should be interested in supporting CCIs to create sustainable societies and liveable communities, which is in line with several SDGs.*

Based on our understanding, which is supported by limited academic discussion (see indicatively Gao et al., 2024), and our own ongoing research efforts in this field, the CCIs already contribute to these SDGs and related targets (UN, 2017), as noted in Table 1.1, which lists only some indicatively:

Table 1.1 illustrates a selection of SDGs and targets and how the CCIs have been contributing to them, perhaps silently, with their business offers. Chapters in volumes 18A and 18B are referenced to indicate where these kinds of offers are discussed in more detail, though connections to specific SDGs may not necessarily be explicit in those chapters. What we conclude from this brief overview is that many CCI enterprises (including the self-employed), despite often going unnoticed, have contributed to meeting what we call today the SDGs in their ways of working. While admittedly the often-precarious working conditions within the CCIs are challenging, this does not devalue the sustainability effect of their economic activities and their significant social impact.

Indicatively, a case study of a Council run creative hub demonstrates how a micro-business with studios, a cafe, and a retail area, contributes to developing a local economy and meets the SDGs (Hill & Scott, 2024, p. 266):

- Low fees for studio rental to local creatives enable residents to remain local and to reach out to more customers via the hub's marketing activities, providing quality and sustainable infrastructure to support economic development and human well-being through affordable access (SDG 9.1).
- Seasonal events offered by the hub bring local residents and families together to enjoy shared activities, developing creative skills (SDG 8.3) and supporting healthy lives and well-being (SDG 3).
- The use of recycled paper in the shop for packing purchases within the creative hub aligns with sustainable consumption and production patterns (SDGs 12.5 and 12.7).

While we know about the relevance of cultural heritage and culture for society and economic development, this knowledge is 'somehow' lacking depth about *how* the CCIs matter for increasing or accelerating sustainable development. As we demonstrate below, the insight into how the CCIs operate, 'think', and practice sustainable business under the pressure of enormous resource constraints is one important strand of research we need for policymaking within the CCIs, both

Table 1.1. How CCIs have been Contributing to Meeting the SDGs (The Authors).

SDG Number	SDG Title	Target NumBer	Target Description	Contributions by CCIs
4	Ensure inclusive and equitable quality education and promote lifelong learning opportunities for all	4.3/ 4.7a	4.3 By 2030, ensure equal access for all women and men to affordable and quality technical, vocational and tertiary education, including university; 4.7a Build and upgrade education facilities that are child, disability and gender sensitive and provide safe, non-violent, inclusive and effective learning environments for all.	Workshops, co-curricular and outside of formal education, that develop creativity and craft skills (pottery, jewellery making, wood turning, etc.); mask-making by women during COVID-19 (Grannemann et al., 2023, in volume 18A); innovative organisational forms of support to develop training and skilling, arising from professionalisation difficulties in the music sector, and marginalisation of young artists in France (Schieb-Bienfait & Emin, 2023, in volume 18A)
8	Promote sustained, inclusive and sustainable economic growth, full and productive employment and decent work for all	8.3/ 8.9	8.3 Promote development-oriented policies that support productive activities, decent job creation, entrepreneurship, creativity and innovation, and encourage the formalisation and growth of micro-, small- and medium-sized enterprises, including through access to financial services; 8.9 By 2030, devise and implement policies to promote sustainable tourism that creates jobs and promotes local culture and products.	Employment and self-employment in CCIs, not only for women (Gowling's chapter 9 in this volume 18B), but also disadvantaged societal groups; workshops aimed at developing creativity in citizens of all ages; supply chain to CCIs offering jobs, often on a self-employed basis

(Continued)

Table 1.1. (Continued)

SDG Number	SDG Title	Target Number	Target Description	Contributions by CCIs
9	Build resilient infrastructure, promote inclusive and sustainable industrialisation and foster innovation	9.4	By 2030, upgrade infrastructure and retrofit industries to make them sustainable, with increased resource-use efficiency and greater adoption of clean and environmentally sound technologies and industrial processes, with all countries taking action in accordance with their respective capabilities.	Fostering innovation through workshops and skills development (as above); improved contributions to the economy through discussion of the challenges popular and folk music artists in Cameroon face (Ning, 2023, in volume 18A)
10	Reduce inequality within and among countries	10.2	By 2030, empower and promote the social, economic and political inclusion of all, irrespective of age, sex, disability, race, ethnicity, origin, religion or economic or other status.	While employment in crafts is often precarious, it can be a stepping stone for women's empowerment to earn an income and move on afterwards to more profitable income streams (Grannemann et al., 2023 in volume 18A)
11	Make cities and human settlements inclusive, safe, resilient and sustainable	11.4	Strengthen efforts to protect and safeguard the world's cultural and natural heritage.	Heritage craft (Jevnaker & Hill, chapter 15 in this volume 18B.) across the world focuses on maintaining traditional skills and using local/regional materials for craft production
12	Ensure sustainable consumption and production patterns	12.8	By 2030, ensure that people everywhere have the relevant information and awareness for sustainable development and lifestyles in harmony with nature	Self-help groups in the Himachal Pradesh region in India during and after the COVID-19 pandemic (Bhardwaj et al., 2023, in volume 18A, see also Goal 11 above)

locally and regionally. The CCIs have often developed positive ways of working that are less resource intensive (Balfour et al., 2018; Hill et al., 2021), and have been shown to engage in co-opetition much more positively and productively than other industry sectors (Flanagan et al., 2017; Galloway et al., 2019; Kuhn et al., 2015). Indeed, a shared mission for social change or commitment to sharing a passion or skills with the wider population can override the for-profit 'dog-eats-dog' competitive business atmosphere displayed in well-known TV series and business realities for some types of business owners.

THE CHAPTERS IN THIS VOLUME 18B

The first section, entitled '*Unusual and temporary places for CCI entrepreneurship*', brings together three chapters that explore the temporariness of spaces for art to be exhibited and enacted. Chapter 2, by *Hayley Reid* and colleagues, offers a valuable new conceptual framework to help identify the various configurations of temporary art spaces in the United Kingdom and how these may impact practice. Temporary art spaces seem to offer an attractive proposition, both for the self-employed artist finding it increasingly challenging to access suitable workspaces to conduct their practice, and indeed the local authorities are dealing with the decline of the high street and the increase of empty commercial properties. This chapter explores an under-researched area of entrepreneurship scholarship by highlighting the lack of lasting and permanent solutions and uneven power dynamics endemic to this aspect of the sector.

In Chapter 3, *Saskia de Klerk and Nada Endrissat* explore temporary performances of art in an arts festival in South Africa. This chapter provides an exploration of the notion of productive entrepreneurship in the context of the social and cultural impact that cultural enterprises can deliver. The focus is on the entrepreneurial ecosystem surrounding the 'Aardklop' ('Earthbeat') Arts Festival, in Potchefstroom, South Africa. Festivals generate social value in the form of networks and social cohesion and, as such, their impact extends far beyond the economic aspects of such events. The research presented in this chapter explores value creation from a cultural entrepreneurship perspective and asks what value does participation in the festival creates and, most importantly, how this value is experienced.

Chapter 4, by *Leigh Morland and Ekaterina Sheat*, provides readers with exciting insights into creative practice, as one of the authors in the team is an artist practitioner. An art form rarely written about, street art, is explored with exciting images giving insight into how during COVID-19 the street became a stage for exhibiting art. Honing in on media box murals and window installations, the chapter uses a variety of means, including artist self-reflection and artwork analysis, to illustrate how street art can contribute to wider regeneration and community-building agendas.

The next three chapters increase understanding on '*Economic perspectives on CCI entrepreneurship*'. *Kristiina Urb* explores, in Chapter 5, mental models of useful collaborations between CCI managers and non-CCIs in Estonia, the United Kingdom, and the United States. Based on an interpretative phenomenological analysis of semi-structured interviews with CCI experts, she develops a concept map illustrating potential themes of CCI managers' mental models for collaborations with non-CCI firms.

In Chapter 6, we gain exciting insights into Zimbabwe's CCIs with the work of *Tafadzwa Masiye* and colleagues, who explore entrepreneurial performance and competition in Zimbabwe. Employing critical reflection, the authors offer an in-depth exploration of the specificity of performance management and competition in this sector. A lived experience approach enables them to highlight some distinct contrasts between creatives from developed and developing countries. In this case, the influence of high unemployment, low demand for creative products, and oversupply due to the high concentration of creative producers in the Zimbabwean CCI market, all shape the performance criteria greatly.

Nanne Migchels and Milou van der Linden explore, in Chapter 7, how creative entrepreneurs integrate economic and artistic logics in their day-to-day practices. The authors conduct a qualitative study of 19 creative entrepreneurs based in the Netherlands. An analysis of semi-structured interviews shows that creative entrepreneurs experience multiple logics, leading them to implement coping strategies while requiring flexibility in the use of such strategies. Recognising that these findings have implications for both policy and practice, the authors highlight several important directions for future research, with the aim of gaining a richer understanding of how creative entrepreneurs experience and deal with the tension between the creation of economic and cultural value.

The section '*Organising clustering of CCI entrepreneurs*' explores, online and offline, how entrepreneurs organise while doing business and are organised by programmes and incubators. In Chapter 8, *Stephen Dobson* and colleagues explore, through their research into the transformative processes of cross-sectoral and cross-disciplinary collaboration, the role that Higher Education Institutions can play in the local creative economy. Their work focuses on a Creative Labs programme aimed at bringing together artists and scientists to develop new collaborative relationships, and as a catalyst for creative innovation. Within a context of creative clusters and communities of practice, the research explores the importance of building the capacity to collaborate amongst micro creative organisations and individuals through creative lab hosting. The role of social, cultural and intellectual closeness (propinquity) rather than solely geographic proximity or co-location is an important contribution for policymakers and initiatives aimed at supporting the local creative economy.

The COVID-19 pandemic provides an important context in *Beki Gowling*'s research, presented in Chapter 9, which explores the particular challenges faced by women creative entrepreneurs. The development of online communities to support women throughout this difficult time offers valuable insights into the dynamics of communities. The study compares both in-person and virtual business support for women creatives through four cycles of action research, with two held in-person pre-pandemic and two held online during the pandemic. The chapter explores how previous studies have identified issues particularly faced by women entrepreneurs, such as isolation, low income, burnout, mental health concerns, exploitation, and lack of state support. Given the importance of the creative sector in providing solutions to such problems, it is critical to better understand how communities might emerge to mitigate these effects for women entrepreneurs. The value of online support is foregrounded and the research helps to demonstrate that this type of support is in many ways of equal value to in-person mentoring.

In Chapter 10, *Adeyinka Adewale* and colleagues showcase research in Nigeria on a prototype innovative platform labelled the 'Creative Village'. They explore practically one of Africa's biggest Music reality TV shows. This chapter identifies that 'as the African music business continues to grow, so does the need for disruptive innovation and new ways of doing things'. Here, the authors present The Creative Village, an app designed to support and strengthen the collaboration and creative outputs of the music industry ecosystem of Nigeria. More widely, the literature around African CCIs has identified innovation capacity, poverty reduction, job creation, and cultural value as significant areas for research focus. This chapter considers that African creatives must (1) understand the business of their craft; (2) build businesses with sustainable and scalable business models, and; (3) be connected to the local, regional and global ecosystems for improved market access. The Creative Village is an innovative virtual platform designed to offer a systematic approach to talent discovery, education, and market linkage processes. The research employs end-user focus groups and in-depth stakeholder interviews to establish three key areas of challenge: A weak infrastructure, underdeveloped value chain, and a lack of artiste and consumer education. Overall, the potential impact of The Creative Village offers valuable insights for interventional work.

The next section, entitled '*Cognitive aspects of doing CCI entrepreneurship*', consists of two chapters. Chapter 11, by *Lei Jian Qiang* and colleagues, analyses the effects of entrepreneurship education (EE) on innovative talent training models using a mixed-method methodology comprising a survey of 400 students from three Chinese universities and semi-structured interviews with 12 students and three instructors. The findings reveal a significant direct effect of the institutional environment and supporting infrastructure on innovation capability. Of note is the presence of peer input as a moderator, with the effect of the EE programme on innovation capability being positively significant. The findings from the qualitative study highlight that students enjoy acquiring entrepreneurship experience from peers. Evidence suggests a desire for students to employ entrepreneurial skills and social capital. Students acquiring entrepreneurial capital from EE programmes is important for the cultivation of innovation capability. The study identifies two dimensions of EE, namely institutional environment and supporting infrastructure, having a significant direct effect on student innovation capability. The results highlight that learning institutions should combine innovation-driven entrepreneurial ecosystem cultivation with EE programmes, while strengthening support of institutional environment and infrastructure to enhance student innovation practice ability with both human and social capital. In addition, practice-oriented innovative EE should be encouraged to enhance innovation capability in the economic environment.

In Chapter 12, *Rajat Sharma and Rita Devi* offer a unique exploration of creativity from a neuroscience perspective. This chapter helps to identify the conditions of creativity that lie at the heart of entrepreneurial behaviour. The chapter reviews research employing techniques such as electroencephalogram (EEG), which measures electroactivity in the brain, and functional magnetic resonance imaging (fMRI), which measures changes in blood flow and how this relates to decision-making. EEG findings, for example, demonstrate that entrepreneurs are more effective than others when controlling feelings and responding to external stimuli, resulting in enhanced opportunity judgement. Discussions about the creative industries have often focussed purely on the role of creative output in the economy, however, research into the nature of creativity itself is an important contribution to the field.

The section '*Social spaces and placemaking for CCI entrepreneurs*' comprises three chapters, in which the authors discuss how spatial units, towns and villages can be transformed into active living places, using a variety of theoretical approaches, and how rural development can be fostered via heritage craft revitalisation even in remote locations. In Chapter 13, *Annette Naudin* discusses how community and creative entrepreneurship are intertwined and investigates a small group of CCI entrepreneurs based in studios in a post-industrial heritage building, in a co-working space. Her research suggests that workspaces and personal values play a significant role in shaping entrepreneurial practices, entangled with a sense of responsibility to locality and community.

David Rae, in Chapter 14, analyses book festivals in two Scottish rural towns, in the United Kingdom, with the lens of creative placemaking. Creative placemaking is a medium-to-long term activity involving community and collaborative entrepreneurship between stakeholders to demonstrate sustainability and resilience. However, creative places need to be or become distinctive in some respects for the ingredients and enabling factors of placemaking to combine and sustain effectively as a destination. The chapter explores the feasibility and effectiveness of creative placemaking in small rural towns, offering useful discussion points for rural creativity. His findings suggest that the process of 'creative placemaking' should be seen, temporally, as a medium-to-long term activity.

Finally, in Chapter 15, *Birgit Helene Jevnaker and Inge Hill*, explore heritage craft entrepreneuring in rural contexts in Norway and the United Kingdom. Viewing entrepreneurship as the ongoing accomplishment of entrepreneurial activities, or as entrepreneuring, the authors conduct comparative case study research of two rural heritage craft businesses in Norway and the United Kingdom that use traditional natural materials local to their country and region. Through a process-relational lens, the authors explore different ways of collaborating and entrepreneurial placemaking, highlighting three important entrepreneurial practices: connecting, organising, and co-developing. The authors conclude with important theoretical implications for the entrepreneurship-as-practice and creative industries literatures. Policy implications address the need for business support for creative and heritage businesses in rural areas to maintain their financial sustainability in providing local employment and network building.

POLICY AND PRACTICE IMPLICATIONS OF RESEARCH IN VOLUMES 18A AND 18B

The chapters in both volumes 18A and 18B address a wide range of policy and management insights that are of relevance to creative entrepreneurs. We include such insights in this section for easy access by policymakers, creative professionals, and those supporting them. While some insights in these two volumes were indeed gained through research specific to a variety of countries and continents and diverse cultural and socio-political contexts, they, nevertheless, have relevance beyond the explicit research context of each chapter. Creativity is rooted in community, society, and the linkages between location and people. Table 1.2 provides an overview of selected significant policy implications, which may be transferable to other regions and locations. We encourage readers to browse all the chapters in these two volumes for more details on these–and other–important policy implications.

DIRECTIONS FOR FUTURE RESEARCH: INFORMING POLICYMAKERS AND ENCOURAGING IMPACTFUL RESEARCH

Having outlined the direction of travel and the need to direct policymakers towards the potentially significant role of CCIs in the development of more sustainable ways of living, we suggest a research programme for much-needed novel insights. There is a dearth of knowledge on the business support needs of creative firms, with most of the existing findings discussing technical or skills support for the craft and much less so business support needs (Watson, 2023). Watson (2023) discusses the link between cultural policy and business support applied to music production clusters, based on post-COVID-19 challenges for music businesses to capitalise on digital innovations. The author notes a range of examples where, at the local level, urban policy aiming to produce place branding strategies uses music to support such place branding as 'music capital' or 'music city'. His suggested framework focuses on mentoring, financial support, and strategies to build networks, and promises to address the needed wider economic sustainability of music businesses. Worldwide, there is a trend of 'creative cities' strategies, conceptualised as sets of urban cultural policies anticipating economic and social benefits from growing cultural and creative urban economies (Watson & Taylor, 2014). Yet, what is currently missing is wider research on business support to creative industry professionals and firms outside of the digital sector within the creative industries. Perhaps unsurprisingly, even less research exists on business support for rural creative industries (Hill et al., 2021). Similarly, the role of peer support within the creative industries remains under-researched (Galloway et al., 2019; Hill, 2021; Merrell et al., 2021).

As discussed earlier in this chapter, policymakers do not yet understand the actual and potential role of CCIs for *developing sustainable societies*. In particular, we need further research on how creative professionals already meet many targets

Table 1.2. Selected Policy Implications from Volumes 18A and 18B: Some Key Learnings.

Topic of policy implications	Content of policy implications	Authors and volume
Community engagement and projects to create products for the wider community – to reach out to hard-to-reach groups, in particular women	Local governments or nonprofits supporting new venture creation in communities may take note of social entrepreneurs with high levels of entrepreneurial readiness (with many of them being women) for example on how to empower and engage some potential entrepreneurs locally. Many women engaged in social efforts (e.g., mask making) in groups ultimately develop an entrepreneurial identity.	Grannemann et al., 2023, 18A
Working with women-only groups to reach out to hard-to-reach groups	Online peer coaching and community building, as well as in-person sessions, are successful and more cost-effective, enabling a greater reach to particular groups (e.g., women).	Gowling, 2024, 18B*
Self-help groups	Women's self-support groups bridge the gap between formal support not-fit-for-purpose and no support.	Bhardwaj et al., 2023 18A
Online support, events, and workshops	Online networks and exchange events are needed to keep an ecosystem alive.	Armstrong-Gibbs and Brown, 2023, 18A
Enterprise/entrepreneurship education	Improvement of entrepreneurship policy and continued support of teachers with teacher training.	Lei et al., 2024, 18B
Placemaking and cultural heritage	Creative 'heritage craft placemakers' and their continued co-creative entrepreneurial placemaking by using local natural resources and products connect people, locations, and material products. They provide employment and work in the supply chain. Supporting them in network building and local supply chain development increases the stickiness of residents and placemaking, reducing the out-migration of young people in particular.	Jevnaker and Hill, 2024, 18B
Creative placemaking	Creative placemaking as medium-to-long term activity with joint engagement of all stakeholders (support providers, entrepreneurs, local government, customers) to demonstrate sustainability and resilience. Distinctiveness needs to be developed so that a creative place can become a destination for others.	Rae, 2024, 18B

* 18B = this volume

of the SDGs (UN, 2015) and contribute locally to sustainable communities in running infrastructure institutions, particularly, in community ownership in rural areas, such as running pubs and shops (Plunkett Foundation, 2022a, 2022b) and community centres or creative hubs (Hill et al., 2021; Merrell et al., 2021; Pratt, 2021). Hence, we need future research to demonstrate to policymakers how creative professionals have already contributed (perhaps even for decades) to which SDG targets, making visible their important contributions and impact. Doing so will make the demands for business support more convincing and aligned with evidence of specific needs within the CCIs.

Widening the lens from supporting the business development of creatives and sustainable local communities, policymakers need a deeper understanding and evidence that highlights how important the *supply chain for creative businesses* already is. Specifically, we need insights into more than just 'social impact': While supply chain management is an established research area, the loose network of freelancers contributing to a variety of larger creative and non-creative firms is less explored. Furthermore, self-employed creatives usually have a network of their own, consisting of associates and/or partners with whom they temporarily collaborate on focused projects. This form of 'supply chain' means that spill over effects are a normal result of creative firms, not only those visibly clustered in buildings or sites or areas (Velez-Ospina et al., 2023). While the framework for measuring the value of culture and heritage capital is a step in the right direction (DCMS, 2021), the outputs and few outcomes captured leave open how, ideally, resources are combined and enacted to create these outcomes. Hence, we encourage more process-theory informed research that portrays tactics and practices that inform creative professionals and local policymakers on how to support network building and management to develop cohesive thriving creative economies.

Demonstrating the social impact of CCI firms, particularly in craft businesses and creative hubs (Bell et al., 2019; Blundel, 2019; Hill et al., 2021; Pratt, 2021), is very much required to provide evidence of how local economic development is achieved more holistically. Multi-level studies covering settings, social groups, and individuals and how they interlink are essential to be able to capture how craft is enacted and contributes to local development.

We finish with *a manifesto for more policy research* that creates socio-economic change for CCI entrepreneurs to contribute to the sustainability of societies worldwide. We do not argue for simplified 'cause and effect research' with ever more surveys, as this kind of research cannot capture the nuanced processes of how CCI entrepreneurship is enacted. Rather, we encourage scholars to engage with communities and governments so that impactful research and policies may be developed through ongoing collaboration.

We call for three important actions by the research community:

(1) Conducting more research informed by process theory and a process-relational theory, investigating the practices (Elias et al., 2018, 2022; Hill, 2021) and routines (Court, 2020) of CCI ventures and individuals and how these relate to the SDGs. This kind of research can unveil significant insights

into how CCI entrepreneurs operate sustainably and how it could be supported more effectively.
(2) Collaborating in country-wide studies that combine local level studies with macro-lenses and investigate various types of impact and their ripple effects. Multiple studies are required to account for multi-level in-depth approaches and to capture business and regional development processes.
(3) Developing the intersection of policymaking and CCI entrepreneurship as a research field. Once we gain an enhanced understanding of policymaking in this context, we can then tailor our research and insights towards making a difference and supporting policymakers with actionable insights. The impact achieved by CCI-specific policies needs to be explored and evaluated, and best practices reported.

We hope that these actions pave the way for greater attention to policy-focused research aimed at improving the working conditions of CCI entrepreneurs in a global context. We encourage building from the chapters in both volumes 18A and 18B to develop improved socio-economic conditions for CCI entrepreneurship so that we can create sustainable and thriving communities and economies worldwide. There is a clear need to continue capturing and sharing best practices.

REFERENCES

Apostolopoulos, N., Al-Dajani, H., Holt, D., Jones, P., & Newbery, R. (Eds.) (2018). Entrepreneurship and the sustainable development goals. In *Entrepreneurship and the Sustainable Development Goals (Contemporary Issues in Entrepreneurship Research, Vol. 8)* (pp. 1–7). Emerald Publishing Ltd.

Armstrong-Gibbs, F., & Brown, J. (2023). The resilience and adaptability of an innovative eco-system of creative entrepreneurs during crisis times: Baltic creative CIC - as case study. In I. Hill, S.R.S.T.A. Elias, P. Jones, & S. Dobson (Eds.), *Creative (and Cultural) industry entrepreneurship in the 21st century* (Contemporary issues in entrepreneurship research, Vol. 18A) (pp. 105–120). Emerald Publishing Ltd.

Balfour, B., Fortunato, M. W-P., & Alter, T. R. (2018). The creative fire: An interactional framework for rural arts-based development. *Journal of Rural Studies, 63*(1), 229–239.

Becker, H. (1978). Arts and crafts. *American Journal of Sociology, 83*(4), 862–889.

Bell, E., Mangia, G., Taylor, S., & Toraldo, M. L. (2019). Introduction: Understanding contemporary craft work. In E. Bell, G. Mangia, S. Taylor, & M. L. Toraldo (Eds.), *The organisation of craft work. Identities, meanings, and materiality* (pp. 1–19). Routledge Studies in Management, Organisation and Society, Routledge.

Bhardwaj, B., Blakrishan, & Sharma, D. (2023). Fostering creating entrepreneurship through self-help groups. Post-COVID-19 resilience. In I. Hill, S.R.S.T.A. Elias, P. Jones & S. Dobson (Eds.), *Creative (and Cultural) industry entrepreneurship in the 21st Century* (Contemporary *issues in entrepreneurship research*, Vol. 18A) (pp. 91–104). Emerald Publishing Ltd.

Blundel, R. (2019). Reflecting on the relationship between craft and history. In Bell, E., Mangia, G., Taylor, S. & Toraldo, M. L. (Eds.), *The organisation of craft work. Identities, meanings, and materiality* (pp. 255–270). Routledge Studies in Management, Organisation and Society,Routledge.

Burford, G., Hoover, E., Velasco, I., Janouskova, S., Jimenez, A., Poggot, G., Podger, D., & Harder, M. K. (2013). Bringing the 'missing pillar into sustainable development goals. Towards intersubjective values-based indicators. *Sustainability, 5*(7), 3035–3059.

Cattaneo, T., Giorgio, E., Flores, M., & Barequero, V. (2020). Territorial effects of shared living heritage regeneration. *Sustainability, 12*(20), 86816.

Court, K. (2020). A grounded theory approach to studying craft: The serious work and leisure of knitting. *Craft Research, 11*(1), 79–95.

Department for Culture, Media and Sport (DCMS) and Department for Science, Innovation and Technology. (2023a). *DCMS and digital economic estimates: Business demographics, 2023.* Gov.uk. https://www.gov.uk/government/statistics/dcms-and-digital-economic-estimates-business-demographics-2023)

Department for Culture, Media and Sport (DCMS) and Department for Science, Innovation and Technology. (2023b). *Creative industries sector vision: A joint plan to drive growth, build talent and develop skills.* Gov.uk. https://assets.publishing.service.gov.uk/media/64898de2b32b9e000ca96712/Creative_Industries_Sector_Vision__accessible_version_.pdf

Department of Canadian Heritage. (2017). *Creative Canada: Policy Framework.* https://www.canada.ca/content/dam/pch/documents/campaigns/creative-canada/CCCadreFramework-EN.pdf

Dobson, S., Quaye, D., & Jones, P., (2020). Globalisation and enterprise support in African arts and culture: A Ghanaian context. In S. Dobson, P. Jones, D. Agyapong & G. Maas (Eds.), *Enterprising Africa: Transformation through Entrepreneurship* (pp. 128–141). Routledge.

Eikhof, D., & Haunschild, A. (2007). For art's sake! Artistic and economic logics in creative production. *Journal of Organizational Behavior, 28*(5), 523–538.

Elias, S. R. S. T. A., Chiles, T. H., Duncan, C. M., & Vultee, D. M. (2018). The aesthetics of entrepreneurship: How arts entrepreneurs and their customers co-create aesthetic value. *Organisation Studies, 39*(2–3), 345–372.

Elias, S. R. S. T. A., Chiles, T. H., & Crawford, B. (2022). Entrepreneurial imagining: How a small team of arts entrepreneurs created the world's largest traveling carillon. *Organization Studies, 43*(2), 203–226.

Elias, S. R. S. T. A., Peticca-Harris, A., & deGama, N. (2024). Truly, madly, deeply: Strategic entrepreneuring and the aesthetic practices of craft entrepreneurs. *Strategic Entrepreneurship Journal.* https://doi.org/10.1002/sej.1498

Flanagan, D. J., Lepisto, D. A., & Ofstein, L. F. (2017). Coopetition among nascent craft breweries: A value chain analysis. *Journal of Small Business and Enterprise Development, 25*(1), 2–16.

Fodor, M., Komorowski, M., & Lewis, J. (2023). *Report update: The size and composition of the creative industries in Wales in 2022.* Clwstwr.

Galloway, T. L., Kuhn, K., & Collins-Williams, M. (2019). Competitors as advisors: Peer assistance among small business entrepreneurs. *Long Range Planning, 54*(2), 101929.

Gao, Y., Turkina, E., & Van Assche, A. (2024). The nexus between the cultural and creative industries and the sustainable development goals: A network perspective. *Regional Studies, 58*(4), 841–859.

Grannemann, H., Reis, J., Murphy, M., & Segares, M. (2023). Mask-makers as emerging creative entrepreneurs during COVID-19. In I. Hill, S.R.S.T.A. Elias, P. Jones & S. Dobson (Eds.), *Creative (and Cultural) Industry Entrepreneurship in the 21st Century (Contemporary Issues in Entrepreneurship Research)*, Vol. 18A) (pp. 75–89). Emerald Publishing Ltd.

Hill, I. (2021). Spotlight on UK artisan entrepreneurs' situated collaborations: Through the lens of entrepreneurial capitals and their conversion, *International Journal of Entrepreneurial Behavior & Research, 27*(1), 99–121.

Hill, I., & Scott, J. (with Wahga, A.) (2024). Sustainable entrepreneurship: Sustainability and the circular economy. In Deakins, D. & Scott, J. (Eds.), *Entrepreneurship. A contemporary and Global Approach* (2nd Edn.) (pp. 249–273). Sage Publishing Ltd.

Hill, I., Manning, L, & Frost, R. (2021). Rural arts entrepreneurs' placemaking - how entrepreneurial placemaking explains creative hub evolution during COVID-19 lockdown. *Local Economy, 36*(7–8), 627–649.

Hill, I., Elias, S., Jones, P., & Dobson, S. (2023). Creative (and cultural) industry entrepreneurship in the 21st century - State of the art. In I. Hill, S.R.S.T.A. Elias, P. Jones & S. Dobson (Eds.), *Creative (and Cultural) industry entrepreneurship in the 21st century (Contemporary issues in entrepreneurship research,* Vol. 18A) (pp. 1–14). Emerald Publishing Ltd.

Jevnaker, B. H., & Hill, I. (2024). Heritage craft entrepreneuring in the wild: the role of entrepreneurial placemaking for rural development. In I. Hill, S. Elias, S. Dobson, & P. Jones (Eds.), *Creative (and Cultural) Industry Entrepreneurship in the 21st Century* (Contemporary Issues in Entrepreneurship Research, Vol. 18B). Emerald Publishing Limited.

Jones, P., Klapper, R., Ratten, V., & Fayolle, A. (2018). Emerging themes in entrepreneurial behaviours, identities and contexts. *International Journal of Entrepreneurship and Innovation*, 19(4), 233–236.

Kim, T. (2021). Understanding creative economy policies in the Canadian context: A case study of 'Creative Canada.' *Cultural Trends*, 30(5), 425–441.

Klein, M., Gerlitz, L., & Spychalska-Wojtkiewicz, M. (2021). Cultural and creative industries as boost for innovation and sustainable development of companies in cross innovation process. *Procedia: Computer Science*, 192, 4218–4226. https://doi.org/10.1016/j.procs.2021.09.198

Kuhn, K. M., & Galloway, T. L. (2015). With a little help from my competitors: Peer networking among artisan entrepreneurs. *Entrepreneurship Theory and Practice*, 39(3), 571–600.

Li, W., Zhou, Y., & Zhang, Z. W. (2021). Culture-led plan for peri-urban agricultural sustainability: A case of Pu'an village in China. *Land*, 10(3), 242.

Marsh, C. (2017 October 11). *In the era of Netflix, what do we want Canadian Content to be?* National Post. https://nationalpost.com/entertainment/in-the-era-of-netflix-what-do-we-wantcanadian-content-to-be

Merrell, I., Fuzi, A., Russell, E., & Bosworth, G. (2021). How rural coworking hubs can facilitate well-being through the satisfaction of key psychological needs. *Local Economy*, 36(7–8), 606–626.

Ning, E. N. (2023). Creative industries in Cameroon: Problems and prospects. In I. Hill, S.R.S.T.A. Elias, P. Jones & S. Dobson (Eds.), *Creative (and Cultural) industry entrepreneurship in the 21st century (Contemporary issues in entrepreneurship research, Vol. 18A)* (pp. 165–177). Emerald Publishing Ltd.

Pagan, R. (2020). How important are holiday trips in preventing loneliness? Evidence for people without and with self-reported moderate and severe disabilities. *Current Issues in Tourism*, 23(11), 1394–1406.

Palanivel, T. (2019) *How cultural and creative industries can power human development in the 21st century*. Human Development Reports. https://hdr.undp.org/content/how-cultural-and-creative-industries-can-power-human-development-21st-century

Plunkett Foundation. (2022a). Better form of business community shops. *Report 2022*. Woodstock.

Plunkett Foundation. (2022b). Better form of business community pubs. *Report 2022*.Woodstock.

Pratt, A. (2021). Creative hubs: A critical evaluation. *City, Culture and Society*, 24, 100384.

Putland, C. (2008). Lost in translation: the question of evidence linking community-based arts and health promotion. *Journal of Health Psychology*, 13(2), 265–76.

Schieb-Bienfait, N., & Emin, S. (2023) Between professionalisation and marginalisation in the creative (and cultures) industries: A new look of the work of musicians in a French large creative city. In I. Hill, S.R.S.T.A. Elias, P. Jones, & S. Dobson (Eds.), *Creative (and Cultural) Industry Entrepreneurship in the 21st Century (Contemporary Issues in Entrepreneurship Research, Vol. 18A)* (pp. 135–149). Emerald Publishing Ltd.

Stickley, A., Koyanagi, A., Leinsalu, M., Ferlander, S., Sabawoon, W., & McKee, M. (2015). Loneliness and health in Eastern Europe: findings from Moscow, Russia. *Public health*, 129(4), 403–410.

UNESCO & World Bank. (2021). *Cities, culture, creativity: Leveraging culture & creativity for sustainable urban development & inclusive growth*. https://documents1.worldbank.org/curated/en/104121621556036559/pdf/Cities-Culture-Creativity-Leveraging-Culture-and-Creativity-for-Sustainable-Urban-Development-and-Inclusive-Growth.pdf

UN (United Nations). (2015). The sustainable development goals. https://sdgs.un.org/goals

UN (United Nations). (2017). SDG indicators. Global indicator framework for the Sustainable Development Goals and targets of the 2030 Agenda for Sustainable Development. https://unstats.un.org/sdgs/indicators/indicators-list/

Velez-Ospina, J., Siepel, J., Hill, I., & Rowe, F. (2022). How can policy makers help rural creative businesses contribute to Levelling Up? Creative industries Policy and Evidence Centre. https://pec.ac.uk/blog_entries/how-can-policy-makers-help-rural-creative-businesses-contribute-to-levelling-up/

Velez-Ospina, J., Siepel, J., Hill, I., & Rowe, F. (2023). Determinants of rural creative microclustering: Evidence from web-scraped data for England. *Papers in Regional Science, 102*(5), 903–943.

Watson, A. (2023). Supporting regional music production clusters in the post-pandemic era: Placing business support at the heart of the local cultural policy. *International Journal of Cultural Policy*, 1–15. https://doi.org/10.1080/10286632.2023.2251034

Watson, A., & Taylor, C. (2014). Invisible agents and hidden protagonists: Rethinking creative cities policy. *European Planning Studies, 22*(12), 2429–2435.

Welsh Government. (2022). *New plan to help develop Wales' creative talent, New plan to help develop Wales' creative talent*. GOV.WALES.

UNUSUAL AND TEMPORARY PLACES FOR CCI ENTREPRENEURSHIP

CHAPTER 2

TEMPORARY ART SPACES: A CONCEPTUAL FRAMEWORK

Hayley Reid[a], Andreana Drencheva[b] and Malcolm Patterson[a]

[a]*The University of Sheffield, UK*
[b]*King's College London, UK*

ABSTRACT

This chapter offers a conceptual framework to explicate the current configurations of temporary art spaces in the United Kingdom and how they seek to support the interests of artists as self-employed individuals. This chapter begins with a review of the literature on artists' (temporary) spaces. Next, we present a conceptual framework of the dimensions of temporary art spaces and explore how they support or hinder entrepreneurs in the cultural and creative industries to create and sustain their businesses and their wellbeing. The framework questions notions of temporary art space design that are often taken for granted by putting the most fundamental facets of the space (time and use) under a microscope. It can be used as a basis for future research into temporary art spaces and as a way to design better spaces that prioritise artists and their ways of working.

Keywords: Art space; pop-up; creative enterprise; place; temporary art spaces

INTRODUCTION

Thirty-two percent of the workforce of creative industries is self-employed (DCMS, 2021), thus acting on their own account and risk as entrepreneurs (Gorgievski & Stephan, 2016). Self-employed artists are finding it increasingly difficult to access affordable, convenient, and suitable workspaces that meet their needs and allow them to produce work in their artistic practice. At the same time, the United Kingdom high street is in decline with shops closing at an alarming rate and empty commercial buildings becoming a recognisable feature in town and city centres (Butler, 2021). Temporary art spaces offer a solution to both problems by filling empty spaces between commercial tenants, often at little to no cost to the artist. The building owner can gain from the security and economic benefit of having a space temporarily filled, while localities benefit from a sense of vibrancy and additional cultural value. The benefits of temporary art spaces are well documented and endorsed by policy makers and arts organisations (Bolsetti & Colthorpe, 2018).

However, what remains problematic is both the compensatory nature of temporary spaces, which neglects lasting and permanent solutions to the problems that artists face, and the jilted power dynamics, which favour landlords and developers above the artist. Little academic attention has been devoted to supporting artists who occupy temporary art spaces and how such support may differ based on the configurations of the spaces on offer. Similarly, the academic literature does not indicate whether temporary spaces benefit or limit artists based on the arrangements of the space. Temporary spaces are diverse and vary based on time and different types of artistic practice, yet these nuances in their configurations and diversity are often neglected. Consequently, our understanding of how temporary art spaces help or hinder artists to develop and sustain their businesses and their wellbeing is limited. This chapter makes contributions to the emerging study of temporary art spaces by providing a framework through which to understand the range of configurations across two essential dimensions: time and usage, and their potential impact on artists. We will begin with an overview of artist spaces and temporary art spaces, exploring why these spaces are important and examining their limitations. We then present our conceptual framework for understanding temporary art spaces and how they can help or hinder artists' work and wellbeing, providing examples from arts organisations in the North of England.

WHAT ARE ARTIST SPACES?

Artists inhabit different types of physical spaces for the purpose of inspiring, creating and presenting the product(s) of their artistic practice. These spaces look like shared or private studios, galleries within museums or art spaces, public places, such as murals on the side of buildings or sculptures in parks, and sometimes the artists' own home. Places of presenting artwork can be separate to places where work is created, but now often these places are linked. Artists use studio spaces as places to research, experiment, create and present their work.

They use them to teach new skills by hosting workshops and classes, and to learn new skills from other artists with whom they might share a space. Studio spaces can become gallery spaces, and host opening parties and events.

Historically the artist studio has been afforded the position of the 'unique space of production' (Buren & Repensek, 1979, p. 51), which is as important to the constitution of art as both the materials that compose it and the gallery that, traditionally, presents it. It is a secure, safe and enclosed place where artists have the freedom and space to experiment and create (Tuan, 1977), where ideas begin, and things are born. Within studio set-ups, artists can share ideas and create a sense of community and kinship with fellow artists, especially as they operate in a role that can be isolating and lonely (Bain, 2004; Bain, 2005). Beyond idea and relationship building, the studio also becomes a marker of identity for the artist as a physical place that has an intimate relationship with their work and is intertwined with their practice (Bain, 2004; Kelly, 1974; Skrapits, 2000; Zakin, 1978). One distinct way this happens is through recognising that the art studio is more than a place of production, but rather an archive for the artists' past and a catalyst for their future trajectory (Sjoholm, 2014).

WHAT ARE TEMPORARY ART SPACES?

The need for and use of temporary spaces is intertwined with the changing position of artists in society. Artists of the past held esteemed positions through links to academies, where they were provided with grand studio spaces (Bain, 2005). As artists' position in society began to shift to that of outsiders or struggling bohemians, so too did their studios shift towards lofts in forgotten areas of town (Bain, 2005). Now, as rent costs rise and places such as London that have been seen as cultural centres lose their fringe areas through gentrification and commercialisation (Bolsetti & Colthorpe, 2018), artists have immense difficulty finding suitable space for their work. Artists face accessibility issues to permanent studio spaces by either being priced out by high rents, or simply living in an area without access to viable studio spaces. Working from home is often not a suitable working environment because it does not meet the space requirements or equipment needs conducive to experimental work.

In this context, spaces that are temporarily used by individuals or collectives to inspire, create and present the product(s) of their artistic practice compensate for the limited accessibility of permanent spaces. Temporary spaces have existed in some form across the United Kingdom for around 15 years (Brooks et al., 2021), although this is an estimate as unreliable data and fragmented reporting by organisations make it difficult to quantify. Temporary art spaces are not just a UK phenomenon with well-established schemes in European cultural centres, like Berlin (Colomb, 2012) and Ghent (City of Ghent, 2018). While temporary spaces are not a new phenomenon, they are increasingly used as a mechanism to support artists and their practice in the United Kingdom. Despite this, they are academically under-researched, with existing literature on artist spaces focussing solely on the benefits they provide for neighbouring communities (Florida, 2012) or the negative associations with the gentrification of neighbourhoods (Grodach et al., 2014).

We suggest that artists can benefit from temporary art spaces in several ways: by assisting in the production of work, through facilitating experimentation and the development of their personal practices, by creating a sense of community and avoiding loneliness, and by supporting artists in remaining as authentic public actors.

Temporary art spaces are new civic spaces that allow for affordable experimentation and learning. For example, the Empty Shop CIC runs The Empty Shop Think Tank (TESTT), a large artist studio and event space above the bus station in the Durham city centre, designed as a place where the Empty Shop can run pilots related to vacant properties. TESTT, as the acronym suggests, is a place for new and experimental ideas to be tested before some are taken forward and others are abandoned. Hudson and Donkin (2019) suggest that the temporary nature of the space is the very thing that allows it to be 'a new civic space, a new vista of utopia which tests out art and models of social and aesthetic forms (some of which are taken forwards, some abandoned)' (p.194). This type of space provides an environment where risks can easily be taken with no repercussions from any potential failures (Carnegie & Drencheva, 2019).

When temporary art spaces are used to highlight social issues, allowing artists to be authentic and to promote issues important to them and their identity, they can also begin to build links to local communities. In 2014, architecture social enterprise Studio Polpo engaged in a programme of performances in an empty space in Sheffield titled Open Public Experimental Residential Activity (OPERA). During these performances, co-producers from the public were invited to spend a night in the space, which had been set up as a residential property, and to discuss alternative ways of living and 'further collective action in vacant buildings' (Orlek et al., 2014, p. 705). In this way, temporary space was used to raise awareness and encourage conversation around issues of housing and empty spaces in town and city centres, and to build links between the artists occupying the space and the local community.

WHAT ARE THE LIMITATIONS OF TEMPORARY ART SPACES?

The multiple uses and benefits of temporary spaces are clear; however, there remain several drawbacks which could impact on artists and make the programmes across the United Kingdom difficult to implement and maintain. While temporary spaces allow artists to take risks and experiment, their unstable and precarious nature can also create anxieties around the uncertainty of the space, which can be destabilising for artists. Among artists, there are high levels of poor mental health, which may be a pre-disposed condition, or the result of isolating working environments (Moore, 2014). It has also been suggested that the 'increasingly temporary arrangements and high uncertainty' of temporary spaces could have further detrimental effects on the mental health and wellbeing of artists

(Carnegie & Drencheva, 2019, p. 13). Artists also experience feelings of loneliness from periods of isolation and a tendency towards alienation (Bain, 2005; Bridgstock, 2005) which can be countered through fostering a sense of community. However, by creating a community based around a temporary space there is a risk of destabilising, displacing and ultimately destroying the carefully crafted community dynamic when the space is no longer in use, all of which extract personal time, money and energy from the individual artists working there (Brooks et al., 2021), affecting their future resilience.

Finally, the power dynamics of temporary art spaces is rarely in favour of the individual artists or art collectives (Harris, 2020). Building owners can remove artists from the premises at their behest, despite any remaining works in progress or events that are outstanding, thus potentially damaging artists' wellbeing and work.

In the next section, we introduce and explore a conceptual framework through which to understand past, current and future configurations of temporary art spaces.

TEMPORARY ART SPACES: A CONCEPTUAL FRAMEWORK

What is currently missing in the academic literature on temporary spaces is when artists in these types of spaces experience specific benefits or limitations based on the arrangements of the space. We offer a framework for the configuration of temporary spaces based on two dimensions: openness and time in operation and discuss how these dimensions can help or hinder artists' work and wellbeing (see Fig. 2.1). Openness refers to the extent to which space is open to the public versus its use as a closed and private studio space for the occupying artists. Time in operation refers to the amount of time that the space is occupied by artists. Based on our framework, we identify four ideal types of temporary spaces: short-term open, short-term closed, long-term open, and long-term closed. In this section, we elaborate on each one of the dimensions and provide examples of temporary art spaces operating in the last ten years in the North of England, which have been facilitated by different organisations[1].

OPEN AND CLOSED SPACE

Despite the many variations in the materiality of spaces, a common dimension is the degree of openness of the space. Open spaces are those which regularly open to the public for events, exhibitions, performances, or workshops. They are spaces in which artists work on their practice but also regularly facilitate wider participation from visitors, contributing to the important footfall numbers that are factored into council reports and funding bids. They do not need to be entirely open to the public during artist working hours, but opportunities for the public to attend the space make up most of the time that artists spend there.

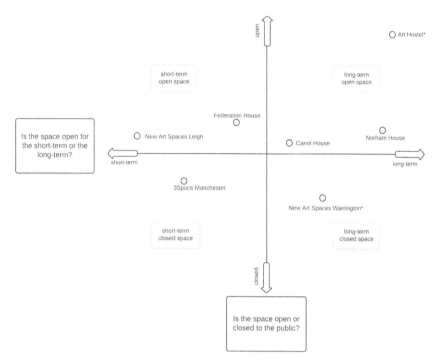

Fig. 2.1. Conceptual Framework for Understanding Temporary Art Space Configurations (The Authors). *Note(s)*: * indicates a temporary space that is still open at the time of writing, thus changes to its approach, time in operation, and consequently placement in the framework are possible.

An example of an open temporary art space that operated almost entirely based on public exhibition, events or workshops is East Street Arts' (ESA) Art Hostel as a 34 bed, backpacker style hostel in the heart of the Leeds City Centre, where each room was designed by individual artists or art collectives. While it functioned as a commercial, hospitality space, it also acted as an exhibition for the commissioned rooms and offered event and exhibition space in the basement and lobby/kitchen area. The Art Hostel is no longer in its original location on the historic Leeds Street, Kirkgate, but its arrangement was so successful, hosting around 10K guests over two and a half years, that it was moved in 2022 to a larger, permanent home. The success of pop-up spaces that are open to the public often results in their demise, as the increased interest in a building or area that is generated by pop-up lures developers and prospective commercial buyers (Harris, 2020). An open space means that there will likely be more communication and dialogue between artists' and local communities, limiting loneliness and providing outside exposure to their work, potentially broadening future opportunities to create within a locality. Open spaces may also limit opportunities for experimentation as any art (production) must be neat, safe and fit for the purpose of the public entering the building.

Closed, private spaces are those in which the main activity is undertaken by artists either in isolation by themselves or with one another, without participation or visitation from the public. The main way that closed spaces are utilised is through artists' private studios, which often operate in temporary spaces in a similar way to their traditional orientation in more permanent studios. In closed spaces, artists are often in a room of their own or occupy a desk in a shared and open plan space where there is still opportunity to collaborate and work together with other artists, and exhibitions or events with the public still happen but are not part of the main programming or activity which takes place in the space.

While a temporary art space may spend much of its life closed to the public, it is unusual to find one which operates almost entirely on a closed basis. This is likely due to public attendance, participation and community involvement in artist-run initiatives being a major part of the charitable missions of many temporary space hosting organisations. Despite this, it can be beneficial for artists to have a private space, shared with other artists, where they can develop their practices. This is often seen in permanent artist studios which often take the more traditional form of creative space as separate from exhibition space. London-based pop-up space provider, 3Space, launched a large temporary space in the former headquarters for London Scottish Bank in central Manchester, over a period of 10 months from 2015 to 2016. Although the building housed several commercial endeavours and events which made it open to the public (3Space, 2022) it also provided a home and private studio and makerspace for three artist collectives. This type of space differs from the dual open/closed space (discussed below) as the area where the artists' work is distinctly separate to the public/presenting space. It allows artists to experiment and be messy without needing to make the space palatable and presentable to the public. This might also influence the length of time that the space is open for as, on the one hand, the space may not have visibility to potential buyers, but on the other hand, the space may not be viable for continued upkeep by the brokering arts organisation if the space has little outwards community and public impact. While the closed space configuration can provide a concentrated place to produce work, it may also create difficulty around artists to interact with one another, perpetuating alienation, and poor artist wellbeing.

As openness is a continuum, some temporary arts spaces operate a dual function of spending most of their time close to the public, but regularly opening to allow the artists working there to present and exhibit their work. This dual, open/closed model is not unusual for temporary art spaces as supporting organisations seek to help artists in their private practice but also meet their goals as a charitable organisation to bring footfall, community interest and participation to their cultural endeavours. Examples of temporary spaces with dual functions are Castlefield Gallery's New Art Spaces programme and NewBridge Project's Cariol House.

The NewBridge Project's Cariol House in Newcastle upon Tyne opened in 2017 and during its 2-year lifespan provided studio space for up to 80 artists at a time, had a co-working space for collaborative work and project, workshop and event space (The NewBridge Project, 2022). The art space was built around the idea that the local community and the artists' who live there should have places where they can develop work and help to improve their locality together. Similarly, Castlefield Gallery's New Art Spaces operate a dual model across their current sites in Warrington, Bolton and Wigan. For instance, the artists who have worked in New Art Spaces Warrington, a cavernous former Marks and Spencer store in the town centre, since its opening in early 2020 have used it as a place to create and experiment in their practice privately, setting up makeshift workspaces on the shop floor and often creating site-specific work with the end goal of exhibiting in the space to the public.

Dual spaces allow artists the freedom to produce, develop and experiment in their practice, and also provide them a framework and purpose for the work by opening the space regularly to the public.

TIME IN OPERATION

The time that an artist or arts organisation can spend in a temporary art space is mostly a question of when a new commercial tenant will take over the space, likely turning it back to its original use of retail or office space, or sometimes demolishing the building entirely to create something new. Sometimes the spaces may be less temporary than anticipated. While most temporary spaces are active for a few months, Navigator North, an artist-led organisation in Middlesbrough, took over a temporary space at Dundas House almost 10 years ago and remains in that same space today, paying only for utilities. Similarly, but on a smaller basis, Castlefield Gallery offered artists an initial six-month space agreement for what was previously a large, four story Marks and Spencer shop in Warrington town centre, and the artists remain present in the building today, over a year later. Some organisations may also take over a space for many years but have specific time limits on how long individual artists or art collectives can spend in that space, so as to maximise the number of artists who work with them. For the purpose of this chapter, we will focus on the overall time that a temporary art space is in operation.

The temporality of these spaces can be problematic in a landscape where the power dynamic is firmly in favour of landlords who can give notice on a property at any time, levelling the same flexibility that is marketed to artists as beneficial to their practice against them (Harris, 2020). The amount of time that an artist spends in a temporary space can often be uncertain, subject to sudden change and independent and unsympathetic of how far into a project or piece of work an artist might be. This is due to short-term contracts and quick break clauses between arts organisations and property owners being the norm within the temporary space market, to enable property owners to bring in commercial tenants on short notice. East Street Arts' website (2021) states that temporary spaces 'allow for experimentation' and 'offer incubator options for new projects' while Castlefield Gallery (2021) describes their New Art Spaces as offering a 'unique testing ground for experimental and large-scale creative project development'. These two temporary space providers point to the impermanence of the spaces as allowing for, on the one hand, a pressurised and time-sensitive environment in which creativity, particularly when work is project-based with fast turnaround times, can flourish, yet also a no-pressure space where mistakes are allowed to happen. This paradoxical relationship with the temporary space, and the contradictory ideas posited on it by the arts organisations, could provide a fractured and confusing relationship between the space and the artist. Temporary art spaces currently provide much needed and mutually beneficial opportunities for a number of stakeholders during these times when property is expensive and difficult to come by. But, recognising the differing periods of time that are spent in these spaces and how this creates further opportunity or tension for artists is essential to understanding temporary art spaces. In this section, we offer a few examples of temporary art spaces which have been and are currently operational for different periods of time.

Short-term use of a space allows artists to develop resilience, produce more experimental work, and reach new audiences. Some temporary art spaces last little more than a week, but this shortness of time means that their relatively small impact is not well documented online or in the literature. Instead, the precarious nature of temporary art spaces is highlighted in Castlefield Gallery's 2014 launch of the Federation House, the former, eight storey Cooperative office building near Victoria Train Station in Manchester. The space housed 'exhibition spaces, artist workspaces, an experimental theatre space for developing new work, a film making and screening space, and classrooms for training events' and saw 700 people attend its opening event in 2014, with talks from cultural leaders in Manchester and nationwide (Castlefield Gallery, 2014). The Federation House was provided to Castlefield Gallery with a 5-year lease, but after just one year in the space, notice was given and the artists moved out. This relatively short-term arrangement, disguised initially as a longer-term solution, points to the precarity of temporary art space agreements, where Neo-liberalism's cruel optimism tricks artists into believing that the flexibility of temporary spaces is in their best interests, when in fact it may impede their future progress (Harris, 2020). Despite this, during its short time in operation, Federation House was a place where lots of different types of welcome addition to Manchester's thriving artist artists could come together and interact, forming a welcome addition to Manchester's thriving artist scene and proving opportunity, if brief, to the city's artists.

Long-term use of a space means that artists can move beyond the surface level to create deep- during its seven years level positive social change in a community (Stephan et al., 2016). They can also develop their sense of belonging to a community by having more exposure over time. For example, the NewBridge Project's Norham House, in Newcastle upon Tyne, developed a deep bond with the local community during its seven years of operation from 2010 to 2017 (Whetstone, 2017). Norham House benefitted artists by providing studios, exhibition space, and workspaces such as a dark room and a rehearsal room, and it supported the local community through the bookshop, gallery and regular workshops hosted there. It helped the local council reinvigorate an area dilapidated by the 2008 crash, and brought enough footfall from the building users to eventually see the area return to retail use. The artists and other building users described leaving the building as feeling a sense of loss for a place that they dedicated so much time and energy, especially as The NewBridge Project downsized when they moved to their next building at Cariol House, but also described feeling positive about the work that had been achieved there (Whetstone, 2017). Being able to linger for such a length of time in a temporary art space allowed the resident artists at Norham House to thrive and develop their practice in such a way that was free from the financial constraints and overheads of traditional, permanent studios. Norham House also created a community around the space where artists were able to work collaboratively with each other and local people, limiting isolation and increasing the spread of ideas and inspiration. However, when it was time to leave the building, it was not the organisations' terms, but rather the terms of the building owners who gave a six month notice period. To cease seven years of work in six months is likely a jarring experience for the artists in the building. Artist Charlotte Gregory indicated that during those seven years at Norham House, people built a community and network of peers, and experienced a sense of loss when leaving (Whetstone, 2017).

Through the dimensions which make up the framework we have identified four configurations of spaces which constitute the temporary art space landscape. The first configuration is one which is short-term open. These are spaces, such as Castlefield Gallery's Federation House and New Art Spaces Leigh which both had a dual function as offering private space to their artists at some times, while being open as an exhibition, workshop, or practice space for most of the time. These spaces are characterised as being mostly open to the public but operating for a short period of time. The second configuration is short-term closed which can be seen in 3Space Manchester where the artist activity occurring there mostly took place behind doors closed to the public, and which occurred during the short-term. The third configuration is long-term open, with spaces such as The NewBridge Project's Norham House, open for seven years with public bookshops and workshop space, and East Street Art's Art Hostel, fully open to the public in 2016, and moving to a new location in 2022. The fourth configuration is long-term closed with examples found in Castlefield Gallery's New Art Spaces Warrington and The NewBridge Project's Cariol House which both offer dual functions as open/closed space but mostly offer environments for artists to work privately.

CONCLUSION

Temporary art spaces in the United Kingdom are taking on new importance in the post-Brexit and post-pandemic landscape. The world of artists is changing as a result of these new challenges. Individual artists' identity is challenged during a time when demand and availability for artistic work is scarce and increased feelings of isolation and loneliness are present (Szostak & Sułkowski, 2021; Stuckey et al., 2021). Uncertainty about the post-pandemic future has created tensions which are expected to manifest in increased mental health issues, particularly among artists who already suffer disproportionately with mental health when compared to the general population (Stuckey et al., 2021). As a combined result of Brexit and COVID-19 lockdowns, the United Kingdom high street is facing unprecedented change with retail and hospitality units closing rapidly due to a combined result of consumer preferences switching to online shopping, less in-person spending, Brexit related supply chain issues and staff shortages (Partington & Partridge, 2021). An increased uptake of temporary art space programmes across the United Kingdom would assist in revitalising high streets by increasing footfalls to town and city centres and would help artists to find affordable spaces to make work and retain their artistic identity.

The conceptual framework posed in this chapter questions notions of temporary art space design that are often taken for granted, by putting the most fundamental facets of space (time and use) under a microscope. The framework can be used as a basis for future research into temporary art spaces, and as a way to design better spaces which prioritise artists and their ways of working. There are a number of additional factors that could help us to refine our understanding of temporary art spaces in future research. These could include the types of practice that artists undertake in the space, the intersectional identities of the occupying artists, the location of the space (in relation to the rest of the country and in its rural or urban locality) and the monetary cost of the space both for artists and for the arts organisations who sometimes invest in renovations and additional costs such as key making and bills.

NOTE

1. The examples given are based on information that is publicly available, compiled by the authors through news articles, the organisations' websites and through the authors' personal experiences within certain spaces. It is possible that the information that is publicly available does not fully reflect the finer nuances, details and uses of the space which may not have been documented. This could be due to the nature of temporary space work within arts organisations which often results in a large amount of work taking place without being fully documented, recorded or archived by the organisation. This is not an oversight but rather speaks to the difficulties and restrictions around the amount of time and funding that the organisation is able to dedicate to recording the spaces as opposed to delivering the temporary art space offering to the artists it serves. While the temporality of the spaces is set, how open or closed a space is has been reviewed qualitatively using information available online and is therefore subjective, using the authors' interpretation of the information publicly available. It is also worth noting that the spaces' positions in the framework is flexible, and those spaces that are still open may change their position after the time of writing.

REFERENCES

3Space. (2022). 3Space Manchester. [online]. http://www.3space.org/3space-manchester.
Bain, A. (2005). Constructing an artistic identity. *Work Employment Society*, *19*(25), 25–46.
Bain, A. L. (2004). Female artistic identity in place: The studio. *Social & Cultural Geography*, *5*(2), 171–193.
Bolsetti, N., & Colthorpe, T. (2018). Meanwhile, in London: Making use of London's empty spaces. Centre for London. https://www.centreforlondon.org/reader/meanwhile-use-london/
Bridgstock, R. (2005). Australian artists, starving and well-nourished: What can we learn from the prototypical protean career? *Australian Journal of Career Development*, *14*(3), 40–47.

Brooks, L., Darnley, F., Furness, C., Rahman, M., Wilson, A. (2021). Reform of meanwhile use: Arts & culture on the high street. Same Skies. https://sameskiesthinktank.com/reform-meanwhile-use-arts-culture-high-street/

Buren, D., & Repensek, T. (1979). The function of the studio. *October, 10,* 51–58.

Butler, S. (2021). One in seven shops now vacant across the UK. The Guardian [online]. https://www.theguardian.com/business/2021/jul/30/one-in-seven-shops-now-vacant-across-the-uk

Carnegie, E., & Drencheva, A. (2019). Mission-driven arts organisations and initiatives: Surviving and thriving locally in a time of rupture. *Arts and the Market, 9*(2), 178–187.

Castlefield Gallery. (2014). Castlefield Gallery launches New Art Spaces Federation House in city centre Manchester. [online]. https://www.castlefieldgallery.co.uk/news/5799/

Castlefield Gallery. (2021). New *art spaces.* https://www.castlefieldgallery.co.uk/associates/newartspaces/

City of Ghent. (2018). Refill: A *journey through temporary use.* [online]. http://urbact.eu/sites/default/files/media/refill_final_publication.pdf

Colomb, C. (2012). Pushing the urban frontier: Temporary uses of space, city marketing, and the creative city discourse in 2000s Berlin. *Journal of Urban Affairs, 34*(2), 131–152.

Department for Digital, Culture, Media & Sport UK. (2021). *DCMS sector economic estimates: Employment Oct 2019 - Sep 2020.* GOV.UK [Online]. https://www.gov.uk/government/statistics/dcms-sector-economic-estimates-employment-oct-2019-sep-2020

East Street Arts. (2021). *Temporary spaces.* https://www.eaststreetarts.org.uk/2021/02/24/temporary-space/

Florida, R. L. (2012). *The rise of the creative class: Revisited.* Basic Books.

Gorgievski, M. J., & Stephan, U. (2016). Advancing the psychology of entrepreneurship: A review of the psychological literature and an introduction. *Applied Psychology, 65*(3), 437–468.

Grodach, C., Foster, N., & Murdoch, J. (2014). Gentrification and the artistic dividend: The role of the arts in neighborhood change. *Journal of the American Planning Association, 80*(1), 21–35.

Harris, E. (2020). *Rebranding precarity: Pop-up culture as the seductive new normal.* Zed Books.

Hudson, M., & Donkin, H. (2019). TESTT space: Groundwork and experiment in a complex arts organisation. *Arts and the Market, 9*(2), 188–201.

Kelly, F. (1974). *The studio and the artist.* David and Charles.

Moore, M. D., Recker, N. L., & Heirigs, M. (2014). Suicide and the creative class. *Social Indicators Research, 119*(3), 1613–1626.

Orlek, J., Parsons, M., & Cerulli, C. (2015). Collective residential experiments: Prototyping shared living through the Reuse of Vacant Buildings (Conference paper) (pp. 705–715). [online]. https://www.researchgate.net/publication/291148243_Collective_Residential_Experiments_Prototyping_Shared_Living_through_the_Reuse_of_Vacant_Buildings

Partington, R., & Partridge, J. (2021, August 24). UK plunges towards supply chain crisis due to staff and transport disruption. The Guardian [online]. https://www.theguardian.com/business/2021/aug/24/uk-retailers-stock-supply-shortages-covid- pingdemic

Sjoholm, J. (2014). The art studio as archive. *Cultural Geographies, 21*(3), 505–514.

Skrapits, J. C. (2000). The studio as subject from Vermeer to Vuillard. *American Artist, 64,* 28–35.

Stephan, U., Patterson, M., & Kelly, C. (2016). Organizations driving positive social change: A review and an integrative framework of change processes. *Journal of Management, 42*(5), 1250–1281.

Stuckey, M., Richard, V., Decker, A., Aubertin, P., & Kriellaars, D. (2021). Supporting holistic well-being for performing artists during the COVID-19 pandemic and recovery: Study protocol. *Frontiers in Psychology, 12,* 577882–577882.

Szostak, M., & Sułkowski, Ł. (2021). Identity crisis of artists during the Covid-19 pandemic and shift towards entrepreneurship. *Entrepreneurial Business and Economics Review, 9*(3), 87–102.

The NewBridge Project. (2022). *Our history.* [online]. https://thenewbridgeproject.com/history/

Tuan. Y. F. (1977). *Space and place: The perspective of experience.* Edward Arnold.

Whetstone, D. (2017, March 3). Why a Newcastle city centre building colonised by artists will soon be empty again. Chronicle Live [online]. https://www.chroniclelive.co.uk/whats-on/arts-culture-news/newcastle-city-centre-building-colonised-12687355

Zakin. R. L. (1978). *The artist and the studio: In the eighteenth and nineteenth centuries.* Cleveland Museum of Art.

CHAPTER 3

CULTURAL ENTREPRENEURSHIP AT THE AARDKLOP ARTS FESTIVAL: AN ECOSYSTEM PERSPECTIVE

Saskia de Klerk[a] and Nada Endrissat[b]

[a]*University of the Sunshine Coast, Australia; North-West University, South Africa*
[b]*Bern Business School, Switzerland*

ABSTRACT

Arts festivals provide fertile ground for cultural entrepreneurs to access a marketplace and to grow and sustain their businesses. Yet, festivals also generate social value in the form of networks and social cohesion that extends far beyond economic means. Building on entrepreneurial ecosystem (EE) theory, we explore the collective effort of dealing with social and physical constraints in building a sustainable ecosystem that enables cultural entrepreneurs to make a living. To do so, we study cultural entrepreneurs who participate in the 'Aardklop' ('Earthbeat') Arts Festival, held annually in Potchefstroom, South Africa. The festival is built upon the Afrikaner culture and provides a temporary place for cultural entrepreneurs to express this culture using language, art, food, dance, and music. Our research questions were directed to get a deeper understanding of what motivated the cultural entrepreneurs to participate in the festival. Other research questions asked about 'what' value they perceive that they create at the festival and 'how' this value is experienced. Our findings suggest that cultural entrepreneurs negotiate a dynamic and resource-constrained environment by creating economic and social value through networking, social support, and the preservation of their cultural values. We contribute to a better understanding of cultural entrepreneurship and entrepreneurship ecosystem theory in particular, by highlighting the opportunities festivals offer to cultural entrepreneurs and by specifying their reasons to participate in them. We discuss the implications of our findings and give recommendations to guide local stakeholders, organisers, and business support organisations on how to increase the capacity of cultural entrepreneurs in the festival ecosystem.

Keywords: Cultural entrepreneurship; entrepreneurial ecosystem; network; social capital; community

INTRODUCTION

Culture and arts festivals are temporary, cultural events that support micro and small businesses in rural and regional areas to build relationships with a variety of stakeholders to survive, thrive, and enhance their competitiveness (Baron & Shane, 2005; Quinn, 2013). Although festivals can vary in character and scope, they are typically taking place for a limited time and held at a particular location with a program that consists of specific themes, productions, and planned shows as well as activities that promote engagement (Getz, 2008; Getz & Page, 2016). Put differently, festivals are cultural events that constitute seasonal regional ecosystems (Guercini & Runfola, 2012) to deliver products that resonate with their audience (Bendixen, 2000). Post-Covid these events have become even more important being described as the 'fabric of global society' (Davies, 2021). In South Africa, festivals have increased countrywide from nearly 100 in 1996 to 600 in 2012 (Loots et al., 2012). The importance of these festivals, as part of the creative and cultural industries in general, does not go unsupported by the government, and their impact on job creation and regional growth is considered an important area for the future (Government Communication and Information System (GCIS), 2015). While the economic impact of festivals on regional development is well documented (Duffy, 2018; Mair & Duffy, 2018), the reasons for participation and the outcome of such participation for the cultural entrepreneurs leave room for further exploration. Also, how different cultures translate into creative industries need to be better understood (Dobson et al., 2020). To address this question theoretically, we employ the entrepreneurial ecosystem (EE) theory. Empirically, we focus on the Aardklop ('Earth beat') festival (https://aardklop.co.za/), which takes place annually in the rural town of Potchefstroom, in the North-West Province, of South Africa. This Festival started in 1998 and has developed into the third-largest Arts festival in South Africa, annually attracting crowds of approximately 150 000 people from the neighbouring Gauteng and Free State provinces, as well as residents from Potchefstroom and surrounding North-West Province towns (Saayman et al., 2009). Aardklop is scheduled at approximately the same time every year to coincide with the September/October school holidays. The province of 3.7 million people in which it takes place is characterised by higher than the national average unemployment of 52.5% (Lehohla, 2015). Entrepreneurship and the collective effort in the regional town are not only seen as a vehicle to provide economic benefits but to diversify and grow the impact of the festival (Saayman & Rossouw, 2011) while preserving the local culture. Aardklop showcases mostly Afrikaans music, theatre, dance, cabaret, children's theatre, visual arts, and a large craft market (Meyer, 2015). Drawing from both qualitative and quantitative data, we offer an inside-out perspective of the motivation why the entrepreneurs trade at this festival and the perceived impact of their involvement at the festival. In doing so, we contribute to the literature on cultural entrepreneurship and EE theory. We start by outlining our theoretical framework before we move to our empirical case and its findings. This research addresses the gap in research where predominantly urban and mainstream events are included when investigating cultural entrepreneurship (Borin & Jolivet, 2021). In this research, we focus on the festival as an EE in a regional area. We end by discussing the implications of our research for theory and practice.

CULTURAL ENTREPRENEURSHIP

The field of cultural entrepreneurship is rapidly expanding addressing a variety of questions such as the making of culture, the deployment of culture (e.g., storytelling) for entrepreneurial activities, the culture of entrepreneurship, and the focus on entrepreneurship as cultural practice (for an overview see e.g., Endrissat & Tokarski, 2017; Gehman & Soublière, 2017). Among those, the focus on the process of creating new products and services in the creative industries is the most used.

Cultural entrepreneurs are mostly seen to be micro to small enterprise entrepreneurs who manage resource constraints (Laing, 2018; Loots et al., 2021), such as the lack of capacity and space to grow or expand operations (Rentschler & Radbourne, 2009), as well as lack of personal support (Soetanto, 2017). Cultural entrepreneurs also face specific constraints such as not being able to deliver commercialised and high-volumes, servicing niche markets and having limited outlets for their products. Craft-making as a form of cultural entrepreneurship is often associated with not being commercially viable or having a high mainstream return on investment (Jakob, 2012).

ENTREPRENEURIAL ECOSYSTEM

Entrepreneurial ecosystems (EE) are defined in various ways according to Malecki (2018) but most emphasise the interaction of elements, for example, networks, and cultural values. We use Stam and Spigel's (2016, p. 1) definition that defines the EE 'as a set of interdependent actors and factors coordinated in such a way that they enable productive entrepreneurship within a particular territory' This EE is composed of various elements 'that, ... are idiosyncratic because they interact in very complex ways, are always present if entrepreneurship is self-sustaining. ...although the combinations are always unique, ... to be self-sustaining entrepreneurship, you need conducive policy, markets, capital, human skills, culture, and supports' (Isenberg, 2010, p. 6). According to

Maroufkhani et al. (2018), the elements of the EE then also could either support or hinder the efforts of the entrepreneur.

Literature suggests that festivals can become temporary ecosystems where the stakeholders (organisers, entrepreneurs, local government, investors, sponsors, creatives, festivalgoers, and local community) participate in the event, and 'enable productive entrepreneurship' (Stam & Van de Ven, 2021). At the same time, the literature calls for a better understanding of the context in which the entrepreneur operates and to describe the value that can be derived from it (Autio et al., 2014; Müller & Korsgaard, 2018). In environments characterised by limited resources, marketing opportunities (Fillis, 2003), seasonal changes, strong competition, and high demand for new and innovative craft products (Ellmeier, 2003) the motivation to access actual and potential resources through community capital (Emery & Flora, 2006) is high. The lack of formal structures, support, and available resources makes the strategic use of community capital, such as human, social, financial, political, cultural, and built capital all the more important to sustain entrepreneurship (Bliemel et al, 2019; Emery & Flora, 2006). A successful EE is thought to consist of all the supporting elements (Emery & Flora, 2006) but will be offered and accessed in different ways depending on the environment in which it takes place. Following this line of argument, festivals can play the role of an agent, and it offers structure to the rural ecosystem (Miles & Morrison, 2020). A structured event offers access and exposure to large crowds at one time, extended networks, and opportunities to collaborate (Andersson & Getz, 2008). Moreover, the contribution of the revenue and hype (large crowds and publicity) (Botha et al., 2012), stimulates trade and encourages local businesses to be more competitive (Cabiddu et al., 2013; Getz, 2008), and to produce at a higher quality (de Klerk & Saayman, 2012). Festivals are also socially bound and 'expressions of people, information, ideas, money, and culture' (Quinn, 2006, p. 301).

We build on this research and wish to explore further how festivals offer the infrastructure that can support the development of community and social capital (Svendsen & Svendsen, 2004). Our research question asks: 'why' do cultural entrepreneurs participate in the festival, 'what' value do they create, and 'how' is this value experienced?

Methodology

To address our research questions, we follow an interpretive phenomenological approach (Cope, 2011) that provides us with a deeper understanding of the benefits of festival participation from the perspective of cultural entrepreneurs. We used a two-step process where we first conducted a quantitative survey (self-administered survey) to gather more information on the context and profile of the cultural entrepreneurs and then a second qualitative step where we conducted individual telephone interviews to explore the experiences that participants had concerning the benefits of participation. Data was collected in October 2015 in Potchefstroom, South Africa. The sample includes the cultural entrepreneurs who offered their products and services (including selling craft products and performing art) during the festival except food stall owners as they are operational only. For the self-administered survey, we gave each entrepreneur a survey and then collected the survey at the end of the first day. We repeated this every day until we had reached almost all the entrepreneurs summing up to 155 self-administered surveys in total. Of these, we selected a random sample of 25 entrepreneurs to conduct follow-up telephone interviews. Each interview lasted between 30 and 45 minutes and was conducted in Afrikaans. All interviews followed the same semi-structured interview guideline that was inspired by Oakley's (2014) study, exploring three different areas of interest.

- their 'story' of why they became a cultural entrepreneur including their demographic profiles (i.e., age and education) nature and size of their business, and exhibiting history at this festival including the rationale for their participation;
- their evaluation of the festival as the business environment for sustaining and growing their business;
- the opportunity for social interactions and their way of interacting and networking with others during the festival.

The interviews were electronically recorded and transcribed by an independent transcriber. For the presentation of the findings, selected quotations were translated from Afrikaans into English (own translation by the first author). Following this initial data collection, we kept a close eye on the further developments of the festival and followed social media updates such as Facebook (2022), and local newspapers (e.g., the *Potchefstroom Herald*, 2022). The festival management changed in 2016, and the model continued to reap success (Strachan, 2022a). A prominent festival director passed away in 2019, and he served as an important link between the local university and the festival management (Strachan, 2022a) which impacted the stakeholder relationships.

FINDINGS

The festival has grown and adapted to market trends and changes in customer demands as well as responded to the environmental changes, for example, the recent adjustments to the COVID-19 pandemic restrictions. Festivalgoers also had to adapt and more recently had to get used to an online component of the festival as well as this year the diversification of offerings and venues (Pienaar, 2022). The cultural entrepreneurs had to pivot their business models and the festival management and sponsorship also changed during this time. The festival evolved over the years from 1998 when it was held over four days and 25,000 tickets were sold (Coetzee, 2018) to changes in the venue, management, sponsors (Blackburn, 2016) and the rebranding and repositioning in 2017 to bring R50 million (A$4.45 million, AS$3.06 million) to the Potchefstroom region (Coetzee, 2018).

The cultural connection of Potchefstroom, as well as the vital marketplace for cultural entrepreneurs that was developed over the years, made the policymakers rethink their economic strategy. Mrs. Strachan mentioned 'We would like to thank each Potchefstromer for their hospitality and the remarkable role that they play in the success of Aardklop. Aardklop belongs at the Bult, in the heart of Potchefstroom, but we can't roll out the red carpet for thousands of festivalgoers, that is what Potchefstromers do with us' (translated from Afrikaans) (Blackburn, 2016). The decision by the Aardklop leadership at the time in 2016 to terminate the festival because of internal political and economic reasons made the stakeholders realise the inherent value of the festival to preserve the culture, and economic income of the entrepreneurs as well as for the town and broader region. New festival scenes and diversified offerings were the focus in 2019 (Kruger & Saayman, 2019). In 2020 the COVID-19 pandemic heavily impacted the country, especially the North-West Province and the Gauteng provinces making it impossible for Aardklop to go ahead in 2020, and they resorted to a limited online 'pop-up' version in 2021 (Hattingh, 2022; Pienaar, 2022). In more recent developments in 2022, a new sponsor came on board (Wetdewich, 2022) and the festival diversified to offer more online content as well as expand the festival over two weeks and in three Afrikaans-speaking demographic areas that are closer to the major cities (Strachan, 2022a). At first, the festival management received a lot of resistance from Potchefstromers, but since the festival is not aligned with the school or university holidays this year in Potchefstroom, people are starting to accept the outcome (Strachan, 2022b). There is also a renewed focus on children's theatre and commissioned pieces. Hence, the festival continues to operate along with the same principles as it did during our data collection. What remains to be seen is to what degree the online version will change onsite attendance in the coming years.

The profile of the cultural entrepreneurs has remained the same throughout the lifecycle of the festival. Most cultural entrepreneurs identify as artists or craftsmen with a large percentage of them manufacturing their products including wooden toys; leather products (belts, shoes, handbags, and ornaments); children's and women's clothing; artwork (paintings, pottery, and cast-iron works); handmade teddy bears, organic products (olives and oils), inlaid products, hair accessories, ornaments, and outdoor furniture. The business size ranges from one person (the owner) to 10 employees. This means that businesses can thus be roughly classified as micro and very small enterprises. Micro-enterprises range from one to four employees and generate an annual turnover of between R25000 and R50000 (1875.74USD to 3752.05USD at an exchange rate of 13.32 South African Rand buying 1USD),[1] and are mostly owner-managed (Mahembe, 2011). Most entrepreneurs attend at least two festival markets annually. What follows is a description of the main benefits of attending the festival from the cultural entrepreneurs' point of view. Table 3.1 provides an overview and unpacks the main themes briefly before we describe each and support them with relevant quotes from the interviews.

Table 3.1 Main Themes.

Motivation (Why do cultural entrepreneurs participate?)	Economic Social	Earn a living Feel part of something
Interaction and networks (What activities do cultural entrepreneurs engage in?)	Support their business development Support one another in the operations during the festival	Leads to cohesion Promoting each other's offering
Impact of the interactions and networks (How are cultural entrepreneurs impacted?)	The stability of the annual event leads to economic and social value and stability	Leads to cultural value and preservation

THEME 1: MOTIVATION FOR PARTICIPATION

The environment in which these events take place is often known for limited job opportunities, therefore, pushing the participants to trade at these events. Africa (Dobson et al., 2020), struggles with many social and economic problems including low employment rates and economic growth. Entrepreneurship is a means by which opportunities can be sought and exploited to overcome this and culturally and socially, there have been many changes in how entrepreneurship evolved and continues to develop in this region. Post-COVID-19 also brought about some innovations and some of these 'places' where these events would take place, moved to a digital or hybrid marketplace to continue to trade and support creative entrepreneurs despite the restrictions and challenges (Hill et al., 2021). The attractiveness of these events to conduct their business independently also pulls the entrepreneurs towards the event and provides structure and promotional support. This is emphasised, for example, in the many notions that 'to earn a living' was an important rationale to attend the festival as it offered a central (sometimes even only) opportunity to make some money: 'This festival is our main income and helps us to make something as our bread and butter' (p. 11); and 'We have to make it work since we need to make the money, everyone wants to make a profit and have some fun in the process, learn from each other' (p. 20).

The economic impact of having the opportunity to generate a financial gain is part of the 'fabric' and attractiveness of the festival: 'To supplement my income. My hobby became my sole income, and this event provides an opportunity to sell my products' (p. 6); 'People are there for the same reason to make money, to enjoy the event and we share the culture the background. A lot of us have the background that we either lost our permanent employment or we need to do this to supplement our income to survive' (p. 22).

On the other hand, interactions with the public and other creative people help them to stay informed and increase their creativity by opening their perspectives and getting fresh ideas. The community of all ventures having to adapt to new business models or embrace the transition to new platforms to trade and present their products also motivated most entrepreneurs to continue and find ways to overcome unprecedented situations.

THEME 2: INTERACTIONS AND NETWORKS

The second main theme is the value cultural entrepreneurs derive from interactions and networking at the festival also known as social capital. The businesses are micro to small, with only the owner/artist and maybe their partner, or a family member. The value of this ecosystem is the access to resources and social capital that can realize the economic value in terms of marketing, informational and financial benefits. By tapping into this EE extends their ability to stay up to date on market trends and product innovation. Some of the resources that they access through this ecosystem include, gaining access to and sharing market information (96%); industry information (89%); access to product knowledge (92%), and identifying market trends (92%). One remarked that 'The diversity of the products and ideas is always refreshing. You can learn about new things or how to do things differently' (p. 3). Referring to these interactions as supporting their innovations and creative ideas.

In a similar vein, another one emphasises the benefit of having direct contact with his customers at the festival. It serves as a form of customer/market research that he would otherwise have no resources available for: 'A lot of repeat business is generated by my involvement at this event; I would not be able to do this any other way. I think my products also bring a lot of people to the event since it is so unique and one of a kind' (p. 9).

Likewise, another entrepreneur stressed the importance of having direct interactions with the customers, getting their feedback, and communicating the value and uniqueness of the products to them: 'I am very relaxed, I chat and do business my way, I like to interact with others and especially chat with my supporters and customers' (p. 5). These interactions also allow him to improve the service delivery, and to understand their needs and preferences better.

Most entrepreneurs strive to take advantage of the opportunity and tap into a new market. From the literature, we know that festivals hold positive marketing and financial (Colbert, 2003) as well as networking opportunities for micro to small businesses (Johansson & Kociatkiewicz, 2011). In the interviews, it became clear that participants willingly shared advice, and offered as well as received personal support. They willingly shared their experiences through mentoring, supporting, and collaborating with others: 'We all want to make it work; we share the idea of if we do not work together it is going to be harder to make a success' (p. 9) and 'I have a good relationship with my fellow stall owners, and we crack jokes and make it enjoyable for each other' (p. 18).

Social capital is described as having solidarity (Coleman, 1990) and gaining a strong competitive advantage through combined efforts (Ihlen, 2005; de Klerk, 2015). To be a part of the social structure of the event and have repeat customers year after year supports the development of social capital and the customization of product offerings since the customer feedback is personal and immediate (Viswanathan et al., 2014): 'People learn from each other by observing how they display their products or the selling process of talking to the customer, so newcomers can learn from observing established businesses' (p. 7) and 'We learn from each other about business. They would say this works or that worked for me, so then you can learn from this' (p. 22).

THEME 3: COMMUNITY AND SHARED IDENTITY

Not all the cultural entrepreneurs associated their relationships at the festival with networking or a means to build social capital, but mentioned that they value the social interactions and the sense of cohesion that develops from it: 'On day one of the festival we do our own thing, but by the end of the week we are friends and after that, we look forward to meeting up again year after year' (p. 5); 'Repeat exhibitors become family we look forward to seeing each other year after year' (p. 7) and 'We share a few laughs look after each other's stall and take turns to go and buy some food or a have a toilet break. It is really like looking out for each other' (p. 3).

The entrepreneurs mentioned that to feel part of something (86%) and to feel part of the festival (79%) as important reasons to attend the festival. They associate their experience with notions of becoming 'friends' and even 'family' (see quotes above) which suggests a strong sense of identification and social cohesion. This was also repeated as one of the highlights of their involvement at the festival: 'We feel as if everyone (the entrepreneurs and fellow stall owners) is in this together so the sense of solidarity and being brothers working side by side is very special and gives you a sense of purpose' (p. 5).

The repeat encounters contribute to the trust and strength of the connections among festival participants. Social cohesion and a sense of community are developed at this festival where people feel solidarity and share values; this was mentioned as being instrumental in the overall success of the businesses and the festival. Over 23% of the entrepreneurs indicated that they have been operating their business as part of the last 11 or more festivals. The feeling of being part of a community and socially connected leads to further 'bonding' as described by Holzmann and Jorgensen (1999), which is directly linked to the development of social capital (see Theme above).

CONCLUSIONS

By taking an EE perspective we wanted to highlight the value festivals offer to cultural entrepreneurs in South Africa. Our findings suggest that festivals can be understood as structured events for sustainable entrepreneurial practices. A basic understanding of the main motivations; perceived value derived and how this value can be articulated supports the ecosystem analogy where the ecosystem as much as the entrepreneurial orientation is needed to create ongoing and sustainable outcomes. The ecosystem allows for creativity by selling directly to the public and interacting much closer than through intermediaries, webpages, and shopfront stores. By facilitating access to the human, social, financial, environmental, and economic resources, the festival offers the context to develop and thrive through social networks and community leading to social cohesion and a shared identity that motivates repeated participation. There should be a continuous acknowledgment of the economic role, but more specifically the social and community role that these events can play in developing cultural entrepreneurs. The centrality of repeated personal interactions was also emphasised during the

COVID-19 pandemic during which the festival was moved into an online/virtual space leading to practical implications to sustain their efforts.

Practically, entrepreneurs had to adjust their business practices to embrace the use of a digital platform. This research adds to calls for a better understanding of how entrepreneurs deal with unprecedented situations to exploit synergies to sustain themselves (Rashid & Ratten, 2021). The pivoting and steep learning curve could have been supported more by the EE. Future planning, proactiveness, and innovation in how the social space of the festival can be expanded to include a hybrid or virtual component as well could be considered. Future research can explore how the social space should be recreated to resemble a 'real presence' and future innovation around the use and expansion of virtual opportunities for these cultural entrepreneurs to increase their reach, for example creating a support network and sense of community (e.g., a business webpage listing; electronic newsletter; and showcase business profiles online). How Cultural entrepreneurs can utilize virtual spaces and new innovations, to enhance their business strategy and the experience of their customers can be explored. A deeper understanding of how technology can be utilised to achieve cultural, social, and community outcomes should be investigated in different contexts and industries.

To conclude, the multicultural society of South Africa lends itself to the development of a multitude of culturally themed festivals. Different cultures want to feel as if they belong to and share their culture by being involved in the variety of art and cultural performances, experiences and culinary traditions offered at such an outlet (Paldam, 2000). This provides an excellent opportunity for cultural entrepreneurs not only to make a living but also to create social support networks, interact and learn from each other, thereby overcoming known resource constraints in the cultural industries (Loots et al., 2021; Rentschler & Radbourne, 2009).

NOTE

1. See http://www.xe.com/currencyconverter/convert/?Amount=25000&From=ZAR&To=USD.

REFERENCES

Andersson, T.A., & D. Getz. (2008). Stakeholder management strategies of festivals. *Journal of Convention & Event Tourism*, 9(3), 199–220.

Autio, E., Kenney, M., Mustar, P., Siegel, D., & Wright, M.(2014). Entrepreneurial innovation: The importance of context. *Research Policy*, 43(7), 1097–1108.

Baron, R. A., & Shane, S. A. (2005). *Entrepreneurship: A process perspective* (1st ed.). Thomson South-Western.

Bendixen, P. (2000). Skills and roles: Concepts of modern arts management. *International Journal of Arts Management*, 2(3), 4–13.

Blackburn, C. (2016). *MaroelaMedia. Aardklop 2016: Ou gronde en spotgoedkoop kaartjies*. Retrieved August 17, 2016, from https://maroelamedia.co.za/vermaak/geleenthede/aardklop-2016-ou-gronde-en-spotgoedkoop-kaartjies/

Bliemel, M., Flores, R., De Klerk, S, & Miles, M. P. (2019). Accelerators as start-up infrastructure for entrepreneurial clusters. *Entrepreneurship & Regional Development, 31*(1–2), 133–149.

Borin, E., & Jolivet, C. (2021). Entrepreneurial cultural ecosystems in rural contexts: Some insights from rural cultural centers in France. In P. Demartini, L. Marchegiani, M. Marchiori, & G. Schiuma (Eds.), *Cultural initiatives for sustainable development. Contributions to management science*. Springer. https://doi.org/10.1007/978-3-030-65687-4_15

Botha, K., Viviers, P., & Slabbert, E. (2012). What really matters to the audience: Analysing the key factors contributing to arts festival ticket purchases. *South African Theatre Journal, 26*(1), 22–44.

Cabiddu, F., Liu, T., & Piccoli, G. (2013). Managing value co-creation in the tourism industry. *Annals of Tourism Research, 42*, 86–107.

Coetzee, M. (2018). *Festivalgoers' perception about the quality of products and services at Aardklop* [Mini dissertation for the degree Master of Business Administration at the North-West University]. http://repository.nwu.ac.za/handle/10394/30745

Colbert, F. (2003). Entrepreneurship and leadership in marketing the arts. *International Journal of Arts Management, 6*(1), 30–39.

Coleman, J. S. (1990). *Foundations of social theory*. Harvard University Press.

Cope, J. (2011). Entrepreneurial learning from failure: An interpretative phenomenological analysis. *Journal of Business Venturing, 26*(6), 604–623.

Davies, K. (2021). Festivals post COVID-19. *Leisure Sciences, 43*(1–2), 184–189.

Dobson, S., Jones, P., Agyapong, D., & Maas, G. (Eds.). (2020). *Enterprising Africa: Transformation through entrepreneurship*. Routledge.

Duffy, M. (2018). Music events and festivals: Identity and experience. In *The Routledge handbook of festivals* (pp. 304–312). Routledge.

Emery, M., & Flora, C. (2006). Spiraling-up: Mapping community transformation with community capitals framework. *Community Development, 37*(1), 19–35.

Ellmeier, A. (2003). Cultural entrepreneurialism: On the changing relationship between the arts, culture and employment. *The International Journal of Cultural Policy, 9*(1), 3–16.

Endrissat, N., & Tokarski, K. O. (2017). Editorial. *International Journal of Entrepreneurial Venturing, Special Issue on Cultural Entrepreneurship, 9*(3), 203–208.

Fillis, I. (2003). Image, reputation and identity issues in the arts and crafts organization. *Corporate Reputation Review, 6*(3), 239–251.

Gehman, J., & Soublière, J. F. (2017). Cultural entrepreneurship: From making culture to cultural making. *Innovation, 19*(1), 61–73. https://doi.org/10.1080/14479338.2016.1268521

Getz, D. (2008). Event tourism: Definition, evolution, and research. *Tourism Management, 29*(3), 403–428.

Getz, D., & Page, S. J. (2016). *Event studies: Theory, research and policy for planned events* (3rd ed.). Routledge.

Government Communication and Information System (GCIS). (2015). *Pocketguide to South Africa 2014/2015*. https://www.gcis.gov.za/sites/default/files/docs/resourcecentre/pocketguide/PocketGuide-arts-updated.pdf

Guercini, S., & Runfola, A. (2012). Relational paths in business network dynamics: Evidence from the fashion industry. *Industrial Marketing Management, 41*(5), 807–815.

Hattingh, I. (2022). *Aardklop wip weer op in nuwe stel vere*. MaroelaMedia. https://maroelamedia.co.za/vermaak/musiek/aardklop-wip-weer-op-in-nuwe-stel-vere/

Hill, I., Manning, L., & Frost, R. (2021). Rural arts entrepreneurs' placemaking–How 'entrepreneurial placemaking' explain rural creative hub evolution during COVID-19 lockdown. *Local Economy, 36*(7–8), 627–649. https://www.ncbi.nlm.nih.gov/pmc/articles/PMC8971967/

Holzmann, R., & Jorgensen, S. (1999). *Social protection as social risk management*: Conceptual underpinnings for the social protection sector strategy paper. *Journal of International Development, 11*(7), 1005–1027.

Ihlen, Ø. (2005). The power of social capital: Adapting Bourdieu to the study of public relations. *Public Relations Review, 31*(4), 492–496.

Isenberg, D. J. (2010). How to start an entrepreneurial revolution. *Harvard Business Review, 88*(6), 40–50.

Jakob, D. (2012). Crafting your way out of the recession? New craft entrepreneurs and the global economic downturn. *Cambridge Journal of Regions, Economy, and Society*, 6(1), 127–140.
Johansson, M., & Kociatkiewicz, J. (2011). City festivals: Creativity and control in staged urban experiences. *European Urban and Regional Studies*, 18(4), 392–405.
de Klerk, S. (2015). The creative industries: An entrepreneurial bricolage perspective. *Management Decision*, 53(4), 828–842.
de Klerk, S., & M. Saayman. (2012). Networking as key factor in artpreneurial success. *European Business Review*, 24(5), 382–399.
Kruger, M., & Saayman, M. (2019). The relationship between decision-making factors and 'festivalscapes' with visitor loyalty: Evidence from a South African national arts festival. *Acta Commercii*, 19(1), 1–10. https://journals.co.za/doi/epdf/10.4102/ac.v19i1.765
Laing, J. (2018). Festival and event tourism research: Current and future perspectives. *Tourism Management Perspectives*, 25, 165–168.
Lehohla, P. J. (2015, July 23). Mid-year population estimates. Statistics South Africa: Statistical Release P0302. Pretoria. https://www.statssa.gov.za/publications/P0302/P03022015.pdf
Loots, I., Ellis, S., & Slabbert, E. (2012). Factors predicting community support: The case of a South African arts festival. *Tourism & Management Studies*, 7, 121–130.
Loots, E., Neiva, M., Carvalho, L., & Lavanga, M. (2021). The entrepreneurial ecosystem of cultural and creative industries in Porto: A sub-ecosystem approach. *Growth and Change*, 52(2), 641–662.
Mahembe, E. (2011). Literature review on small and medium enterprises' access to credit and support in South Africa. *National Credit Regulator (NCR): Pretoria, South Africa*. Underhill Corporate Solutions.
Mair, J., & Duffy, M. (2018). The role of festivals in strengthening social capital in rural communities. *Event Management*, 22(6), 875–889.
Meyer, B. (2015). *Aardklop 2015 is hier*. Maroela Media. Retrieved July 25, 2015, from https://maroelamedia.co.za/vermaak/musiek/aardklop-2015-is-hier/
Miles, M. P., & Morrison, M. (2020). An effectual leadership perspective for developing rural entrepreneurial ecosystems. *Small Business Economics*, 54(4), 933–949. https://doi.org/10.1007/s11187-018-0128-z
Müller, S., & Korsgaard, S. (2018). Resources and bridging: The role of spatial context in rural entrepreneurship. *Entrepreneurship & Regional Development*, 30(1–2), 224–255.
Oakley, K. (2014). Good work? Rethinking cultural entrepreneurship. In C. Bilton & S. Cummings (Eds.), *Handbook of management and creativity* (pp. 145–159). Edward Elgar Publishing.
Paldam, M. (2000). Social capital: One or many? Definition and measurement. *Journal of Economic Surveys*, 14(5), 629–653.
Pienaar, W. (2022). Aardklop 2022 se feesterrein op die Joolplaas. *Potchefstroom Herald*. Retrieved September 5, 2022, from https://www.citizen.co.za/potchefstroom-herald/news/2022/09/05/aardklop-2022-se-feesterrein-op-die-joolplaas/
Quinn, B. (2006). Problematising festival tourism': Arts festivals and sustainable development in Ireland. *Journal of Sustainable Tourism*, 14(3), 288–306.
Quinn, B. (2013). Arts festivals, urban tourism, and cultural policy. In *Culture and the city* (pp. 77–92). Routledge.
Rashid, S., & Ratten, V. (2021). Entrepreneurial ecosystems during COVID-19: The survival of small businesses using dynamic capabilities. *World Journal of Entrepreneurship, Management and Sustainable Development*, 17(3), 457–476. https://doi.org/10.1108/WJEMSD-09-2020-0110
Reddit. (2022). *Potch artists turn to online platforms*. https://www.reddit.com/r/autotldr/comments/j61rxv/covid19_potch_artists_turn_to_online_platforms/
Rentschler, R., & Radbourne, J. (2009). Size does matter: The impact of size on governance in arts organizations. In *AIMAC 2009: Proceedings: 10th international conference on arts & cultural management* (pp. 1–14). SMU.
Saayman, M., Douglas, M., & de Klerk, S. (2009). Attributes of entrepreneurs at an arts festival. *Southern African Journal of Entrepreneurship and Small Business Management*, 2(1), 17–29.
Saayman, M., & Rossouw, R. (2011). The significance of festivals to regional economies: Measuring the economic value of the Grahamstown national arts festival in South Africa. *Tourism Economics*, 17(3), 603–624. https://doi.org/10.5367/te.2011.0049

Soetanto, D. (2017). Networks and entrepreneurial learning: Coping with difficulties. *International Journal of Entrepreneurial Behavior & Research, 23*(3), 547–565.

Sproule, S. (2022). Aardklop is coming to Pretoria. *Pretoria Record*. Retrieved September 12, 2022, from https://www.citizen.co.za/rekord/news-headlines/local-news/2022/09/12/aardklop-is-coming-to-pretoria/

Strachan, A. (2022a). *Momentum Belegggings Aardklop keer terug na Potch*. https://aardklop.co.za/2023/03/16/momentum-beleggings-aardklop-terug-in-potch/

Strachan, A. (2022b, June 29). Aardklopbrief aan inwoners van Potchefstroom. Earthbeat letter to Potchefstroom residents (Trans.). *Potchefstroom Herald*. https://potchefstroomherald.co.za/109471/aardklopbrief-aan-inwoners-van-potchefstroom/

Stam, E., & Spigel, B. (2016). Entrepreneurial ecosystems. *USE Discussion Paper Series.*, *16*(13), 1–15

Stam, E., & Van de Ven, A. (2021). Entrepreneurial ecosystem elements. *Small Business Economics, 56*(2), 809–832.

Svendsen, G., & Svendsen, G. T. (2004). *The creation and destruction of social capital: Entrepreneurship, co-operative movements and institutions*. Edward Elgar.

Viswanathan, M., Echambadi, R., Venugopal, S., & Sridharan, S. (2014). Subsistence entrepreneurship, value creation, and community exchange systems: A social capital explanation. *Journal of Macromarketing, 34*(2), 213–226.

Wetdewich, D. (2022, April 11). Aardklop kom draai weer in Potch vanjaar. *Potchefstroom Herald*. https://potchefstroomherald.co.za/105293/aardklop-kom-draai-weer-in-potch-vanjaar/

Wyrley-Birch, J.-N. (2022). *Aardklop moes aanpas om te oorleef*. Retrieved June 29, 2022, from https://maroelamedia.co.za/nuus/sa-nuus/aardklop-moes-aanpas-om-te-oorleef/

CHAPTER 4

OUT OF THE STUDIO AND INTO THE STREET: A CASE STUDY OF STREET ART OPPORTUNITIES DURING COVID-19

Leigh Morland[a] and Ekaterina Sheath[b]

[a]*The University of Huddersfield, UK*
[b]*Freelance Illustrator, UK*

ABSTRACT

This chapter explores street art as a form of creative and cultural entrepreneurship from two perspectives. Firstly, in relation to placemaking during a pandemic (COVID-19) and secondly, from the experiences of the artist-entrepreneur, in terms of taking opportunities. Drawing on a single, in-depth case study, it analyses how the art entrepreneur is able to take opportunities through 'necessary combined capabilities' (Wilson & Martin, 2015). Further reflection from the artist then explains how internal capabilities are used to sustain the entrepreneurial process. The discussion gives insight into how creative entrepreneurship is enabled by context and the entrepreneur's self-motivation and learning during COVID-19. It has implications for how art entrepreneurs can develop their skills and reputation through taking placemaking opportunities.

Keywords: Art entrepreneurship; street art; opportunities; placemaking; entrepreneurial capabilities

INTRODUCTION

This chapter considers opportunities for art in the public realm, informed by the experiences of one UK-based illustrator. It explores the relationship between external conditions and entrepreneurial capabilities (Wilson & Martin, 2015) that enable opportunities, noting that the situation of street art (or murals) in the public realm supports stakeholder commitments and access to networks, leading to further opportunities and new venture creation (Comunian et al., 2010; Read et al., 2016).

The chapter starts with a brief overview of public art and placemaking during COVID-19, and then reflects upon creative entrepreneurship in relation to street art opportunities. Then an in-depth case study tells the story of how one freelance illustrator produced their first murals and then found opportunities in paid commissions. It details the entrepreneurial process and determines how 'necessary combined capabilities' (Wilson & Martin, 2015) and engagement with place support opportunity taking. Finally, the art entrepreneur reflects on their ability to explore and take opportunities by moving out of the studio and working in the public realm, thereby enhancing commercial skills and extending their artistic specialisms (Carey, 2015).

Art Opportunities in the Public Realm During Covid-19

Street art takes many forms; this case study focuses on media box murals and window installations. Media box murals refer to visual images produced for a public purpose using brush and paint. This differs from graffiti, a form of self-expression that may not reflect the intended use of space (Fuentes, 2018). The window installations refer to illustrations displayed on vinyls in vacant retail and commercial properties. Both painted murals and window vinyls contribute to placemaking, through the artist seeking permission and/or undertaking commissions to situate art in the public realm. These artworks can create positive connections between people and place, as well as contribute to wider regeneration and community-building agendas (Matthews & Gadaloff, 2022).

Street art is viewed in the pattern of everyday life, and comprises of distinctive images that contribute to place identity. It brings meaning-making into public spaces, such that walking to the shops, going to school, or looking out of a café window, offers the possibility of viewing art and making sense of own experiences. Murals are typically adapted for different spaces (McKelvey & Lassen, 2018), presenting celebratory or uplifting images for communities, from the creative interpretation of place. Therefore, street art can be associated with placemaking, being a purpose-led creative output that enables and reflects stakeholder engagement (Bobadilla et al., 2019; Callander & Cummings, 2021; Matthews & Gadaloff, 2022). Notably, some locations are more conducive to creative placemaking in providing infrastructure, civic and community governance, and networks, that support collaborative projects between artists and communities (Comunian et al., 2010).

Opportunities are integral to the creative entrepreneurial process (Hechavarria & Welter, 2015). There is much conceptual debate concerning the nature of opportunities, but limited situational understanding of decisions and actions, as perceived by the entrepreneur (Dimov, 2011). For this study, opportunities are determined as situations that can be seen and sensed by the art entrepreneur, who is able to act and create value. It proposes that COVID-19 created a context of social and economic change (in one city region in the United Kingdom), to foster such opportunities.

During the first UK lockdown (26 March 2020–10 May 2020) people were limited in how long they were out of the home and where they could go. For some, restrictions led to boredom, anxiety, and loneliness, impacting on physical and mental wellbeing (Banerjee & Rai, 2020). COVID-19 highlighted the importance of creating spaces for wellbeing wherever people are resident. Subsequently, councils and community groups responded with art projects (Hill et al., 2021). Specifically, street art initiatives provide the means to make spaces more vibrant and inspiring, and bring a sense of connection to public areas; but who can take these creative place-making opportunities?

Necessary Combined Capabilities for Entrepreneurship

According to Wilson and Martin (2015), entrepreneurial capabilities enable an individual to pursue opportunities within their context, they stress the importance of 'necessary combined capabilities' (p. 162) summarised as:

- The possibility of recombining resources
- The possibility of transaction
- The possibility of appropriating value.

Reflecting on each in relation to art entrepreneurship in the public realm. For the studio-based artist, street art can be a novel experience. They may need to recombine technical resources and networks, as well as develop new skills. In terms of transactions, the entrepreneur must engage stakeholders in placemaking to create social value. The skill of 'translation' – and the ability to manage stakeholder interests – is required to do this (Bobadilla et al., 2019). Finally, value must be appropriated by the artist to sustain their output and develop a positive reputation. While some places are more conducive to supporting creative entrepreneurship (Comunian et al., 2010), little is known about the interplay between these contextual capabilities and the practice of individual art entrepreneurs, from a process perspective. Therefore, a qualitative case study is proposed to give a deeper understanding of the relationship between art entrepreneurship and opportunities, and in terms of theoretical contribution, illuminate the interrelationship between context and capabilities within the entrepreneurial process.

ART ENTREPRENEURSHIP IN THE PUBLIC REALM

Creative and cultural entrepreneurship typically combines economic, social and environmental goals, resulting in the creation and utilisation of intellectual property and cultural output (Wright et al., 2019). Art entrepreneurs may seek opportunities that are viable, impactful, and personally meaningful, either through necessity or from a desire to undertake self-directed work (Carey, 2015). (In the context of street art, the entrepreneur attunes their creative vision to the placemaking agenda). Opportunities can be time and place-bound, small or large scale, and collaborative; with commissions and projects arising from community groups, commercial organisations, and local authorities. The entrepreneur must understand, and reconcile, different stakeholder interests in the artistic process (Bobadilla et al., 2019), and in the expression of their creative intent (Carey, 2015). Painted murals bring an additional dimension to collaborative placemaking, as they are formed 'in public'. Stakeholder interests can be expressed directly to the artist, or via social media. Therefore, producing and displaying street art provides the entrepreneurial means to attract stakeholder support, and potentially further opportunities for generating artistic output and paid commissions.

METHODOLOGY

During COVID-19 the researcher took daily walks in her neighbourhood and later the nearby city centre; she saw the street artist's work displayed in two locations. A curiosity arose concerning the motivation to produce the art and whether there was a link between these outputs. Did one project lead to another? Using the contact details painted on the art, the researcher reached out to the artist to find out how the opportunities arose, and what had been learned in the process. The case study is co-produced by the researcher and the artist, constructed from field notes, observations, walking interviews (Jones et al., 2008), and reflective writing. This 'situated' approach enables a deeper understanding of the interplay between capabilities and context (Henry & Foss, 2015; Yin, 2008) from the art entrepreneur's perspective. Walking interviews, conducted between February and April in 2022, enabled the researcher and artist to view the art from different physical and sensory perspectives (Wünderlich, 2008).

Taking a socially constructed view of opportunities, the case study tells the story of three successive projects, all located within a UK city region, undertaken during COVID-19. Interview questions explore artistic and entrepreneurial processes, giving insight into the nature of opportunities and how the entrepreneur engages with them. The discussion then analyses the cases by applying 'necessary combined capabilities' for opportunities (Wilson & Martin, 2015), to gain a deeper appreciation of how opportunities manifest within this context for the entrepreneur. Finally, the artist provides a written reflective response to the case study, informing an assessment of their internal capabilities. The research design represents a reflexive qualitative study (Cumming-Potvin, 2013), combining researcher and artist perspectives in constructing and analysing the case. Through this approach, the entrepreneur engages in self-questioning by reflecting on their story (Mauthner & Doucet, 2003), yielding a contextual understanding of 'their opportunities' and associated skills.

CASE STUDY: OUT OF THE STUDIO AND INTO THE STREET

Project 1: Suburban Media Boxes

We walk to a city suburb to view media boxes painted by Ekaterina. These are typically dark green metal units that house media cables. A common site on many streets.

The media box project started in Spring 2020, when the United Kingdom was in lockdown. Although still a University student, Ekaterina was keen to develop her portfolio. Looking through Facebook, she responded to a community group post, seeking artists for the project. Her response was immediate:

> [...] I don't know what it was ... something about it ... I really want to do that, and I remember messaging them instantly ...

It was the first time she considered using her design ideas to produce painted murals, which would require new technical skills and materials to work on exterior metal surfaces. She contacted paint shops and local street artists for advice and learned new techniques through practice. Ekaterina walked around the area and researched online to inform her designs (see Fig. 4.1). Her mural includes images referring to: Surrounding businesses, local people, social practices, and hobbies; each illustration is directly inspired by the area.

Images reflect her inspiration and the audience.

> [...] when I get tired or the painting is taking ages, it just reminds me that people will literally walk past this every single day ... so you want to put a lot of energy and time into it.

The next media box is close by. The colour palette is the same, but her artistic style has evolved, to communicate a stronger sense of movement into her characters.

> [...] it's really fun to push it ... you are communicating energy and tone more than you are communicating realism.

These media box murals need maintaining as birds and plants can damage the finish. Ekaterina also relies on people using social media to let her know if illustrations are defaced. (Her Instagram is referenced on the box.) She feels a strong sense of responsibility to maintain her artwork, returning to remove or conceal defacement.

Two further media box commissions arose, perhaps as a result of her first efforts, and she began to feel more assured in her ability as a mural artist.

> This was when I was learning more and more about working with metal paint and getting a lot more confident with it .... It was fun ....

The timing of the commission matters. Ideally, the mural artist works in dry weather (media box compositions typically take four days) including time for cleaning, painting, and drying. However, some commissions may not afford this flexibility and if wet paint is affected by rain, the finish is impaired. As we look at the art, Ekaterina reflects that some people do object to street art. It might not be the design per se, but rather a concern that neighbourhoods are altered by art. While there is consultation, no one mural can meet the interests of all those who view it.

Fig. 4.1. Suburban Media Box (Photograph: Ekaterina Sheath).

From this project, Ekaterina developed a style of 'boxing off' individual illustrations, allowing her to alter scale and detail within one composition. Practically, she worked outside in new physical and social surroundings, gaining a new perspective on creative placemaking and producing art for a specific public location. Importantly, the accessibility of the art (physically and digitally) enabled further opportunities.

> These basically kickstarted everything that I am now.

As a result of successive projects, Ekaterina was shortlisted for the World Illustration Awards 2021, which involves showcasing her work on a global platform.

> [...] the reason why I reapply is marketing strategy rather than anything else ... you are on a platform that people respect and look for.

(She reapplied and was shortlisted for the 2022 Awards.)

Project 2: 52 Window Installations

We visit a small town within the city region. The scale of this project is a significant departure from painting media boxes, but people who viewed the murals encouraged her to respond to this commission for a once thriving – but now vacant – property. Ekaterina would need to produce images for all 52 former windows, a daunting proposition as she was still completing her degree. Her tutors encouraged her to undertake the work and integrate the learning into her studies. The challenge was to create a concept and make it happen.

She would need to produce digital illustrations, which could then be printed onto metal panels. Although unfamiliar with digital tools, using them would enable her designs to be scaled and printed at different sizes, without pixilation.

The building is located on a corner, with two facades on different streets. Going around the building, we view the illustrative story of a 'walk through time', created by Ekaterina. One side shows past uses of the building, such as theatre, cinema, bingo hall, and nightclub; the other depicts contemporary scenes. Ekaterina embarked on extensive research to inform the historical images, which combine visitors' personal memories with prominent personalities of the time. In the period leading up to the 1960s, the building was a centre for live performance and film (see Fig. 4.2).

Her design ideas were informed by a local archivist, their contacts, and outreach research conducted through Facebook (the best way to reach older generations). Referring to images in Fig 4.2:

> [...] so many people got back to me and one of them said that they had met their wife at the cinema and so there are two hands starting to inch together, then they are holding hands, and then at the end we imagine they are having a cheeky kiss.

Gathered stories are represented in the characters and objects, all fragments of different memories shared by the local community.

Fig. 4.2. 52 Window Installations (Photographs: Hove & Co https://hvcophotography.com/).

> [...] there were lots of snippets of what people told me ... tiny details ... tiny things that I really wanted to include but it didn't create a wider narrative.

In creative placemaking, the artist must determine how to portray the past and make it relevant and meaningful for the present in order to create positive connections with the local community (Matthews & Gadoloff, 2022). Ekaterina appreciates that the sources and artefacts she accesses can't give the full story; they may not be inclusive of everyone who used the building, or representative of who engages with the art today. She brings diversity into her designs through situated observation and continued learning.

> It is about context, your work is on the street, where communities are walking past every single day ....

As we turn the corner to look at the other façade, we consider how contemporary images bring vibrancy and imagination for the future. The art gives the building both a sense of history and, potentially, a new lease of life. Ekaterina reflects upon the artistic freedom she had in developing her illustrations; working digitally enhanced this creative process.

> [...] because it was done digitally and I was on my laptop, so I wasn't affected by the weather or being on location so I could spend so much time pouring detail into it.

She also acted as project manager, learning how to gain public liability insurance and liaise with suppliers to generate the final outputs. Throughout this process, she called on University tutors and a network of fellow artists for help. She was able to reconfigure resources and exercise her creativity as a result of this support. Much of her enjoyment came from connecting with the community to do the research, and in receiving their positive feedback.

Project 3: City Centre Vinyls

As lockdown restrictions were lifting, Ekaterina submitted a proposal to produce window vinyls for empty shops in the city centre. The rapid turnaround time, from proposal to completion, was aligned with the re-opening of non-essential retail. She won the commission for five properties (with sizable windows) and further commissions followed. Her characters are based on the people she saw whilst drawing on location (see Fig 4.3).

The images are diverse and detailed; the designs also reference the ornate city buildings to bring variety to the compositions.

> [...] some of them have the most incredible facades ... so I really wanted to include that because I think sometimes people get too caught up looking at the shop windows ....

Imminent deadlines meant that Ekaterina created digital images without clear window measurements; these could be adjusted later. Moreover, working digitally facilitated efficient workflow between printers and installers.

> I could never have taken on this Commission with such a short deadline if I hadn't developed those skills.

Out of the Studio and into the Street

Fig. 4.3. City Centre Vinyls (Photographs: Hove & Co https://hvcophotography.com/).

Reflecting on her successful commissions, Ekaterina notes that taking time to submit detailed visuals for her proposals, not just written statements, helps to communicate the vision. From her perspective, producing a detailed proposal generates design work that can be used in the commission (should she be successful); as well as enabling the client to understand her creative approach.

Interestingly, the success of Project 3 results in vacant properties being re-opened for commercial use; therefore her illustrations are temporary and will eventually be removed.

On reflection, this illustrator has engaged with – and emerged from – a series of art opportunities in the public realm and developed skills and a sense of purpose through the process.

DISCUSSION OF NECESSARY COMBINED CAPABILITIES

Street art opportunities arise from the interplay between context and capabilities. Specifically, the placemaking opportunities in this case are time-bound, at times temporary, and require a swift response. What does this case reveal about 'necessary combined capabilities' (Wilson & Martin, 2015) and the art entrepreneur's ability to pursue opportunities?

Applying each capability in turn:

The Possibility of Recombining Resources

During the pandemic, the art entrepreneur had the freedom to paint media boxes, although considerable learning was required. This was addressed through research, networking and practical advice, as well as taking action. In addition, the feedback from passers-by – and through social media – provided both inspiration and connection.

> [...] illustration is quite a solitary career you just work at home in your room ... whereas when you are out and about people will come at chat to you ... it was part of the reason why I chose mural painting.

These actions reflect Carey's view (2015) of the self-motivated art entrepreneur, adapting their specialism to a new context. There is technical support including advice from artists and tutors, but also practical support to assist working outside (Ekaterina had an assistant for the media box projects).

Over three projects, the entrepreneur gains skills and confidence, as well as an expanding support network. Projects 2 and 3 are designed on digital platforms but showcased out of the studio. Working digitally allows the artist to capture community research data and create more detailed designs.

The Possibility of Transaction (Creating Value)

For successful commissions, the artist must contribute to the placemaking agenda. In all projects, designs are informed by observation and community engagement, leading to new skills and expertise in placemaking processes (McKelvey & Lassen, 2018). Research skills involve observation as well as social media outreach and archival analysis. The artist's way of looking and researching is integral to what is being commissioned. Larger projects require the entrepreneur to work with multiple stakeholders: including printers, archivists, and governance groups. The skill of 'translation' must extend across a broader community to ensure inclusion and completion. Knowing how to get the job done and on time, is important.

Due to the time-bound nature of opportunities, her approach to creating detailed visuals in her proposals paid off and was suitable for ambitious deadlines, hastened by the end of COVID-19 restrictions.

The Possibility of Appropriating Value

Over time the scale of commissions and the impact of this artist has increased. The initial media boxes reflect 'affordable loss' (Read et al., 2016), which then leads to paid commissions. Street art is accessible, and its' display helps to market the artist both in terms of creative output, and how they contribute to placemaking. In addition, the art can be viewed 'in production', and via social media, and therefore promoted in different ways, by multiple stakeholders.

In this case, the street art provides the entrepreneurial means for self-marketing (Carey, 2015) and creating connections. The initial media boxes led to accolades and awards, which support finding and forming opportunities (Hechavarria & Welter, 2015). The artistic output also contributes academic 'value', as the art entrepreneur is supported to integrate her learning into the degree programme.

Reflecting on the context, the impact of COVID-19 in this city region instigated new placemaking opportunities (Comunian et al., 2010). The entrepreneur gains knowledge of commissions through connections, there is public money available, and an urgency to bring artistic output into public spaces, to which the entrepreneur responds (Cnossen et al., 2019). The necessary capabilities are met but how is this art entrepreneur enabled to act? Wilson and Martin (2015) refer to necessary internal capabilities, questioning if opportunities are available for all?

REFLECTIONS OF ENTREPRENEURIAL INTERNAL CAPABILITIES

The following section draws upon a reflective statement, written by the entrepreneur after reading the case study. Their reflections show how internal capabilities (adapted from Wilson & Martin, 2015) of: 'intent'; 'taking action', and 'learning' are needed to engage with opportunities.

Intent – Exploring Opportunities

This entrepreneur can see and intends to explore opportunities that arise during COVID-19. They were inspired to respond to a community placemaking project.

> [...] the pandemic had an interesting effect on how people now view our local areas. Suddenly confined to the places we live, unable to commute or travel, we looked around and were inspired by what we could change.

Operating commercially - and for social impact - requires the motivation to develop new skills. The ability to translate ideas and the interests of different stakeholders plays a key role (Bobadilla et al., 2019). Moreover, the entrepreneur must engage with new language to situate themselves in this context.

> [...] I began to collect terms that resonated with me; public realm, community, representation, situational illustration, heritage, contemporary illustration, street art. Each project began to piece together the creative I am.

Adopting this language enables the entrepreneur to communicate what they do and who they are as a creative, as well as help build relationships with others.

Taking Action – Engaging with the Opportunities

Technical and entrepreneurial skills are gained through action, and a support network is integral to this process.

> Through the support of my tutors, contacting professionals and the Careers Department I was able to manoeuvre my way through large commissions ....

The research process is critical to the development of the art entrepreneur's creative approach. Their values and desire for positive social impact are reflected in the research approach and designs.

> Representation sits at the heart of my work. Seeking ways to celebrate diversity and equality of ethnicities, religion, ability, gender and sexuality in a culturally aware and sensitive way. Research and on-location drawing are core to my process and continued learning.

Learning – Emerging from Opportunities

Situated in a new context, the entrepreneur is challenged and motivated to learn and develop the requisite skills (Carey, 2015).

> University gives you the luxury of making mistakes, overthinking, experimenting, and the freedom to fall back on your original goal. On a live brief, however, you were hired on set visuals for a specific job and you need to complete a certain number of outcomes to a strict deadline. This was a shock to the system.

The entrepreneur associates taking opportunities with creative placemaking and situating their practice. There is a sense of finding oneself through opportunities; undertaking learning informs and develops this new identity.

> These commissions allowed me to find the sector I want to dedicate my practice to, space to develop a process, and have helped me establish an in-depth knowledge of relevant business skills. They were my way of finding out what my practice meant to me and where I wanted to see my work. ... Through taking opportunities that were unknown and new I was able to find a way of working that I never knew was available to illustrators.

This entrepreneur's experiences have led to reflexivity and a contextualised understanding of what they do. They have extended their specialist creative skills, working physically and digitally in public spaces to create cultural assets.

Interestingly, street art situates the public as an audience, they too experience opportunities for connection and contribution through placemaking (Hill et al., 2021).

> Public art ... breaks the mould of presenting culture inside four walls and brings artwork to the streets. Allowing people who would never necessarily consider themselves artists, or even enjoy art, to engage with it.

CONCLUSION

This case study has given a detailed account of how an entrepreneur engages with street art opportunities. 'Necessary combined capabilities' (Wilson & Martin, 2015) allude to the complex and conducive relationship between context and internal capabilities discussed in this case. In addition, it shows that skills and identity can also develop through opportunities. The art entrepreneur creates the potential for future action by taking initial 'low risk' opportunities. Their development, from action, has resulted in self-marketing, increased entrepreneurial means, and enhanced specialist skills.

The case also reveals how COVID-19 has created new placemaking opportunities. Mural artists 'put themselves out there' and in this case, each project has led to recognition and stakeholder commitments for further opportunities. Perhaps counter to other industries, COVID-19 has created new street art possibilities outside of city centres, in both suburban and town locations. Equally, it can be seen as a time during which the art entrepreneur is free to act; she is both self-motivated and supported to engage with opportunities (Wilson & Martin, 2015). However, it should be questioned as to whether all degree students can take this path?

Can art degree programmes support students to take freelance opportunities and integrate the learning into their studies? What opportunities exist post COVID-19? There are notable benefits; producing street art can provide artists with exposure, feedback, and the means to build a network, quickly (in this case, within a year). For this entrepreneur, being an illustrator is redefined through placemaking opportunities as business skills and artistic specialisms are developed.

To conclude, external and internal capabilities are dynamic and intertwined in complex ways (Wilson & Martin, 2015). This study proposes a further outcome, that identity is changed through taking opportunities in a new context. In this story, moving from the studio and engaging in public art projects introduces a new network, a new artistic identity, and the potential to grow the local creative community.

LIMITATIONS AND FUTURE RESEARCH

There is more to say about collaboration and the relationship between art entrepreneurs and stakeholders (including digital connections) in the context of placemaking during COVID-19. Furthermore, while art entrepreneurship contributes to placemaking, can the street art commissions and opportunities help to grow the local creative community (Comunian et al., 2010)? Finally, more comparative studies of new graduates undertaking street art, in alternative locations, can give insight into how necessary combined capabilities may vary, with implications for how degree programmes support nascent art entrepreneurs to take placemaking opportunities.

REFERENCES

Banerjee, D., & Rai, M. (2020). Social isolation in Covid-19: The impact of loneliness. *International Journal of Social Psychiatry*, 66(6), 525–527.

Bobadilla, N., Goransson, M., & Pichault, F. (2019). Urban entrepreneurship through art-based intervention: Unveiling a translation process. *Entrepreneurship & Regional Development*, 31(5/6), 378–399.

Callander, A., & Cummings, M. E. (2021). Liminal spaces: A review of the art in entrepreneurship and the entrepreneurship in art. *Small Business Economics*, 57, 739–754.

Carey, C. (2015). The careers of fine artists and the embedded creative. *Journal of Education and Work*, 28(4), 407–421.

Cnossen, B., Loots, E., & van Witteloostuijn, A. (2019). Individual motivation among entrepreneurs in the creative and cultural industries: A self-determination perspective. *Creativity and Innovation Management*, 28(3), 389–402.

Comunian, R., Chapain, C., & Clifton, N. (2010). Location, location, location: Exploring the complex relationship between creative industries and place. *Creative Industries Journal*, 3(1), 5–10.

Cumming-Potvin, W. (2013). "New basics" and literacies: Deepening reflexivity in qualitative research. *Qualitative Research Journal*, 13(2), 214–230.

Dimov, D. (2011). Grappling with the unbearable elusiveness of entrepreneurial opportunities. *Entrepreneurship Theory and Practice*, 35(1), 57–81.

Fuentes, E. (2018). The abstraction of content and intent between murals and street art. *Visual Inquiry: Learning and Teaching Art*, 7(1), 9–17.

Hechavarria, D. M., & Welter, C. (2015). Opportunity types, social entrepreneurship and innovation: Evidence from the panel study of entrepreneurial dynamics. *International Journal of Entrepreneurship and Innovation*, 16(4), 237–252.

Henry, C., & Foss, L. (2015). Case sensitive? A review of the literature on the use of case method in entrepreneurship research. *International Journal of Entrepreneurial Behavior & Research, 21*(3), 389–409.

Hill, I., Manning, L., & Frost, R. (2021). Rural arts entrepreneurs' placemaking – how 'entrepreneurial placemaking' explains rural creative hub evolution during COVID-19 lockdown. *Local Economy, 36*(7–8), 627–649.

Jones, P., Bunce, G., Evans, J., Gibbs, H., & Hein, J. R. (2008). Exploring space and place with walking interviews. *Journal of Research Practice, 4*(2), D2.

Matthews, T., & Gadaloff, S. (2022). Public art for placemaking and urban renewal: Insights from three regional Australian cities. *Cities, 127*, 1–14.

Mauthner, N. S., & Doucet, A. (2003). Reflexive accounts and accounts of reflexivity in qualitative data analysis. *Sociology, 37*(3), 413–431.

McElvey, M., & Lassen, A. H. (2018). Knowledge, meaning and identity: Key characteristics of entrepreneurship in cultural and creative industries. *Creative Innovation Management, 27*, 281–283.

Read, S., Sarasvathy, S., Dew, N., & Whitlock, R. (2016). Effectual entrepreneurship.Taylor & Francis Group. https://ebookcentral.proquest.com/lib/HUD/detail.action?docID=4694360

Sheath, E. (2022, July 18). https://ekaterinasheath.com/

Wilson, N., & Martin, L. (2015). Entrepreneurial opportunities for all? Entrepreneurial capability and capabilities approach. *International Journal of Entrepreneurship and Innovation, 16*(3), 159–169.

Wright, A., Marsh, D., & McArdle, L. (2019, April 10–12). A darker side of creative entrepreneurship. *The Design Journal, 22*(sup1), 177–188.

Wünderlich, F. M. (2008). Walking and rhythmicity: Sensing urban space. *Journal of Urban Design, 13*(1), 125–139.

Yin, R. (2008). *Case study research: Design and methods*. Sage Publications.

ECONOMIC PERSPECTIVES ON CCI ENTREPRENEURSHIP

CHAPTER 5

ESSENTIAL PUZZLE PIECE FOR CCI ENTREPRENEURSHIP: CCI MANAGERS' MENTAL MODELS CONCERNING COLLABORATIVE PROCESSES WITH NONCCI

Kristiina Urb

Estonian Business School, Estonia

ABSTRACT

Creative industry entrepreneurs successfully exploiting the identified new business opportunities depends on creative and cultural industry (CCI) managers and their collaboration with other sectors (nonCCI). The chapter offers a contribution to the creative industry entrepreneurs' collaboration literature. It strives to understand and exhibit potential themes underlying cognitive mental models of CCI managers concerning collaboration processes with nonCCI. This novel knowledge may be an enabler for smoother and more effective collaboration processes between CCI and nonCCI organisations. The chapter employs an explorative abductive approach with interviews as the primary research method and uses an interpretative phenomenological analysis (IPA). Based on the findings, the chapter proposes a concept map illustrating potential themes of CCI managers' mental models for collaborations.

Keywords: Collaboration; cognitive enablers; mental models; interpretative phenomenological analysis; creative and cultural firms

1. INTRODUCTION

Cultural and creative industry (CCI) entrepreneurs depend upon managers who help turn entrepreneurs' visions into realities and successfully exploit the identified new business opportunities (Bilton, 2007). However, the literature shows that some of the main challenges and skills gaps in CCI enterprises are related to strategic management (Sassi et al., 2020). Furthermore, there is a gap in the literature regarding managerial performance in CCI enterprises (Hadida, 2015).

The chapter distinguishes between CCI managers and nonCCI managers, that is, the term 'CCI managers' stands for managers of companies within cultural and creative industries and 'nonCCI managers' stands for managers of companies within other industries outside of CCI.

Collaborating with other sectors (nonCCI) is beneficial to overcome challenges and skills gaps in CCI enterprises, as CCI needs a mix of a highly skilled workforce, new ideas, and technological and creative innovation to thrive (Siepel et al., 2016). Creative enterprises that combine arts and science skills outperform those that utilise only art skills or science skills; the broader the set of skills a creative enterprise uses, the higher its level of innovative performance and future growth (Siepel et al., 2016). The author of the chapter has been active in the cultural and creative industries field for over fourteen years in different entrepreneurial, managerial, consulting, and expert roles. However, her experience shows that the collaboration between cultural and creative industries (CCI) and other sectors (nonCCI) is often not as fluent as it could be.

Therefore, the author focuses on researching the phenomenon of collaboration between CCI and nonCCI and aims to find potential enablers for smoother and more effective collaboration processes that enhance creative entrepreneurship. The chapter strives to understand and exhibit potential themes of underlying cognitive mental models CCI managers may have concerning collaboration processes with nonCCI. Thus, the chapter contributes to creative industry entrepreneurs' collaboration literature and participates in the empirical discussion about CCI. The research question that guides the study of the phenomenon is 'how do CCI managers make sense of their collaboration experiences with nonCCI?'

The chapter uses an explorative abductive approach to answer the research question. It takes the reader through the journey of studying this important but poorly understood phenomenon, cycling between the empirical findings and literature.

The chapter is positioned in cognitive science and uses constructivism as the underlying philosophy. The governing understanding of the chapter is that the organisational world is socially constructed and that the people constructing their organisational realities are 'knowledgeable agents' (see, e.g. Gioia et al., 2013).

The chapter is divided into six parts. After the introduction, the second part creates context and theoretical framing for the research topic. The third part explains the research methods. The fourth part presents the findings of the empirical analysis, followed by the fifth part, which discusses the research findings and the chapter's contribution. The last part discusses concluding remarks related to the research question.

2. CONTEXT AND THEORETICAL FRAMING

Entrepreneurs can identify new business opportunities but are not always excellent at developing and exploiting them; thus, they depend upon networks, relationships, and supporting teams who help turn entrepreneur visions into realities (Bilton, 2007). Therefore, a crucial part of the creative industries entrepreneurship is managers of CCI companies, plus relationships and strategic collaborations (Bengtsson & Kock, 2000). Firms are simultaneously involved in several different relationships, horizontal and vertical, to defend their position in the business network and collaborate to utilise the company's limited resources in the most efficient way (Bengtsson & Kock, 2000). Only if social relations are managed carefully can the benefits of collaborative working (e.g., cost savings and efficiency) happen (Hill, 2021).

One of the distinctive characteristics of creative industries entrepreneurship is that the creative industries sector comprises a large number of small enterprises and a small number of large enterprises (Küttim et al., 2011). According to the 'Market analysis of the cultural and creative sectors in Europe' by the EIF (2019), there are 2.7 employees per company in the CCI. Thus, in a CCI enterprise, the entrepreneur who uses the scarce resources of individual creativity, skills, and talent to develop and produce goods and services is also in the manager's role.

The chapter contributes to the collaboration of creative industry entrepreneurs' literature as it strives to understand and exhibit potential themes of underlying cognitive mental models CCI managers may have concerning collaboration processes with nonCCI.

According to EIF (2019), most companies within the CCI are SMEs and, on average, employ 2.7 employees per company in Europe. CCI managers often come from art colleges; therefore, the managers within CCI are considered the ones who use the scarce resources of individual creativity, skills, and talent to develop and produce goods and services (Chaston & Sadler-Smith, 2012; Urb, 2019).

2.1. CCI Collaboration with nonCCI

The CCI enterprise stimulates to combination of different resources of technology, arts, business, and culture but is not as monolithic as capacity-oriented industries (e.g. manufacturing) and has a multitude of dimensions as it creates social, cultural, and sustainable development value in addition to economic value (Masalin, 2012; UNCTAD, 2010). Studies show that the CCI has a substantial impact beyond its sector and contributes to numerous nonCCI sectors with its impact on places, society and the economy through the overflow of concepts, ideas, skills, knowledge and different types of capital (Bakhshi et al. 2008; Fleming, 2015; Potts & Cunningham, 2008).

It is essential that CCI managers collaborate with other industries outside of the creative domain, i.e. nonCCI, and overcome the possible communication gap between the CCI and nonCCI companies (Urb, 2019). The collaboration between CCI and nonCCI is necessary for (1) tapping into the potential of the CCI and fostering purposeful growth in society and economy stemming from that, and (2) continuous development within the CCI (Fleming, 2015; Hill et al., 2021).

2.2. The Role of Mental Models

Mental models are personal, internal representations of external reality that people use to interact with the world around them (Jones et al., 2011). These mental templates consist of organised knowledge about an information environment that enables interpretation and action in that environment (Huff, 2005; Walsh, 1995). The psychologist Kenneth Craik (1943) originally introduced the notion of a mental model. Nowadays, it is a widely accepted construct in the social science literature that mental models are used to reason and make decisions and can be the basis of individual behaviours (Jones et al., 2011). In order to successfully achieve objectives, managers must possess sufficient knowledge of their immediate environment in order to compose suitable and fitting responses to a given decision context and in such situations, mental models provide the structures that form the basis of reasoning and decision-making (Gray et al., 2014; Jones et al., 2011; Moore & Golledge, 1976).

In decision-making contexts, the perceived usefulness of internal mental models lies in their simplicity as well as parsimony that allows complex phenomena (e.g. collaboration) to be 'interrogated' and select 'salient components' to form judgments (Gray et al., 2014). The generation of workable explanations of the collaboration processes is facilitated by inferring causal relationships between various factors based on available evidence or beliefs (Gray et al., 2014).

CCI and nonCCI managers employ mental models to mitigate the challenges of an information-rich world to reason and make decisions and can be the basis of individual behaviours (Jones et al., 2011). They are constructed by managers themselves based on their unique life experiences, perceptions, and understandings of the world (Jones et al., 2011). Therefore, mental models may influence CCI and nonCCI managers' decisions and behaviour when it comes to collaboration with each other. Thus, it is fundamental to understand more about the potential themes of underlying cognitive mental models of CCI managers concerning collaboration processes with nonCCI. Understanding themes of CCI managers' cognitive mental models may serve as enablers for smoother and more effective collaboration processes.

3. METHODS

3.1. Research Design and Strategy

To answer the research question of 'how do CCI managers make sense of their collaboration experiences with nonCCI', the chapter employs an explorative abductive approach as the research question emerges from the author's real-life observation of empirical phenomena. The abductive approach studies this essential but poorly understood phenomenon by cycling between the empirical findings and literature (Timmermans & Tavory, 2012).

The author has been involved within the CCI for over fifteen years in different managerial, consulting, and expert roles that provided unique insight and the possibility to observe the phenomenon first-hand. Anecdotal evidence referred to the inferior quality of collaboration between CCI and nonCCI and the potential role of underlying cognitive mental models. The author's observations from the field led to researching literature about mental models and preparing and conducting semi-structured interviews with CCI managers to elicit mental models related to collaboration with nonCCI. In addition, the author conducted structured interviews with CCI experts to understand more about the collaboration between CCI and nonCCI. The final step was conducting an interpretative phenomenological analysis (IPA) of interviews (Smith et al., 2012).

3.2. Data Collection

The unit of analysis is the collaboration behaviours of individuals. Therefore, data samples for this chapter are from established CCI experts known to the author in Europe (UK, Brussels, Estonia; n=6) and the CCI companies managers suggested by the experts: First in the United Kingdom (n=5) and then in the United States (n=6) for triangulation. The author made contact originally via email and later met in person. The United Kingdom was chosen because of its well-developed cultural and creative industries sector. Many countries (e.g., Estonia) base their definition of CCI on the one proposed by the United Kingdom.

The chapter uses theoretical sampling developed by Glaser and Strauss (Flick, 2014), whereby the author jointly collects and analyses the data and decides what data to collect next and where to find it (Glaser & Strauss, 1967, p. 45). The first interviews with CCI managers were held in Liverpool, UK, and following their recommendations the author decided to conduct the next round of interviews in the United States (New York and San Francisco). In both cases, the author used purposive sampling and aimed to select particularly typical cases.

Guiding interview questions for in-depth semi-structured interviews with managers from CCI companies were designed to elicit mental models about collaboration with nonCCI (Fig. 5.1). Structured interviews with CCI experts aimed to generate more profound knowledge regarding collaboration between CCI and nonCCI.

3.3. Data Analysis

Mental models exist within the minds of CCI managers and are, therefore, not available for direct inspection or measurement (Jones et al., 2011). The chapter uses an IPA to get a deeper insight into how CCI managers make sense of their collaboration experiences with nonCCI. IPA allows to open up the phenomena more in-depth and assures rigour in qualitative research by applying an inductive concept development methodology (see Smith et al., 2012; Gioia et al., 2013). The author used Atlas.ti programme for data analysis as it is based on the approach of grounded theory and coding and can process not only texts but also images, graphics, and sounds (Smith et al., 2012).

The IPA was chosen because it allows focusing on people's experiences and understandings of particular phenomena as well as the perceptions and views of participants (Smith et al., 2012). Studies using the IPA approach regularly have a small number of participants, and the aim is to reveal something about the experience of each of those individuals (Smith et al., 2012).

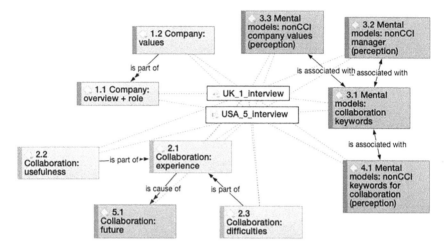

Fig. 5.1. Topics Covered during the Semi-Structured In-Depth Interviews (Illustrated by Two Interviews from the United Kingdom and USA). *Source*: Created by the Author in Atlas.ti.

To understand potential themes of underlying cognitive mental models CCI managers may have concerning collaboration processes with nonCCI, the author considered various passages when analysing interviews with CCI managers that can be seen in Fig. 5.2.

When going through the **IPA** data analysis process, the following steps were taken: (1) author immersing herself in the original data and (2) creating notes, for example, exploratory comments, (3) analysing exploratory comments to identify

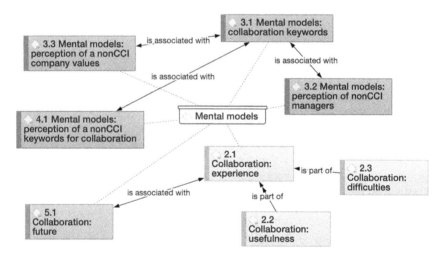

Fig. 5.2. Concept map showing the Passages Considered in Analysing CCI Managers' Interviews. *Source*: Created by the Author in Atlas.ti Program.

Essential Puzzle Piece for CCI Entrepreneurship

emergent themes, and finally, (4) searching for connections across emergent themes and creating super-ordinate themes, and (5) looking for patterns across cases, for example, higher order concepts (Smith et al., 2012).

Following the analytic process of IPA with the CCI managers interviews, the author (1) created exploratory comments for the interviews with CCI managers in the United Kingdom, (2) developed emergent themes and, based on them, super-ordinate themes, and (3) looked for patterns and created higher order concepts (Table 5.1). For triangulation, the author then analysed interviews with CCI managers from the United States to understand and compare the level of developed higher-order concepts.

4. FINDINGS

4.1. Collaboration between CCI and nonCCI

Findings from structured interviews with CCI experts show there are benefits for CCI and nonCCI to collaborate. CCI experts pointed out that the potential benefits for CCI companies from collaboration with nonCCI companies could be related to growth, innovation, sustainability, visibility and reach, and acquisition of skills and knowledge.

> One important aspect of involving new and vivid ideas is to avoid patterns that are based on routine or long-term habits. CCI business models demand constant discussions about various possibilities followed by design-thinking-based action plans. That kind of experience assists companies to raise questions from a new angle and keep the discussions open for new ideas and possible innovations. – Expert 3

Nevertheless, these findings from interviews with CCI experts also show that on a day-to-day basis, the collaboration quality between the CCI and nonCCI is not at the level it could be. When describing the quality of collaboration between CCI and nonCCI companies (1=a collaboration between the two is very challenging, 10=collaboration is very smooth), the average was 4.17. The obstacles to a smoother collaboration between CCI and nonCCI were, for example, the 'capacity to understand each other vocabulary and objectives;' 'lack of preparation for and experience in this kind of collaboration'; 'CCIs are sometimes less structured, and their working methods might not match the internal procedures of other companies'; 'different sectors have a different vocabulary, etiquette, communication styles and assumptions about the meaning of "success"'. When asked what may cause these obstacles, the experts largely agreed it might be due to the following.

> The lack of collaborative cross-disciplinary programs in universities. Lack of general awareness about the working methods of different sectors. Stereotypes about creative people and creative processes. Lack of trust between creative sectors and other sectors. – Expert 7

CCI experts proposed the following possible solutions to overcome obstacles in collaboration between CCI and nonCCI.

> More collaborative cross-disciplinary programs in universities. Teaching creative more entrepreneurial and project management skills and teaching other sectors how to work with creative

Table 5.1. Examples of Exploratory Comments, Relevant Emergent Themes, Super-Ordinate Themes, and Higher Order Concepts from Interviews with CCI Managers. *Source:* Created by the Author.

Examples of exploratory comments by the author	Relevant emergent themes	Super-ordinate themes	Higher order concepts
CCI calls themselves problem solvers. *Embracing mistakes and learning from them is crucial.* *They feel like they are doing the right thing.*	– CCI as a problem solver – embracing learning from mistakes – CCI helping to validate nonCCI	The aspect of higher purpose	Focus on intangible
Giving a seemingly independent voice to nonCCI. *It feels like doing something positive.* *More about the actual values and culture than what is written on the paper.* *Creating the best possible future.*	– liberating nonCCI – enabling nonCCI – actualisation of real values – actualisation of positive values	Actualising elevated values	
Ideal collaboration is symbiotic. *The need for effective communication with the right tools.* *Deconstructing and analysing what is said.* *Good management of communication is essential.* *New project management methods (lean, scrum) - easier and better to collaborate for CCI.* *CCI must fit into the nonCCI project management style: choosing whom they work with.*	– symbiotic collaboration – effective communication tools – communication management + Pareto principle – alignment between CCI and nonCCI project management important	Symbiotic and efficient communication and management	Focus on process
Differentiated: critical that everyone has clear roles. *Needs to be clear-cut and defined: clear boundaries.* *CCI saw collaboration much more as a partnership than nonCCI.* *Taking more significant projects into smaller pieces is suitable for CCI SMEs (agile approach).*	– a clear division of roles – defined boundaries for collaboration – agile partnership	Defined roles and agile partnership	

Essential Puzzle Piece for CCI Entrepreneurship

Different capabilities. *At times, excellent relationship, but it varies greatly.* *Appreciating the sense of community; celebrating the diversity versus being only about getting the best results.* *Is nonCCI actually ready for what they are asking for?*	– variations in relationships – differences in capabilities – differences in expectations	Possibility for fluctuations and misalignment
Possible differences in business culture, understanding it is essential. *Different cultures in companies.*	– misunderstandings in business culture – differences in organisational culture	An array of organisational cultures
NonCCI is more about 'ticking the boxes' *NonCCI envies CCI operational speed (SME).*	– slow versus fast organisations – the level of organisational flexibility	Variations in operational speed and flexibility
NonCCI organisations can have difficult gatekeepers. *NonCCI can have institutional restrictions that halt the collaboration.* *All about people, and people vary.*	– institutional restrictions overcoming the gatekeeper	Possibility of institutional obstacles
People working in nonCCI from whom CCI can learn. *Passing on knowledge to relevant parties.* *The sense of achievement.* *NonCCI is keen to embrace the project.* *Important to disseminate the lessons learned/information gained by older companies to startups.*	– opportunities for learning from nonCCI – networking – the organisational growth – knowledge sharing	Cross-sectorial capacity building and growth
Place marketing, the sense of place. *Reaching a wider audience.* *Collaborations are diverse.*	– community building – reaching a diverse audience	Getting a broader reach in society

Focus on organisation

Focus on self

teams. Using mediators (consultants, coaching, mentors, development centres) to bring together creatives and other sectors. ... Working in cross-disciplinary hubs and clusters would bring together CCIs and companies from other sectors. – Expert 7

Findings from CCI expert interviews show that CCI and nonCCI managers are perceived to be associates of two distinct groups who could benefit from collaboration. Nevertheless, the quality of their collaboration should be better. Thus, we need to understand better CCI managers' potential themes of underlying cognitive mental models as this knowledge may serve as an enabler contributing to their collaboration processes.

4.2. Potential Themes of Underlying Cognitive Mental Models

Findings from interviews with CCI managers reveal four primary focuses that cluster potential themes of underlying cognitive mental models of CCI managers related to collaboration with nonCCI. They can be seen in Table 5.2 together with related super-ordinate themes.

Based on the findings from the IPA of CCI managers interviews, the author created a concept map of potential themes of underlying cognitive mental models of CCI managers related to collaboration with nonCCI consisting of higher-order concepts, super-ordinate themes, and relevant emergent themes (Fig. 5.3).

A systematic approach to triangulation in social research recommends studying phenomena on different dates and places and from different persons (Flick, 2014). Therefore, the author relied on a triangulation of data from multiple sources and analysed findings accordingly. The findings are in Table 5.3 and show how dominant super-ordinate themes in different sources were[1].

5. DISCUSSION AND CONTRIBUTION

As discussed in the theoretical framing, a crucial part of the creative industries are managers of CCI enterprises who help turn entrepreneurs' visions into realities (Bilton, 2007). Also, to overcome challenges and skills gaps in CCI enterprises,

Table 5.2. Master Table of Themes for the CCI Managers.
Source: Created by the Author.

Focus on the intangible	– The aspect of higher purpose
	– Actualising elevated values
Focus on business processes	– Symbiotic and efficient communication and management
	– Defined roles and agile partnership
	– Possibility for fluctuations and misalignment
Focus on an organisation	– An array of organisation cultures
	– Variations in operational speed and flexibility
	– Possibility of institutional obstacles
Focus on self	– Cross-sectorial capacity building and growth
	– Getting a broader reach in society

Essential Puzzle Piece for CCI Entrepreneurship

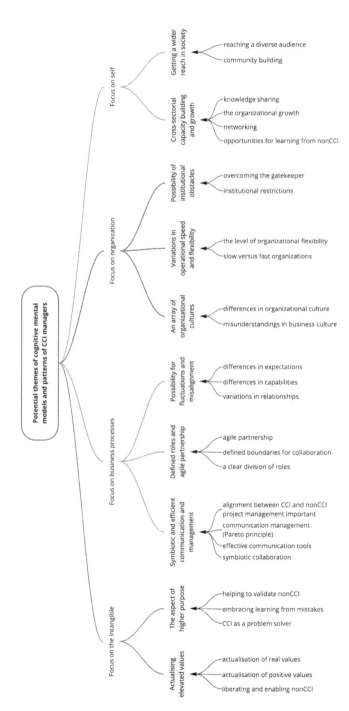

Fig. 5.3. Concept Map for Potential Themes of Underlying Cognitive Mental Models of CCI Managers Concerning Collaboration with nonCCI. *Source:* Created by the Author in Miro.

Table 5.3. Findings from Triangulation. *Source:* Created by the Author.

Super-ordinate themes	Data sources				
	Interviews			CCI experts	Observation
	Liverpool, UK	*New York, USA* (CCI managers)	*San Francisco, USA*		
The aspect of higher purpose	Strong evidence	Strong evidence	Strong evidence	Moderate evidence	Moderate evidence
Actualising elevated values	Strong evidence	Sporadic evidence	Moderate evidence	Moderate evidence	Moderate evidence
Symbiotic and efficient communication and management	Strong evidence	Strong evidence	Strong evidence	Strong evidence	
Defined roles and agile partnership	Strong evidence	Moderate evidence	Strong evidence	Sporadic evidence	Moderate evidence
Possibility for fluctuations and misalignment	Strong evidence	Moderate evidence	Strong evidence	Strong evidence	
An array of organisation cultures	Strong evidence	Moderate evidence	Moderate evidence	Sporadic evidence	Strong evidence
Variations in operational speed and flexibility	Strong evidence	Sporadic evidence	Moderate evidence	Sporadic evidence	
Possibility of institutional obstacles	Strong evidence	Strong evidence	Strong evidence	Moderate evidence	
Cross-sectorial capacity building and growth	Strong evidence	Moderate evidence	Moderate evidence	Strong evidence	Strong evidence
Getting a broader reach in society	Strong evidence	Moderate evidence	Moderate evidence	Moderate evidence	

it is beneficial for CCI managers to collaborate with nonCCI, as CCI enterprises that combine arts and science skills outperform those that utilise only art or science skills (Siepel et al., 2016). Thus, it is essential for creative industries entrepreneurship that CCI and nonCCI managers collaborate and fundamental for the entrepreneurship literature to understand more about the potential themes of underlying cognitive mental models of CCI managers concerning collaboration processes with nonCCI.

The concept map proposed by the chapter may enable more effective collaboration processes between CCI and nonCCI and enhance creative entrepreneurship – it may serve nonCCI managers as a guiding tool when collaborating with CCI managers. Novel knowledge about CCI managers' potential mental models that may guide their actions gives way to understanding how they work and their decisions during collaborations.

Thus, the chapter contributes to the creative industry entrepreneurs' collaboration literature by detecting potential themes of underlying cognitive mental models of CCI managers concerning collaboration processes between CCI and nonCCI. Based on their focus, the potential themes of the named underlying mental models can be clustered into (1) focus on the intangible, (2) focus on business processes, (3) focus on an organisation, and (4) focus on self. However, it is essential to note that concept maps are often used as external representations of internal mental models; these graphical representations and mental models are not the same (Gray et al., 2014).

6. CONCLUSIONS

In conclusion, for successfully exploiting the identified new business opportunities, creative industry entrepreneurs depend upon CCI managers and their collaboration with nonCCI; thus, the chapter draws attention to the role of cognitive mental models CCI managers have concerning collaboration with nonCCI and proposes a concept map illustrating potential themes of CCI managers' mental models in this context. The chapter's findings also provide valuable insight for creative business incubators and other CCI business support organisations supporting creative entrepreneurs collaborating with other industries (nonCCI).

However, caution must be applied with a small sample size pertinent to the IPA. The findings cannot describe underlying cognitive mental models for all CCI managers nor depict them exhaustively.

This research has thrown up many interesting questions in need of further investigation. For example, how the use of new knowledge on CCI managers' mental models ensures more successful collaborative ventures between the two groups in practice. A natural progression of this work is to analyse research findings in more depth in different settings and further elaborate on CCI managers' mental models.

NOTE

1. Strong evidence=dominant theme in the source; Moderate evidence=frequent but the not constant theme in the source; Sporadic evidence=theme appearing occasionally in the source. The empty cell indicates no evidence for theme in the source.

REFERENCES

Bakhshi, H., McVittie, E., & Simmie, J. (2008). Creating innovation: Do the creative industries support innovation in the wider economy? NESTA.

Bengtsson, M., & Kock, S. (2000). Coopetition' in business networks – to cooperate and compete simultaneously. *Industrial Marketing Management*, 29(5), 411–426.

Bilton, C. (2007). Management and creativity: From creative industries to creative management. Wiley-Blackwell.

Chaston, I., & Sadler-Smith, E. (2012). Entrepreneurial cognition, entrepreneurial orientation and firm capability in the creative industries. *British Journal of Management*, 23, 415–432.

Craik, K. J. W. (1943). *The nature of explanation*. Cambridge University Press.

EIF. (2019). *Market analysis of the cultural and creative sectors in Europe*. European Investment Fund. https://www.eif.org/what_we_do/guarantees/cultural_creative_sectors_guarantee_facility/ccs-market-analysis-europe.pdf

Fleming, T. (2015). *Cultural and creative spillovers in Europe: Report on a preliminary evidence review*. Arts Council England.https://www.artscouncil.org.uk/sites/default/files/Cultural_creative_spillovers_in_Europe_full_report.pdf

Flick, U. (2014). An introduction to qualitative research. SAGE Publications.

Glaser, B. G., & Strauss, A. L. (1967). *The discovery of grounded theory: Strategies for qualitative research*. Aldine.

Gray, S. A., Zanre, E., & Gray, S. R. (2014). Fuzzy cognitive maps as representations of mental models and group beliefs. In E. Papageorgiou (Ed.), *Fuzzy cognitive maps for applied sciences and engineering* (pp. 29–48). Springer.

Gioia, D. A., Corley, K. G., & Hamilton, A. L. (2013). Seeking qualitative rigor in inductive research: Notes on the Gioia methodology. *Organizational Research Methods*, 16(1), 15–31.

Hadida, A. (2015). Performance in the creative industries. In C. Jones, M. Lorenzen, & J. Sapsed (Eds.), *The Oxford Handbook of Creative Industries* (pp. 219–250). Oxford University Press.

Hill, I. R. (2021). Spotlight on UK artisan entrepreneurs' situated collaborations: Through the lens of entrepreneurial capitals and their conversion. *International Journal of Entrepreneurial Behavior & Research*, 27(1), 99–121.

Hill, I., Manning, L., & Frost, R. (2021). Rural arts entrepreneurs' placemaking - how 'entrepreneurial placemaking' explains rural creative hub evolution during COVID-19 lockdown. *Local Economy*, 36(7–8), 627–649.

Huff, A. S. (2005). Managerial and organizational cognition islands of coherence. In K. G. Smith, & M. A. Hitt (Eds.), *Great Minds in Management: The Process of Theory Development* (pp. 331–354). Oxford University Press.

Jones, N. A., Ross, H., Lynam, T., Perez, P., & Leitch, A. (2011). Mental models: An interdisciplinary synthesis of theory and methods. *Ecology and Society*, 16(1). [Online]. http://www.ecologyandsociety.org/vol16/iss1/art46/

Küttim, M., Arvola, K., & Venesaar, U. (2011). Development of creative entrepreneurship: Opinion of managers from Estonia, Latvia, Finland and Sweden. *Business: Theory and Practice*, 12(4), 369–378.

Masalin, H. (2012). *Mapping of Nordic creative and cultural industries financial environment*. Nordic Council of Ministers. https://norden.diva-portal.org/smash/get/diva2:843187/FULLTEXT01.pdf

Moore, G. T., & Golledge, R. G. (1976). Environmental knowing: Concepts and theories. In G. T. Moore, & R. G. Golledge (Eds.), *Environmental knowing: Theories, research and methods* (pp. 3–24). Dowden, Hutchinson & Ross, Inc.

Potts, J., & Cunningham, S. (2008). Four models of the creative industries. *International journal of cultural policy*, *14*(3), 233–247.

Sassi, M., Urb, K., & Pihlak, Ü. (2020). The evaluation of organisational performance: Estonian cultural and creative industries organisations. In M. Piber (Ed.), *Management, Participation and Entrepreneurship in the Cultural and Creative Sector* (pp. 189–218). Springer.

Smith, J., Flowers, P., & Larkin, M. (2012). Interpretative *phenomenological analysis: Theory, method and research*. SAGE Publications.

Siepel, J., Camerani, R., Pellegrino, G., & Masucci, M. (2016). The fusion effect: The economic returns to combining arts and science skills. A report for Nesta. Nesta.

Timmermans, S., & Tavory, I. (2012). Theory construction in qualitative research: From grounded theory to abductive analysis. *Sociological theory*, *30*(3), 167–186.

UNCTAD. (2010). *Creative economy report*. United Nations. https://unctad.org/system/files/official-document/ditctab20103_en.pdf

Urb, K. (2019). Creative entrepreneurs' perception of entrepreneurial motivation: A valuable insight for creative business incubators when supporting creative entrepreneurs' cooperation with other industries. *European Journal of Cultural Management and Policy*, *9*(2), 17–30.

Walsh, J. P. (1995). Managerial and organizational cognition: Notes from a trip down memory lane. *Organization Science*, *6*(3), 280–321.

CHAPTER 6

ENTREPRENEURIAL PERFORMANCE AND COMPETITION WITHIN THE CREATIVE AND CULTURAL INDUSTRIES: CHALLENGES FOR CULTURAL ENTREPRENEURS IN A DEVELOPING COUNTRY

Tafadzwa Masiye, Alison Lawson and Kuldeep Banwait

University of Derby, UK

ABSTRACT

This chapter investigates performance management and competition within the creative and cultural industries (CCI) in a developing country like Zimbabwe. The chapter is a critically reflective piece that aims to develop an in-depth understanding of the complexities of performance management and competition in CCI. Lived experiences reveal distinct differences in performance criteria between creatives from developed and developing countries. Zimbabwean creatives' perception of performance, its management and competition are influenced by economic pressures such as high unemployment, low demand for creative products, and oversupply due to high concentration of creative producers in the market. As a result, the application of performance criteria is dynamic and dependent on external pressures beyond the sector. The chapter makes recommendations for future studies in this area.

Keywords: Developing country; African entrepreneurship; performance measurement; cultural entrepreneurship; competition for CCIs

INTRODUCTION

Cultural industries in developing countries provide an outlet for creative expression of a people's culture and heritage as well as being a source of livelihood for the entrepreneurs who create cultural products for sale. Creative and Cultural Industries (CCI), especially in a developing country context include, but are not limited to, handicraft producers, sculptors, painters, singers, poets and rural hosts who create products and services representing local cultures. The creative sector in which we find cultural industries is largely informal which makes it difficult to identify performance and competition indicators, strategies, or targets being used by cultural entrepreneurs operating in the sector. The lack of formal structures in the sector is not uncommon in the CCI especially in developing countries like Zimbabwe (Woyo & Woyo, 2018).

This chapter refers to the authors' lived experiences to critically reflect on how performance is measured and the role of competition in performance strategy formulation by cultural entrepreneurs selling cultural and heritage products. The chapter will examine how cultural entrepreneurs address market conditions and how market conditions influence the relationship between performance and competition, using the results of a small study conducted in Harare, Zimbabwe. The study is designed to answer the following questions:

- Which performance criteria are used by cultural entrepreneurs to guide their day-to-day business?
- How are performance criteria selected, reviewed and at what intervals are they reviewed?
- What is the role of competition in the selection and reviewing of performance criteria for a cultural entrepreneur?

The study observed market dynamics of arts and handicrafts market clusters populated by authentic artisans (artists from families with generations of artisans and concerned with safeguarding their heritage producing artefacts of artistic merit) and entrepreneurial artisans (artisans who are drawn to the industry by its potential to earn a living by selling artistic products and who are not necessarily concerned with artistic merit) selling cultural products. These market clusters comprise a mix of 10–15 authentic artisans and entrepreneurial artisans selling largely homogenous products at similar price ranges. Each of these clusters is a competitive environment where all five of Porter's Five Forces of competition are present. There are high levels of competitive rivalry as characterised by being in a cluster of 10–15 artisans selling cultural products. The threat of substitutes is also high because the variety of cultural products being sold at the same market. Buyers have high bargaining power in this market due to the scarce demand for luxury products in the market. There is an ever-present threat of new entrants because there are little to no barriers to enter the market as a producer of cultural products or a trader. However, previous research (Ardielli, 2017; Chiaravalloti, 2014), suggests that performance in the arts should not just be limited to financial accounting and volume of sales because the cultural sector is a complex ecosystem where quantitative indicators of performance are not the only ones under consideration. The diverse nature of enterprises, institutions and individual operators (as investigated by this chapter) in the cultural sector dictates that to simply evaluate performance by measuring quantitative indicators would fail to produce a representative picture of how performance is perceived in the sector.

Understanding and Measuring Performance in CCI

Managing arts enterprises has evolved from applying mainstream and generic management practices to adopting management practices and strategies developed specifically for managing arts enterprises and artistic products (Chiaravalloti, 2014). Performance measurement as a function of arts management differs significantly from mainstream performance measurement and, especially the criteria or indicators that are measured when evaluating performance in creative enterprises (Turbide & Laurin, 2009). Finding consensus on measuring or evaluating performance in the CCI sector is problematic as every individual artist, creative, enterprise or institution will have unique performance indicators (Hadida, 2015), which hold different importance in different circumstances. For example, performance evaluation in museums could be concerned with repeat visitors whereas an entrepreneurial artist may be more concerned with the quantity of handicrafts they have created for sale in a month. Similarly, a fashion designer may be more concerned with public approval of their designs as much as a theatre company would also be concerned about critical acclaim of their performance. What these examples show is that profit, sales and return on investment are typically not as important performance indicators to the CCI sector as they are to mainstream business sectors (Sassi et al., 2020). Beyond the complexities of what constitutes a performance criterion within the cultural sector, there are also further complexities created by the vast number different types of creatives in the sector and the different types of products they create.

The challenge for performance management in CCI could be narrowed down to two tasks, firstly there is a need to define performance in the CCI entrepreneurship context in which performance is being measured. The second task would be to create a performance measuring framework with criteria that are relevant to the CCI entrepreneurship context. Different authors (Chiaravalloti, 2020; Hadida, 2015; Turbide & Laurin, 2009) have proposed that strategies for measuring performance must first understand the context in which performance is being measured. Labaronne (2017) believes that any definition of performance will vary between publicly funded creative or cultural organisations (CCO) or individuals and private enterprises or entrepreneurs. Indeed, the number of stakeholders with vested interests in public funded CCO or individuals have a bearing on how performance is defined and measured. Impact is often cited as an indicator of performance where organisations are publicly funded to create or produce artistic productions. Labaronne and Tröndle (2021) identified impact as a performance criterion in contexts where public funds are used to support artistic organisations in delivering transformative value in the community.

The complexity of external expectations is less prominent in the context of individual creative entrepreneurs. Critical acclaim, public approval, repeat demand, creative output, creative recognition and freedom are some of the performance criteria that apply to the context of private creative enterprises/ entrepreneurs (Hadida, 2015). However, Höllen et al. (2020) believe that whilst performance measuring for creative enterprises and individual creatives should not or may not mirror mainstream performance management approaches, there are business criteria to consider. Artisans or creatives may not be driven by profit or financial gain, but there is still need for them to strike a balance between the resources they invest into the creative process and the income they derive from the sale of their creative products (Werthes et al., 2017). Indeed, there are frictions between entrepreneurship and the creative process which challenge the application of performance measurement criteria such as trying to create a balance between maintaining creative identify and developing an entrepreneurial identity or brand.

Selecting Criteria for Measuring Performance In CCI

Hadida (2015) reviewed performance criteria across different sectors of the CCI and found that performance criteria can be grouped into the following categories, creative production process, commercial performance, artistic merit and societal impact:

Creative Production Process

Measuring performance in creative production processes allows individuals and organisations in the CCI to monitor and manage their production process from a resource perspective so as to ensure that all the required material inputs and skills, especially the creative contribution of the collective group and/or individuals in the organisation. The creative production process of an arts organisation may require performance reporting of stakeholders to unlock funding that sustain the organisation's creative production (Sassi et al., 2021). Individual creatives operating in the CCI may also be interested in measuring performance of their creative production process to monitor use of resources like time and material inputs to ensure that the production process is sustained (Lee et al., 2022). The consequences of mismanagement can include discontinuation of production with far reaching impact for arts organisations and the communities they serve as well as more immediate implications to the survival or livelihood for the individual creatives (Labaronne & Tröndle, 2021).

Commercial Performance

Whilst the tension between commercial performance and creative freedom is well documented (Chiaravalloti, 2014, 2020; Hadida, 2015; Labaronne, 2017) achieving commercial success is a critical part of CCI. Arts organisations and individual creatives rely on the public's willingness to pay for their creative products for continued existence in the case of arts organisations and livelihood for the individual creatives. Lee et al. (2022) describe willingness to pay as proof that the consuming public sees value in the creative product so much that they can invest their money to own a creative product or to experience an artistic performance. Commercial success, however, does not always reflect the value that the artisans place on their creative product, but rather the price there are willing to accept for their effort in creating the product or performance. Fanelli et al. (2019) believe there is need to strike a balance between expectations for commercial success and accessibility of creative products. Similarly, Lee et al. (2022) suggest that measuring commercial performance of individual creatives must take into consideration a range of fixed and variable indicators, especially in the early phase of a creative career. Measuring commercial performance can include criteria such as cost of product, profit and loss performance and return on investment. All which has a numerical representation. However, there are other criteria like repeat consumption, referrals and commissions which reflect commercial success but are less tangible thus difficult to measure.

Artistic Merit and Societal Impact

The idea of artisans creating products, compositions, and artefacts of artistic merit has been researched numerously (Fillis, 2002, 2011; Ostling, 1978), with each genre of the CCI being defined by a set of criteria that attest to what warrants serious merit. However, defining artistic merit for every artist or artistic product is one that is fraught with difficulty because art in itself is often a very individual expression of an artistic creative process, culture and circumstances amongst many other indicators (Roshchin & Filippova, 2020). Thus, creating a set of criteria for the CCI is almost impossible but perhaps more achievable in specific genres of the industry like music where 10 specific criteria for serious artistic merit have been widely accepted (Ostling, 1978). Elsewhere in the CCI the usual tension between artistic or creative freedom and customer orientation (Purnomo, 2019) influences the perception of what is considered to be of artistic merit. Artisans are forced to balance their pursuit of creative freedom and commercial success which some believe erode the possibility of their work being considered to be of artistic merit by consumers, art critics and other gatekeepers in the CCI (Lee et al. 2022). Archiving the status of being an artist of merit who produces critically acclaimed products gives artisans the freedom to express their individuality in their products, to represent their culture and make societal impact with their work (Jensen & Kim, 2020).

Competition and Performance Measurement In the CCI

Determining the place of competition in performance measurement in CCI is considerably more challenging for some areas than others because of the different nature of the products, artistic identity, artistic motivation and perception of performance from one artist to the next (Cnossen et al., 2019). The role of competition in the sector depends greatly on the form of industry being researched. For example, competition does not feature greatly amongst artisanal producers as this is usually an individualised process in which the artisans' creativity, and pursuit of artistic merit are more important than out-performing other artisans (Loots et al., 2018; Schoales, 2022). However, commercial success, especially in mass media genres such as film, music and television, can result in more direct comparison and therefore competition (Younkin & Kashkooli, 2020). Concentration of creatives in different subsectors of the CCI can also be used as an indicator of competitiveness in each subsector. Kozáková and Bartéková (2020) suggest that whilst market concentration can lead to increased productivity in the market, demand could fall below supply which can put pressure on product pricing amongst creatives. Market concentration is an obvious indicator of competition in conventional industries but this is not always the case in CCI as artisans are not motivated to outperform each other or driven by financial success (Baláž et al., 2022; Cnossen et al., 2019).

Competition can potentially have significant implications for performance of artisans and their products if it leads to changes in personal motivation, pursuit of commercial success instead of artistic merit and imbalance between creative freedom and customer orientation (Loots et al., 2018). Another potential implication of competition in the CCI is that performance fails to benefit from collaboration and co-creation when artisans and the creative process are focussed on out-performing each other (Musgrave, 2017). Uniquely, CCI are a sector in which artisans with similar or different products all compete to be part of the same market's experience (Cnossen et al., 2019), to be chosen as part of a unique single artist collection or a part of generation of artisans. This extends to arts organisations like museums and art galleries who are all present in the same highly competitive experiential market (Loots & van Witteloostuijn, 2018).

Cultural Entrepreneurship in Zimbabwe

The CCI addressed in this chapter comprises producers of handicrafts and cultural artefacts that represent Zimbabwean culture including subcultural products like Shona sculpture, basketry, carpets and fabrics made out of natural fibres derived from tree bark. Arts traders' markets are found in clusters around Harare primarily targeting affluent suburbs in the north of the city where customers can afford luxury products like art and handicrafts. According to UNESCO (2020) CCI contributes about 6.96% to Zimbabwe's GDP and has about 30000 people in formal employment (Woyo & Woyo, 2018).

Research on the characteristics of cultural entrepreneurs or entrepreneurial artisans in Zimbabwe has identified a number of challenging factors in the sector. For example, there is a widespread lack of entrepreneurship training and/or business training amongst creatives, which may be the underlying cause or may also be a result of the lack of business structures in the sector (Shafi et al., 2020). Macro-environmental factors, such as high unemployment and limited access to education or training, prevailing in the general economy are also important, driving new entrants who lack entrepreneurship skills into the CCI sector (Mujeyi & Sadomba, 2019). Zimbabwe has been in the economic decline since the land redistribution programme of the early 2000s which had adverse impact on country's economy in general and for CCI the fall in tourism arrivals has been detrimental because it has reduced income demand from tourists (Makoni & Tichaawa, 2021).

LIVED EXPERIENCE

Personal experience of arts markets and cultural products and services in Zimbabwe over a number of years has led to the gathering of anecdotal evidence from those who work in this sector. Conversations with creatives give interesting personal insights into their work and their experience as entrepreneurs. Discussion of these insights helps to illuminate the literature on the subject.

Which Performance Criteria Are Used by Cultural Entrepreneurs to Guide Their Day-to-Day Business?

Secondary research demonstrates that there are no set criteria for managing performance in CCI (Chiaravalloti, 2014; Hadida, 2015; Labaronne & Tröndle, 2021), because of the diverse nature of the subsectors of CCI in which individual creatives and creative institutions operate. Literature review also revealed that criteria for managing performance in CCI can sometimes be imposed on individual creatives and creative institutions operating in the industry by a range of stakeholders as well the micro and macro environments in which they operate (Purnomo, 2019). Lee et al. (2022) suggested that for individual creatives', performance criteria are often dictated by the personal circumstances of the creatives thus they are likely to differ significantly from one creative to the next. Review of literature found that financial performance (Chiaravalloti, 2014), critical acclaim (Younkin & Kashkooli, 2020), and societal impact (Labaronne & Tröndle, 2021) were some of the performance criteria being used to guide day-to-day business in CCI.

The significance of individual circumstance was also present in the type of performance criteria that were being applied by artisans working at arts markets in Harare, Zimbabwe. Anecdotal evidence gathered during visits to markets revealed that perception of performance differed between artisans as did the criteria that were applied by different artisans. Some artisans regarded monthly sales as a key performance criterion, but others looked at the difference between the asking price of products and agreed price as a more reliable indicator of performance than overall monthly sales. Other performance criteria that were being applied by artisans in Zimbabwe include the number of products produced and sold per month. Critical acclaim was hardly considered as a performance measurement criterion primarily because creatives felt being able to sell products was adequate acclaim for their work.

The difference between secondary data and primary data points towards the difference in the context in which participants in the two sets of data operate. Anecdotally it can be concluded that artisans in developed economies of the Global North in which the majority of the secondary data was found have a wider range of performance criteria than those from a developing economy like Zimbabwe. Additionally, the perception of performance differed in that artisans in Zimbabwe were less concerned about societal impact and critical acclaim than their Global North counterparts.

How Are Performance Criteria Selected, Reviewed and at What Intervals Are They Reviewed?

Hadida (2015) listed creative production process and financial performance as frequently used criteria in the CCI and their selection was largely dependent on the individual artisans' circumstances. Labaronne and Tröndle (2021) found that critical acclaim and societal impact were performance criteria that were imposed on creative institutions by funders and other similar stakeholders. Monitoring and reviewing of performance criteria is a less structured process amongst individual artisans as it is for creative institutions (Labaronne, 2017). Individual artisans largely stick to the same set of criteria unless their personal circumstance change or there are pressures in the market which require them to revise their pricing strategy, product design and/or access to inputs for their creative process (Cnossen et al., 2019).

Conversations with creatives in Zimbabwe revealed that the criteria selection process was much narrower than those revealed by the secondary data. Creatives in Zimbabwe had criteria that centred around production and selling their products which did not change much for the majority of the time. The anecdotal evidence showed that the pricing strategy used to sell products was heavily influenced by market forces like demand for creative products and the prices that customers were willing to pay. This unique relationship between demand and prices forces creatives to regularly review two main criteria namely price of products and rate of production of new products. A specific example of this phenomenon is that artisans at arts market in Harare, Zimbabwe were prepared to negotiate their prices at every sales event and even more so when they have not sold any products for a prolonged period or at specific points of the month like month end or in times when they need to pay for rent, schools fees, medical bills or food. It is not uncommon that artisans are willing to sell products at less than the amount it costs them to produce the products to meet survival needs.

The role of individual circumstance in determining the criteria selection process, the review and frequency of review of criteria is predictably complex in CCI because of the diversity of individual creatives, their chosen genre of creativity, the economies they operate in and the micro/macro factors prevailing in the markets the trade in. The anecdotal evidence suggests that pricing as a performance indicator in Zimbabwe can best be described as being dynamic and extremely sensitive to the personal circumstances of the creatives in that market.

What Is the Role of Competition in the Selection and Reviewing of Performance Criteria for a Cultural Entrepreneur?

Loots et al. (2018) and Schoales (2022) identify motivation or sources of motivation as a key characteristic amongst creatives which influences the place of competition in the CCI, its role in performance and the fact that financial success is not a key motivator for artisans. Baláž et al. (2022) and Cnossen et al. (2019) believe the low-ranking that artisans place on financial success over other motivators like creative freedom and enjoyment of work reduced the importance of competition or being able to compete when artisans select or review performance criteria.

Experiences from the observations and interactions in the arts markets in Harare, Zimbabwe revealed that artisans are not driven to compete, nor do they place much importance in being perceived as being competitive. In fact, a number of them pointed to their presence in those arts markets as an indication that they are not concerned about competition otherwise they would be located elsewhere away from people selling arts and crafts to avoid competition. The few that acknowledged the presence of competition in their performance assessment felt that being in an arts market was indeed competitive especially in a market where demand is low and new entrants can easily enter the cluster. However, their perception of competition did not lead to artisans putting any competitive strategy to outsell each other artisans because they felt each of them had unique products and customers would choose the art they want not because it was competitively priced but rather that it was what they are drawn to.

Competition as a factor on performance figured on one of the arts market clusters where some artisans felt the quality of their products improved or benefitted from being in a creatively competitive environment. Artisans at that arts market felt the quality of their sculptures had to go up in order to distinguish themselves from newcomers who were not from the traditional sculptor families but people who entered the market to make a living. In this case performance, particularly the creative production process, was influenced by competition as the artist sought to demonstrate their artistic merit as authentic artisans over entrepreneurial artisans through the quality of their work.

CONCLUSIONS

This chapter set out to answers the following questions:

- Which performance criteria are used by cultural entrepreneurs to guide their day-to-day business?
- How are performance criteria selected, reviewed and at what intervals are they reviewed?
- What is the role of competition in the selection and reviewing of performance criteria for a cultural entrepreneur?

Answering the three questions has revealed two key conclusions in relation to performance management in CCI. The first key conclusion is that it is difficult to arrive at a generic set of performance criteria in the CCI because of the diverse nature of the industry (Hadida, 2015; Labaronne & Tröndle, 2021) and the creatives within the industry. This diversity extends to the types of products and markets targeted by those products which also have a bearing on perception of performance and the criteria that are used to measure it. The conversations with individual artisans showed that they had distinctly different needs for performance measurement from creative institutions (Purnomo, 2019; Sassi et al., 2020) and this also influenced the type of criteria used to measure performance by these two groups. This chapter found further complexity in measuring performance when looking at artisans from developed countries where macro environmental factors such as the state of the economy have significant influence on performance, especially profit margin and artisans' willingness to accept significantly lower prices for their products due to external pressures. Artisans reviewed their prices to suit their personal circumstances at any given time and often sold products at prices that are lower than the cost of sales if there is a pressing need for cash.

The second key conclusion this chapter makes is that artisans are not motivated by financial success (Baláž et al., 2022; Cnossen et al., 2019) as a performance criterion in intensely competitive markets but they draw motivation from competition to improve their craft and the products they produce in response to that competition. This phenomenon revealed a characteristic in the Zimbabwean CCI where artisans seek to distinguish their artistic merit and heritage of coming from traditionally artistic families by outperforming artisans who do not come from similar artistic background through the quality of their products. Thus, it was their perception of artistic merit and heritage which was at stake in the market rather than sales competition from newcomers which they south to protect.

LIMITATIONS

This chapter's conclusions are limited due to the anecdotal nature of the evidence presented. However, the authors believe there is a valid academic interest in the anecdotal evidence presented here to warrant future research in Zimbabwe's CCI to deepen insight into the performance strategy of individual creatives given the country's macro environment. A second conclusion from this chapter is that there is a need to test whether entrepreneurship training would help artisans in CCIs of developing countries like Zimbabwe to make better decisions on managing the balance between supply and demand especially the impact of oversupply on pricing strategy. Future research could be used to provide entrepreneurship training to a focus group of artisans in order to assess how such training impacts perception of performance, competition and how that could differ from untrained artisans in the same market.

REFERENCES

Ardielli, E. (2017). Performance evaluation of cultural sector in the Czech Republic and EU-member countries. *Theoretical and Practical Aspects of Public Finance 2017*, 92.

Baláž, V., Jeck, T., & Balog, M. (2022). Beyond financial success: Success goals of creative entrepreneurs. *Journal of Innovation and Entrepreneurship*, *11*(1), 1–10.

Chiaravalloti, F. (2014). Performance evaluation in the arts and cultural sector: A story of accounting at its margins. *The Journal of Arts Management, Law, and Society*, *44*(2), 61–89.

Chiaravalloti, F. (2020). Stop measuring, start understanding! An arts policy and management researcher's autobiographic account of the urgency of an ethnographic turn in research on the values of art1. *Art & the Public Sphere, 9*(1–2), 131–143.
Cnossen, B., Loots, E., & van Witteloostuijn, A. (2019). Individual motivation among entrepreneurs in the creative and cultural industries: A self-determination perspective. *Creativity and Innovation Management, 28*(3), 389–402.
Fanelli, S., Donelli, C. C., Zangrandi, A., & Mozzoni, I. (2019). Balancing artistic and financial performance: Is collaborative governance the answer? *International Journal of Public Sector Management, 33*(1), 78–93.
Fillis, I. (2002). Creative marketing and the art organisation: What can the artist offer?. *International Journal of Nonprofit and Voluntary Sector Marketing, 7*(2), 131–145.
Fillis, I. (2011). The evolution and development of arts marketing research. *Arts Marketing: An International Journal, 1*(1), 11–25.
Hadida, A. (2015). Performance in the creative industries. In C. Jones, M. Lorenzen, & J. Sapsed (Eds.), *The Oxford handbook of creative industries*, (pp.219–248). Oxford University Press.
Höllen, M., Lengfeld, C., & Konrad, E. D. (2020). Business success for creative and cultural entrepreneurs: Influences of individual-and firm-related factors on revenue and satisfaction. *International Journal of Arts Management, 22*(2), 52–65.
Jensen, M., & Kim, H. (2020). Reaching for the stars: The importance of reputational rank in creative career development. *Poetics, 80*, 101396.
Kozáková, M., & Barteková, M. K. (2020). Analysis of market concentration in creative industry. In *SHS Web of Conferences, 83*, 01035. EDP Sciences.
Labaronne, L. (2017). Performance measurement and evaluation in arts management. *Zeitschrift für Kulturmanagement, 3*(1), 37–70.
Labaronne, L., & Tröndle, M. (2021). Managing and evaluating the performing arts: Value creation through resource transformation. *The Journal of Arts Management, Law, and Society, 51*(1), 3–18.
Lee, B., Fraser, I., & Fillis, I. (2022). To sell or not to sell? Pricing strategies of newly-graduated artists. *Journal of Business Research, 145*, 595–604.
Loots, E., Cnossen, B., & van Witteloostuijn, A. (2018). Compete or cooperate in the creative industries? A quasi-experimental study with Dutch cultural and creative entrepreneurs. *International Journal of Arts Management, 20*(2), 20–31.
Loots, E., & van Witteloostuijn, A. (2018). The growth puzzle in the creative industries. *Revue del Entrepreneuriat, 17*(1), 39–58.
Makoni, L., & Tichaawa, T. M. (2021). Impact analysis of the COVID-19 pandemic on the informal sector business tourism economy in Zimbabwe. *African Journal of Hospitality, Tourism and Leisure, 10*(1), 165–178.
Mujeyi, K., & Sadomba, W. Z. (2019). Unemployment and informal entrepreneurship in Zimbabwe: Implications for regional integration. In *Innovation, regional integration, and development in Africa* (pp. 251–266). Springer.
Musgrave, G. (2017). Collaborating to compete: The role of cultural intermediaries in hypercompetition. *International Journal of Music Business Research, 6*(2), 41–68.
Ostling, A. E., Jr. (1978). *An evaluation of compositions for wind band according to specific criteria of serious artistic merit*. The University of Iowa.
Purnomo, B. R. (2019). Artistic orientation, financial literacy and entrepreneurial performance. *Journal of Enterprising Communities: People and Places in the Global Economy, 13*(1/2), 105–128.
Roshchin, S. P., & Filippova, L. S. (2020). Artistic literacy in the paradigms of teaching fine arts. *Humanities and Social Sciences Reviews, 8*(S2), 136.
Sassi, M., Pihlak, Ü., & Birnkraut, G. (2021). Organizational performance evaluation and performance paradox in CCI organizations. *International Journal of Productivity and Performance Management, 71*(5), 2009–2030.
Sassi, M., Urb, K., & Pihlak, Ü. (2020). The evaluation of organisational performance: Estonian cultural and creative industries organisations. In *Management, Participation and Entrepreneurship in the Cultural and Creative Sector* (pp. 189–218). Springer.
Schoales, J. (2022). Competing in the creative industries: Two-sided networks and the case of Hollywood. *City, Culture and Society, 28*, 100439.

Shafi, A. A., Sirayi, M., & Abisuga-Oyekunle, O. A. (2020). Issues, challenges and contributions of cultural and creative industries (CCIs) in South African economy. *Creative Industries Journal*, *13*(3), 259–275.

Turbide, J., & Laurin, C. (2009). Performance measurement in the arts sector: The case of the performing arts. *International journal of arts management*, *11*(2), 56–70.

Werthes, D., Mauer, R., & Brettel, M. (2017). Cultural and creative entrepreneurs: Understanding the role of entrepreneurial identity. *International Journal of Entrepreneurial Behavior & Research*, *24*(1), 290–314.

Woyo, E., & Woyo, E. (2018). Creative industries as a stimulant for tourism growth in Zimbabwe–A critical interjection. *Almatourism-Journal of Tourism, Culture and Territorial Development*, *9*(9), 195–211.

Younkin, P., & Kashkooli, K. (2020). Stay true to your roots? Category distance, hierarchy, and the performance of new entrants in the music industry. *Organization Science*, *31*(3), 604–627.

CHAPTER 7

MAKE IT WORK: STRATEGIES OF CREATIVE ENTREPRENEURS FOR COPING WITH THE TENSION FROM ARTISTIC AND ECONOMIC LOGICS

Nanne Migchels and Milou van der Linden

Nijmegen School of Management, Radboud University, Nijmegen, The Netherlands

ABSTRACT

This chapter examines the way creative entrepreneurs integrate artistic and entrepreneurial logics into their daily practice. The existence of multiple logics and their role in decision-making is highlighted by institutional logics theory. Coping strategies can resolve the tension between these logics. This study follows the view of paradox theory that embracing a paradox between logic is the first step in dealing with it. The following research question will be explored: In what way are coping strategies used by creative entrepreneurs to deal with the tension between artistic and economic logics? The empirical foundation of this study is based on a descriptive-interpretive approach. We conducted semi-structured interviews with a sample of 19 creative entrepreneurs based in the Netherlands. The results indicate the acknowledgment of the existence of multiple logics, the deployment of coping strategies and flexibility in the use of coping strategies by creative entrepreneurs. In addition, resolving the tension between logics is experienced as harder when they are regarded as oppositional rather than complementary. Research findings have implications for policy and practice, as it highlight differences in approaches to a widely felt tension.

Keywords: Creative entrepreneurs; coping strategies; paradox; dual logics; mitigation; reconciliation

INTRODUCTION

Entrepreneurs in the creative industries face two major challenges. Like other entrepreneurs, they need to sustain a business to generate an income. In addition, creative entrepreneurs need to find ways for authentic artistic expression (Chang & Wyszomirski, 2015). The tension between the two weighs on the daily practice of the entrepreneur who operates with arts and economic logics in several arenas. This will subsequently shape the identity of the creative entrepreneur (Salder, 2021). When economic logics prevail within the business, there will be less room for artistic expression. A balance thus needs to be found to overcome the tension between both logics and allow the creative entrepreneur to integrate both identities (Werthes et al., 2018). In paradox theory, recognition of contradicting logics is the starting point for reconciling them (Lewis, 2000). Though challenging, the way to make this work can be found in coping strategies that are rooted in strategic literature (DeWitt & Meyer, 2017). This helps to respond to conflicting goals or logics and the resulting tension.

The research question that follows is, in what way are coping strategies used by creative entrepreneurs to deal with the tension between artistic and economic logics? The overarching paradox between artistic and economic logics is visible in the choices that creative entrepreneurs need to make in their business. Therefore, we focus our study to explore how creative entrepreneurs experience paradox when running their businesses and following the strategies for finding a balance. For data collection, we have used semi-structured interviews with 19 entrepreneurs, from different parts of Dutch creative industries. All have extensive experience as entrepreneurs, which allows them to reflect on their actions. In the results, we find that freedom is the most cherished dimension of the artistic logics. All respondents reported looking for ways to create time and space for artistic expression or to create occasions dedicated to such expression. Entrepreneurship is a vehicle that helps to establish the independence to achieve this. The coping strategies employed are person and context-dependent. The main differentiator identified, is the degree to which the entrepreneur is either stalled by or able to overcome the tension between logics. The strategies are foremost a means to cope with the dominance of economic logics, as artistic logics are not regarded as the inhibitors.

LITERATURE REVIEW

Dual Goals

Creative entrepreneurs face the combination of entrepreneurial decision-making with artistic creativity. Both are the essential building blocks of creative entrepreneurship of which the outcome is known as the dual value of arts and culture: Economic and cultural value (Patten, 2016; Throsby 2008). Catering to a dual outcome makes it difficult for creative entrepreneurs to navigate entrepreneurial processes, when primarily trained in achieving artistic goals (Chang & Wyszomirski, 2015). The idea of weighing risks, orchestration of resources and the identification of viable opportunities can be regarded as typically entrepreneurial. Somehow a creative entrepreneur will need to find a balance between both values, in order to run a business (Pearse & Peterlin, 2019; Salder, 2021). Creating multiple types of value in this way is unique for creative entrepreneurship and forms the basis for inherent tension in its execution.

Dual Logics

The tension between the creation of cultural and economic value is posited to exist when the desire to produce art as an aesthetic performance, on the one hand, is not reconciled with a market orientation on the other (Eikhof & Haunschild, 2007). The economic logic promotes a need for economic viability through the exchange of goods and services in a market. In this way, the production of art follows its market potential (Knox & Casulli, 2021). The contrast with the arts logic is stark, since authenticity is of major importance in value creation (Petrides & Fernandes 2020). Besharov and Smith (2014) regard compatibility and centrality as key dimensions to distinguish multiple logics in organisations.

The choices that creative entrepreneurs need to make all the time form the basis for the tension between both logics. When, from an artistic perspective, authenticity is valued over commercial success, spending valuable time and effort on commercial activities can be regarded as a poor choice from the perspective of artistic logics (Hanson, 2021). From economic logics, it becomes clear that creative and artistic orientation can be seen as a leverage for success in the market (Loots & van Bennekom, 2022). The economic logics that creative entrepreneurs may try to avoid becomes inescapable as soon as they enter a market.

Balancing both logics is therefore hard work for creative entrepreneurs, an effort which often aims at reducing the dominance of economic logics (Knox & Casulli, 2021). Creative entrepreneurs prefer to define success on peer recognition and accomplishments in the creative profession (Cnossen et al., 2019). A creative entrepreneur may own a business or be self-employed and still find it hard to be regarded an entrepreneur. As Patten (2016) found, identification comes in first place from the craft or occupation of a creative entrepreneur (designer, sculptor, etc.).

In running a business, a creative entrepreneur would turn inward and choose to limit to an effectuation strategy which makes the most of existing resources and achieves success. The tendency for using effectuation also shows in a preference for autonomy by working independently and thus limit the expansion of the business (Pearse & Peterlin, 2019). An increased role of economic logic in a founder's motivations is seen to have a carry-on effect on the venture. Structure and formal procedures are more likely to be applied to the development of the venture and facilitate growth (Cnossen et al., 2019). Ström et al. (2020) have compiled the tensions that creative entrepreneurs face in dealing with both logics.

Tensions may appear in all areas of the business, from HR to managing network relations. As both logics oppose, tension will mount when economic logics start to prevail as a motivator for action.

ENTREPRENEURIAL IDENTITY

To a creative entrepreneur, the foundation for action has also become a question of identity. From structural identity theory, it is clear that entrepreneurial identities act as a motivator for entrepreneurial action (Patten, 2016). However, tension arises when two identities are opposing but activated together in a given context (Pearse & Peterlin, 2019). Since experience and self-reflection shape behaviour, the entrepreneur has to find direction within the hybridity of identities (Shepherd et al., 2019). Therefore, a creative entrepreneur endures a process of identity reconciliation to avoid being stifled by competition between both identities. This process of becoming a creative entrepreneur would help to assume a new (entrepreneurial) identity to establish a role within the new context, and integrate artistic and entrepreneurial identities through the work produced (Knox & Casulli, 2021). Creative entrepreneurs who struggle to adapt their identities to the demands of their venture, also experience this tension (Werthes et al., 2018). According to Radu-Lefebre et al. (2021), the influence of stakeholders in the social environment may have a significant impact on the integration of identities. Werthes et al. (2018) focus on a self-reflective effort by the creative entrepreneur to achieve a balance between identities. Both identities may co-exist when creative entrepreneurs are aware of the entrepreneurial consequences of their creative behaviour. Conscious action will then form the basis for a creative entrepreneur to make the balance work and cope with the situation.

Coping Strategy

Other than achieving balance, forms of coping can be seen in entrepreneurship literature, such as coping with entrepreneurial failure (Cacciotti & Hayton, 2015), or coping with expectations from different stakeholders in a new venture (Sagiv & Yeheskel, 2020). Resolving identity tensions within creative entrepreneurs has often been described as either rebelling against or integrating the economic logics into their identities as a creative (Nielsen et al., 2018). Either way, a coping strategy will represent a struggle. The entrepreneur is to make the most of both identities, settle on appropriate behavioural adaptations and oversee the implications of venture pursuits (Werthes et al., 2018).

Paradox literature offers a means to resolve the tensions that are inherent to management. There are two components to a paradox: (1) Underlying tensions: Elements that seem logical individually but inconsistent when compared and (2) responses that embrace tensions simultaneously (Lewis, 2000; Waldman et al., 2019). Managing paradoxes implies an active and persistent approach based on acceptance of the paradox and the resolve to overcome its complexity (Manzoni & Caporarello, 2017). DeWit and Meyer (2017) compiled coping strategies for dealing with paradoxes which provide an angle to resolve the tension within the work that is done. These strategies are based on prioritising time, tasks and demands. As priorities are situational, variation in responses can be assumed. Thus, the ways in which creative entrepreneurs cope with the paradox between artistic and economic logics emerge from their reasoning and actions.

METHOD

Research Design

The overall aim of this study is to uncover coping strategies used by creative entrepreneurs for dealing with the tension between arts and economic logics. For the purpose of this study, the creative entrepreneur is defined as an entrepreneur in the creative sectors registered at the Dutch Chamber of Commerce, who marks creative entrepreneurship as their main profession. The entrepreneur is supposed to have a serious commitment to the business and sustain a living from it. To generate respondents, our networks were used, followed by snowballing into second and third tier relations. We take a descriptive-interpretive approach to research, allowing us to tap into the complexity and reality lived by a creative entrepreneur. Qualitative data were generated as verbal accounts of the execution of strategies, as well as the reasoning behind them. A total of 19 in-depth face-to-face interviews with creative entrepreneurs were conducted. We took a wide-angled approach to select respondents and create a sample with variations in profession, industry, conceptual or applied creatives, age, and whether they are self-employed or have employees. Table 7.1 shows the main characteristics of respondents. The gender distribution is in line with industry average in the Netherlands (CBS, 2021).

Table 7.1. Characteristics of Respondents.

NAME	JOB TITLE	NO OF EMPLOYEES	AGE	GENDER	NATIONALITY
B	Allround designer	1	31–40	M	Dutch
P	Interior designer	1	41–50	F	Dutch
R	Photographer	1	20–30	M	Dutch
M	Urban planner	1	41–50	F	Dutch
H	Photographer	1	20–30	F	Belgian
EA	Filmmaker	1	20–30	M	Dutch
P	Conceptual artist	1	51–60	M	Dutch
D	Musician	1	20–30	M	Dutch
S	Graphic designer	1	41–50	F	Dutch
R	Web designer/CEO	15	51–60	M	Dutch
S	Filmmaker	1	20–30	M	Dutch
S	Visual artist	1	51–60	M	Dutch
R	Interior designer	1	41–50	M	Dutch
EF	Filmmaker	1	31–40	F	Dutch
T	Novelist	1	61–70	M	Dutch
G	Photographer	1	41–50	M	Dutch
J	Graphic designer/CEO	12	51–60	F	Dutch
K	Graphic designer	1	41–50	M	Dutch
L	Filmmaker	1	31–40	F	Dutch

Data Collection

The interviews were semi-structured and lasted between one and two hours. All interviews were conducted in 2019 in an informal live setting to allow for a free-flowing conversation. The one-on-one approach puts all focus on the interviewee and provides an opportunity to open up and clarify context or trains of thought (Dilley, 2004).

The interview started with unstructured and open-ended questions on the career story of the interviewee and the purpose and current state of their business. Then the concepts of artistic expression, commercialism and identity were discussed. The interviews gradually became more focussed when touching on the manifestation of the tension between logics, the urgency felt to deal with it, the impact on the manner of work and approaches of dealing with that. When answers became recurring, saturation was assumed and the interview concluded.

All interviews were recorded and transcribed using AmberScript. The chosen method for data extraction is thematic coding using partial template analysis. In accordance to template analysis, some a priori themes were identified which focussed on the definitions of artistic expression, creativity and commercialism, manifestations of the paradox, coping strategies and expressions of adherence to artistic or economic logics. Other codes surfaced and were evaluated for possible novel themes (Galletta, 2013). For coding, Atlas TI was used.

RESULTS

Logics

All respondents in the study report experiencing strain from the tension between artistic and economic logics. The results also show that creative entrepreneurs in our study deploy a variety of coping strategies to reduce this strain. Differences appear in the interpretation of artistic logics by respondents; one view is that artistic logics should make things to be enjoyable or fun to do. Another interpretation is that artistic logics is about minimal restraints to allow maximum (creative) freedom. Although mentioned by all respondents, freedom is not categorised in the literature as part of artistic logics. It acts as a separate logic, one that forms the basis of most life and career choices of the creative entrepreneurs interviewed. Other than that, beauty, quality, emotion and novelty are mentioned as part of artistic logics which means they want to create something that ticks more than one box with their audience.

Freedom is about expressing ideas and emotions, being free of judgement, being free to create whatever one desires, choosing how to spend time, and the ability to choose work and activities one enjoys. Creative entrepreneurs in our sample recognise that being an entrepreneur helps to generate this sought-after freedom. It is a form of independence they all aspire, but the ways they achieve it are based on personal judgement. Thus, the coping strategies deployed will differ according to what serves individual preferences.

For economic logics, we observed a distinction between commercial thinking and financial thinking. All respondents established that financial thinking is a requirement to generate an income. However, commercial thinking is associated with advertising and sales. This is largely rejected as it is seen as detrimental to authenticity. For that reason, even respondents with commercial accounts like web designer/CEO R and interior designer P, appear hesitant to advertise themselves. Economic logics affect all respondents with issues like getting assignments and keeping the business afloat (Eikhof & Haunschild, 2007). Dual logics are recognised by the respondents in our study, who look for opportunities to be involved in creative expression, but find it hard to escape economic logics. All respondents resolve this by focussing on networking; an activity they view as authentic and non-commercial as well as vital.

Identity

While the dual identity is apparent for participants in our study, they seem to be reluctant to give in too much to the economic logics that impact their business. As expected, almost all respondents distance themselves from the desire to make money for the sake of money. They downplay the importance of commercial success or profit in comparison to the importance of honest artistic expression, freedom or enjoyment. The respondents are willing to accept low financial security if they get to spend more time on their passion. The motivation for becoming an entrepreneur is mainly related to this freedom, not to economic benefits.

> Living as an artist means financial insecurity. That is the price we more than willingly pay for satisfaction, for the freedom to create what we want. (T – novelist)
>
> Expressing creativity is something that makes me happy, a big fat bank account in the end does not. (EF – filmmaker)

In line with literature, the identity of a creative professional is firmly rooted in creativity (Patten, 2016). It is key in their way of living and closely associated with freedom and satisfaction. Since this is what makes life worthwhile, financial insecurity can be sacrificed.

Another important motivator for a number of creative entrepreneurs in our study is maintaining authenticity which is regarded uncompromisingly as a driver of creativity and artistic expression. All of the respondents identified money as the main threat to authenticity: the creative process is affected when money is involved.

> If you play only for money, you give up all of your creativity. (D – musician)
>
> That one colleague who was good at selling himself only made unoriginal beach images. (P – conceptual artist)

Both quotes show the classic tension between logics when seen from the creative process; working purely for monetary gain is seen as detrimental to authenticity. Solving tension becomes hard once both logics are regarded as oppositional rather than complementary (Besharov & Smith, 2014). Rather than becoming stalled between opposing logics, part of being an entrepreneur is to make choices to help navigate the situation. Creative entrepreneurs need to celebrate the arts, as well as make a living, as illustrated below.

> Amateurs play for fun. Professionals play for the fun and for the money. (D – musician)

The degree to which an entrepreneur feels restrained by the opposing of logics, will then be decisive for the ability to implement coping strategies. As indicated by Lewis (2000), the ability to embrace both sides are key to resolve the tension caused by a paradox.

Coping Strategies

For coping strategies to work, they should provide tools to bring opposites together as the situation requires. Rather than committing themselves to a single strategy or a single kind of strategy, we have found that creative entrepreneurs in our study mix strategies and let them work alongside each other. Two basic approaches appear from practice: Mitigate interference in the creative process and active reconciliation of both logics.

Mitigation Strategies

Attempts to mitigate interference from the creative process make use of trade-offs to balance the role of economic logics in decision-making (Eikhof & Haunschild, 2007). It assumes a continuous effort to find an optimum between both logics, such as the balance between creating novelty and catering to customer demand. Novelist T expresses the need to be creative even if that may not breed commercial success.

> You have to be cautious to not repeat yourself, once something turns out to be successful with readers. (T – novelist)

Related to this is the choice of web designer/CEO R to reject big projects that would lead him to expand his workforce. Growth would weaken the informal ties that nurture creativity in his company. It would also stretch his managerial responsibilities to the extent that he would not be involved in creative processes. The enterprise thus acts as a support for the creative freedom that entrepreneurs aspire to. In line with the tendency for using effectuation (Pearse & Peterlin, 2019), choices are driven by the desire to retain autonomy which holds for creative entrepreneurs as well as small businesses.

Respondents in our study also report the trade-off to balance customer wishes with personal views or values. After all, creative entrepreneurs choose projects for both financial and artistic reasons. Once working on a project, the customer is still not always king. Respondents who work in applied fields of creativity have developed ways to balance customer involvement with maintaining control in the creative process.

> So, last Thursday I spoke to a new client. He proposed a standard solution, but that is just not going to happen. When we feel like it, we will come up with a better plan. That's the fun of it. Every time a different challenge, that's what I like. (M – urban planner)

> I only ask what the client wants, never how they want it. (R – interior designer)

A creative professional can enjoy a bit of leeway, as becomes clear from the quotes. However, none of the respondents is in a position to ignore customer demands. When the odds are in favour of the paying customer, balancing as a coping strategy is replaced by juxtaposing. As trade-offs become difficult, mitigation aims to give in to opposing demands as much as possible. While the paying client gets served as demanded, respondents in our study report that they are keen on protecting their reputation with peers and prevent alienation of potential clients. In that case, a piece of work will not be added to a website or portfolio or signed with their name. This highlights the tension in the creative process from interaction with customers which leads to mounting tensions should economic logics prevail over artistic vision (Ström et al., 2020). The following quotes serve as illustrations.

> I think you're not really artistically free when you have a customer. (J – Graphic designer/CEO)

> Business and creative make up about fifty-fifty. Yeah, sure I'm pleased with that. I really like doing creative stuff, but I find my earnings suffer from that. So, that is the downside. (B – designer)

Both quotes illustrate the difficulty experienced by creative entrepreneurs in our study to bridge both logics, as there is always a need for a compromise. But once economic logics become more important than the intrinsic motivation to create, frustration will mount. The effort to generate an income will then have overtaken the joy of artistic creation.

> Working hard to produce business movies ruins the joy of film making for yourself in your free time. (E – filmmaker)

> I'm doing too much of what others want me to do and too little of what I want to photograph (.) there are many things I'd like to do but I have to keep in mind that they may not have value for my customers. (R – photographer)

As illustrated by the previous quotes, the motivation to be creative may be gone when activities focus more on income generation than creative expression. The trade-off has gone the wrong way and as a result, the enjoyment and motivation of the creative entrepreneur will suffer. This shows that balancing as a coping strategy requires the reconciliation of opposing logics into a delicate balance.

Reconciliation Strategies

Reconciliation can also take a more active approach by navigating both opposites. This requires creative entrepreneurs to be aware of the consequences of their behaviour as they go about making day-to-day choices (Werthes et al., 2018). Navigation is one of the coping strategies used by all respondents, which focusses on the management of time by separating tasks. By recognising the value of time, the economisation of time automatically follows as a basis for entrepreneurial choices. In this way, the coping strategy provides a clear path to resolve the paradox that surfaced (Lewis, 2000). Navigation requires the ability to shift focus from time to time to give in to one logic over the other. When fully focussed on artist city, this may become a strain on a creative entrepreneur, as observed by web designer/CEO R.

> Real creatives with managerial talent and a business are a rarity. Because real creatives are too focused on creating and protecting their process and results. (R – web designer/CEO)

One way to use navigation is to apply a strict division between time spent on either logic within working hours. This could take place by deliberately scheduling time for creativity without linking it to a possible audience. Respondents who also have commercial and financial activities, dedicate time on a daily or weekly basis and spend the rest of their time on the creative process. Some choose one day per week whereas others schedule one or two hours per day for this. Novelist T has divided a year: Two-thirds on finishing a novel and one-third on PR activities with his publisher and PR assistant. In this way, reconciliation as a coping strategy works for an entrepreneur by managing time through the separation of tasks.

Another coping strategy helps to take the separation of tasks one step further. Parallel processing helps to free up time through collaboration. This coping strategy is based on the division of creative and commercial tasks over different individuals, groups or systems. Outsourcing managerial tasks to a specialist helps to maintain focus on creative processes. These capabilities can also be found within one's inner circle.

> I am really bad with numbers. I know I shouldn't be but it's good that I have someone in my collective who is. (K – designer and DJ)

K's DJ collective is made up of two creatives and one business-minded person. Web designer/CEO R, graphic designer/CEO J and musician D take up managerial tasks to allow others to be more involved in the creative processes. After musician D became involved in management, it turned out an enjoyable experience, aligning commercial activities with the artistic value of enjoyment.

> I see it as a game. That's what makes it fun. (D – musician)

Parallel processing is a strategy to tap into external capabilities and expertise. The entrepreneur can then focus on core capabilities, like a web designer hiring a photographer to take photos for a website to achieve better quality while economising on time and effort. Skills like these are usually delegated to fellow creative entrepreneurs on the basis of trust. As a result, this coping strategy enables mutual partners to generate maximum value.

Resolving is another coping strategy that aims at maximising artistic and economic value within the same activity. The main assumption of the resolving strategy is that authenticity and passion drive 'good' work and that staying true to authenticity and passion will attract the 'right' customers who value the work and pay accordingly.

> We make stuff and people want to listen to that. We produce things and apparently, there's demand for it. That's the most awesome thing I can imagine. (K – designer and DJ)

Some respondents note that the ideal situation is well-paying customers who leave them plenty of artistic freedom. However, graphic designer/CEO J says this is usually reserved for the 'lucky few' or superstars. Undaunted by this, some entrepreneurs in our study assume an outward orientation to their work to make the resolving strategy work for them. They assume there must be people who like their work and they may be willing to pay for it. To find these customers, they actively deploy networking. They report taking deliberate steps to trace desired customers, initiate contact, seek out events or competitions to meet desired customers or media and seek out markets that allow for commercial as well as artistic work. This may look like a commercial activity, but our respondents see it as part of the artistic process, since the outcome enables them to undertake artistic projects.

> I'm not commercial, but I heavily invest in my network. (M – urban planner)

> Photographers are found via informal networks, not via Google. (R – photographer)

Both quotes show that creative entrepreneurs deal with networking to sustain their business and foremost support the creative processes (Ström et al., 2020). Since networking is a basic capability for any entrepreneur, both logics are resolved into activities that fulfil both demands.

Delivering high-quality work to customers as well as for their own satisfaction is another way of resolving. They strongly feel that delivering good work is part of the artistic identity, and this aids in delivering high-value products. However, there is a financial limit to what can be done to improve quality.

> If you spend the majority of your time on doing fun stuff for a low hourly wage, you'll end up with no money at all. (S – visual artist)

> You know, you need to develop your skills in your trade. And then, maybe give away a bit of that freedom. In return you will get to deliver better quality productions. (EA – filmmaker)

Resolving the delivery of quality by a creative entrepreneur requires a clear view of the outcome of entrepreneurial actions as both quotes show (Werthes et al., 2018). Time and effort spent, should be in line with the income earned. Economic reasons to accept lower wages is work promising the improvement of skills or network, thus improving future income.

DISCUSSION

Creative entrepreneurs tend to distance themselves from economic logics but use several ways to cope with or even enact them. Besharov and Smith (2014) regard compatibility and centrality as key dimensions to distinguish multiple logics in organisations. Coping strategies have the capability to bridge the gap between logics and show how complementarity can be created in practice. In the case of creative entrepreneurs, coping strategies are used to free up time and space for creative expression. Most of the coping strategies described by DeWit and Meyer (2017) were clearly recognisable in the data. Navigation is used to deal with opposing demands and is regarded as a means to create a sense of freedom. Parallel processing takes the form of collaboration with all sorts of people and professions in order to make room for the creative process. Resolving both logics in decision-making proves hard for entrepreneurs as it requires hard trade-offs to deal with pricing, accepting projects, and finding the right customers that match their passion and values. If this can be reconciled, then both artistic and entrepreneurial processes can be managed.

Freedom and independence proved to be stronger drivers in creative entrepreneurs than the desire to create beauty or authentic art. It is not unique to creative entrepreneurs to gravitate towards freedom more than towards artistic logics, as seeking freedom is regarded as a general trait of entrepreneurs (Radu-Lefebre et al., 2021). Freedom logics associated with entrepreneurship directly feed artistic as well as economic logics. Conflict arises when logics are treated as oppositional which is the case when entrepreneurs display a negative attitude towards a focus on finance, marketing and sales. This will then lead to a heightened experience of the strain experienced from the tension between artistic and economic logics. The way identities are played out by an entrepreneur will thus prove decisive for the tension experienced (Knox & Casulli, 2021).

CONCLUSION

This paper concludes that creative entrepreneurs use a diverse set of coping strategies to deal with tensions from artistic and economic logics. Coping strategies help to overcome the tension between artistic and economic logics. This confrontation is enacted on a daily basis in entrepreneurial decisions. Creative entrepreneurs benefit from coping strategies by generating time and space for that gives them freedom and independence.

The results show that both CEO's in the sample of respondents gave similar responses as the self-employed creative entrepreneurs. Further research is needed to explore the role of business size in coping with the tension between logics. The larger a business, the more prevalent economic logics may be assumed. However, both entrepreneurs seem to be defiant to this view. Other future research could explore how the difference in experience of the strain between logics plays out in entrepreneurial decision-making. Since not all respondents are equally comfortable in navigating or reconciling both logics, a typology of strategies may be derived from these dimensions. This would generate a better insight into the drivers of actions of creative entrepreneurs.

The sample of respondents could work as a limitation to the study. Although freedom and independence came out as important motives, they are also characteristic for the culture of the Dutch. Further studies should establish that this is not part of a built-in cultural bias. Also, the number of CEO's in the sample is not enough to support conclusions about this part of the entrepreneurial community. This study shows the use of coping strategies by creative entrepreneurs, but does not investigate what determines the choice of strategies or the ability to apply them to practice.

REFERENCES

Besharov, M., & Smith, W. (2014). Multiple institutional logics in organizations: Explaining their varied nature and implications. *Academy of Management Review, 39*(3), 364–381. https://doi.org/10.5465/amr.2011.0431

Cacciotti, G., & Hayton, J. (2015). Fear and entrepreneurship, a review and research agenda. *International Journal of Management Reviews*, 17(2), 165–190. https://doi.org/10.1111/ijmr.12052
Centraal Bureau voor de Statistiek (CBS.nl). (2021, September 6). Monitor Kunstenaars en andere werkenden met een creatief beroep, 2021. Retrieved from https://www.cbs.nl/nl-nl/longread/rapportages/2021/monitor-kunstenaars-en-andere-werkenden-met-een-creatief-beroep-2021
Cnossen, B., Loots, E., & van Witteloostuijn, A. (2019). Individual motivation among entrepreneurs in the creative and cultural industries: A self-determination perspective. *Creativity and Innovation Management*, 28(3), 389–402. https://doi.org/10.1111/caim.12315
Chang, W. J., & Wyszomirski, M. (2015). What is arts entrepreneurship? Tracking the development of its definition in scholarly journals. *Artivate*, 4(2), 33–31. https://doi.org/10.1353/artv.2015.0010
DeWit, B., & Meyer, R. (2017). *Strategy: An international perspective* (6th Edn.). Cengage Learning.
Dilley, P. (2004). Interviews and the philosophy of qualitative research. *The Journal of Higher Education*, 75(1), 127–132. http://www.jstor.org/stable/3838692
Eikhof, D. R., & Haunschild, A. (2007). For art's sake! Artistic and economic logics in creative production. *Journal of Organizational Behavior*, 28(5), 523–538. https://doi.org/10.1002/job.462
Galletta, A. (2013). The semi-structured interview as a repertoire of possibilities. In *Mastering the Semi-Structured Interview and Beyond* (pp. 45–72). New York University Press.
Hanson, J. (2021). Developing and evaluating the arts entrepreneurship profile: A systematic approach. *The Journal of Arts Management, Law, and Society*, 51(5), 307–324. https://doi.org/10.1080/10632921.2021.1919586
Knox, S., & Casulli, L. (2021). Exploring founder identity tension, resolution, and venture pursuit. *Journal of Small Business Management*, 61(6), 1–31. https://doi.org/10.1080/00472778.2021.1905821
Lewis, M. (2000). Exploring paradox: Toward a more comprehensive guide, *The Academy of Management Review*, 25(4), 770–776. https://doi.org/10.5465/amr.2000.3707712
Loots, E., & van Bennekom, S. (2022). Entrepreneurial firm growth in creative industries: Fitting in… and standing out!*Creative Industries Journal*, 16(3), 1–23. https://doi.org/10.1080/17510694.2022.2025710
Manzoni, B., & Caporarello, L. (2017). Managing creative firms by adopting a paradox framework: The case of studio Libeskind. *International Journal of Arts Management*, 20(1), 54–62. https://www.jstor.org/stable/44989725
Nielsen, S. L., Norlyk, B., & Christensen, P. R. (2018). 'Salesman? Hell no!' Identity struggles of nascent design entrepreneurs. *Creativity and Innovation Management*, 27(3), 358–369. https://doi.org/10.1111/caim.12275
Patten, T. (2016). Creative?... Entrepreneur? Understanding the creative industries entrepreneur. *Artivate*. 5(2), 23–42. https://doi.org/10.1353/artv.2016.0006
Pearse, N., & Peterlin, J. (2019). Artistic creative social entrepreneurs and business model innovation. *Journal of Research in Marketing and Entrepreneurship*, 22(2), 149–162. https://doi.org/10.1108/JRME-07-2018-0036
Petrides, L., & Fernandes, A. (2020). The successful visual artist: the building blocks of artistic careers model. *The Journal of Arts Management, Law, and Society*, 50(6), 305–318. https://doi.org/10.1080/10632921.2020.1845892
Radu-Lefebvre, M., Lefebvre, V., Crosina, E., & Hytti, U. (2021). Entrepreneurial identity: A review and research agenda. *Entrepreneurship Theory and Practice*, 45(6), 1550–1590. https://doi.org/10.1177/10422587211013795
Sagiv, T., & Yeheskel, O. (2020). It takes three to tango: Revisiting paradox management in art and culture organizations. *Organizational Aesthetics*, 9(1), 53–71. https://oa.journals.publicknowledgeproject.org/index.php/oa/article/view/155
Salder, J. (2021). The creative business: Enterprise development in the arts-based creative industries. *Creative Industries Journal*, 14(1), 63–80. https://doi.org/10.1080/17510694.2020.1789414
Shepherd, D. A., Williams, T. A., & Zhao, E. Y. (2019). A framework for exploring the degree of hybridity in entrepreneurship. *Academy of Management Perspectives*, 33(4), 491–512. https://doi.org/10.5465/amp.2018.0013
Strøm, H. A., Olsen, T. H., & Foss, L. (2020). Tensions for cultural entrepreneurs managing continuous innovation: A systematic literature review. *International Journal of Arts Management*, 23(1), 61–78.

Throsby, D. (2008). Modelling the cultural industry. *International Journal of Cultural Policy*, *14*(3), 217–232. https://doi.org/10.1080/10286630802281772

Waldman, D. A., Putnam, L. L., Miron-Spektor, E., & Siegel, D. (2019). The role of paradox theory in decision making and management research. *Organizational Behavior and Human Decision Processes*, *155*, 1–6. https://doi.org/10.1016/j.obhdp.2019.04.006

Werthes, D., Mauer, R., & Brettel, M. (2018). Cultural and creative entrepreneurs: Understanding the role of entrepreneurial identity. *International Journal of Entrepreneurial Behaviour and Research*, *24*(1), 290–314.

ORGANISING CLUSTERING OF CCI ENTREPRENEUR

CHAPTER 8

PLAY, EXPERIMENTATION, AND PROXIMITY IN THE CREATIVE INDUSTRIES

Stephen Dobson[a], Lorena Raquel Serrano Tamayo[b] and Sue Hayton[a]

[a]*University of Leeds, UK*
[b]*Cultural Researcher, UK*

ABSTRACT

The creative industries are often perceived as intrinsically creative and innovative, primarily due to the nature of their output. However, the size of many organisations may mean that whilst product innovation is part of their value proposition, process innovation may be more difficult to achieve due to time constraints and relatively small staff sizes. This can lead to short-term 'survival' heuristics rather than a more strategic approach to personal/organisational development and learning. Alliances are an important means to add capacity and build new competencies and foster new ideas, and creative clusters have emerged as an important means to develop and strengthen alliances in the sector. However, research has shown that many small organisations and freelance artists may struggle to adapt practices accordingly to connect with clusters which often have a high growth orientation. This chapter explores a case study of facilitated collaboration between academic and non-academic partnerships in the creative industries as a means to help catalyse transformative strategies for change and innovation amongst micro and small and medium sized creative enterprises. The aim is to understand how practice-based participants of the University of Leeds Creative Labs Programme perceived their involvement over the twelve years of its delivery and to propose a theory of creative collaboration.

Keywords: Proximity; propinquity; innovation, artist; creative lab; collaboration

BACKGROUND

The creative economy is a vital contributor to industry output globally and accounts for 7% of total employment (Deloitte, 2021). In the United Kingdom, the creative industries contributed to 5.8% of Gross Value Added (GVA) and is described as the fastest-growing part of the UK economy providing £101.5 billion GVA contribution (Chung et al., 2018). However, it is also a sector under pressure. The majority (95%) of enterprises in the creative industries are microbusinesses employing fewer than 10 people with a significant proportion (35%) of workers being self-employed.

> Creative enterprises share many of the challenges that are faced by the wider business community - lack of time, finance and funding, business support, and talent came out as top. But these challenges are particularly felt by those in the creative industries due to the high volume of self-employed workers, the microsize of creative enterprises, and the fact that Intellectual Property (IP) is their bread and butter. (Chung et al., 2018, p. 4)

Clustering can support stronger entrepreneurial ecosystems to add capacity to microcreative firms (Delgardo et al., 2010; Garcia et al., 2018; Glaeser et al., 2010; Hill et al., 2021; Siepel et al., 2020; Velez et al., 2022), offering greater access to skills, knowledge, customers, and amenities (Siepel et al., 2020). However, this approach is not without caveats due to: 'a focus on individual firm preferences and a lack of attention to non-economic, situated temporal and spatial variables; [and] a lack of attention to the specificity of particular industries' (Pratt, 2004). The lack of attention is perhaps more a consequence of the fact that our understanding of creative clusters is 'based on foundations that are not always completely understood. Traditional approaches to clustering point to agglomeration economies that come from companies being in close geographic proximity' (Siepel et al., 2020, p. 3). The role of proximity is highly dependent upon the nature of the industry and its regional locality (Hill et al., 2021). As a result, the important role of smaller, often informal clustering of creative entrepreneurs is identified in more recent research into creative and cultural industries in terms of the role of 'microclusters' (Hill et al., 2021; Siepel et al., 2020; Velez et al., 2022). Microclusters are defined as 'smaller clusters, which occur both within and without traditional creative clusters and are made up of much smaller groupings of 50 or more proximate creative organisations within a radius of 1 to 5 kilometers' (Velez et al., 2022, p. 4). The research into the formation of rural microclusters by Velez et al. (2022) outlines that both urban and rural formations share similar determinants. However, whilst geographic proximity is an important factor in formation, research points towards cluster members sharing sector-specific knowledge, or other related diversity similarities (Pratt, 2004; Velez et al., 2022).

Propinquity Versus Proximity

An important role played by microclustering is offering greater industry specificity and lower perceived membership barriers for microcreative organisations and the self-employed than the more formal creative clusters. Larger and more formal creative clusters have a high-growth orientation due to the nature of funding support. Of the 47 primary creative clusters in the United Kingdom outlined in the 2016 NESTA report (Mateos-Garcia & Bakshi, 2016) 40 of these are described as high-growth clusters. In this case, geographic proximity to a formal cluster alone is insufficient for many microcreative enterprises due to the nature and specificity of their industries. Instead, we may consider the role of 'propinquity' as a critical dimension in this instance. Propinquity may be defined in terms of kinship or a level of intellectual or cultural 'closeness' referred to as *functional* distance. This may be influenced by spatial proximity, but is not synonymous.

> Propinquity is usually thought of in terms of functional distance – that is, the likelihood of coming into contact with another person – rather than sheer physical distance. ('Propinquity' Encyclopedia of Social Psychology)

Whilst much entrepreneurship research describes the importance of networks, collaboration and proximity in creative communities and clusters, the role of propinquity in entrepreneurship is restricted to a very small number of studies (e.g. Kacperczyk, 2013; Whittington et al., 2009). Even so, these refer mainly to 'geographic propinquity' and so are more closely linked to notions of proximity as the key determinant for collaboration, as opposed to knowledge or cultural closeness.

In this chapter, we explore the potential role of Higher Education Institutions in supporting (Culkin, 2016; Moreton, 2018) microcreative enterprises and self-employed artists in widening their potential for 'collaborative propinquity' through the act of playful experimentation outside of their usual practice. The research presented here examines the University of Leeds 'Creative Labs' programme through interviews with researcher and practitioner participants spanning eight years of its delivery. A key characteristic of a creative lab is the ability to act as a catalyst and curator of conversations and ideas to emerge and facilitate learning and development through playful 'trial-and-error' (Rittel & Webber, 1973). Petelczyc et al. (2018, pp. 169–170) describe play as an activity that is 'highly interactive'; an 'enthusiastic and in-the-moment attitude'; and 'amusement, enjoyment, and experienced fun'. The playful and experimental nature of a creative lab is considered vital here to build collaborative propinquity between individuals from potentially very different areas of the creative and knowledge economy. Play therefore is an intrinsic component of creativity and therefore the creative lab experience.

Collaboration and Creativity: The Emergence of Labs

A new mode of working encapsulated in more recent shifts towards the rise of creative industries sees 'communities' of innovators co-working (and 'coworking') to reach a common goal: '"community" in this sense no longer describes a closely-knit social constellation of people but rather testifies to the existence of other people's engaging in similar practices elsewhere' (Schmidt & Brinks, 2017 p. 291). For many, the traditional bounded workplace is no longer deemed 'fit for purpose' and collaborative, flexible, creative spaces are rapidly becoming seen as a necessity for ideation (Dobson & McKendrick, 2018; Dobson & Suckley 2015; Gandini 2015; Gibson, 2010) by entrepreneurs, innovators and in industry. Fab labs, co-worker spaces, creative labs, innovation hubs, maker spaces etc. – these are all terms which encapsulate new organisational forms to foster innovation and creative working and have sprung up in many cities globally. They offer both access to a range of materials and tools but most importantly bring social benefits of interactivity and co-creativity (Schmidt & Brinks, 2017). Essentially, they offer propinquity to like-minded creative individuals. Gandini (2015) outlines the origin of the contemporary co-working environment as emerging from San Francisco in the early 2000s. Although, an important distinction is made here between co-working and coworking (i.e. with and without the hyphen). Co-working refers to people, often working independently, but co-located in one workspace complex (in close proximity, but disconnected), whereas coworking refers to the additionality of close collaboration on a shared project or goal (Fost, 2008). The notion of the 'lab' for creative production in many ways originates from the early Fab Lab movement emerging from the Massachusetts Institute of Technology in 2001 (Walter-Herrmann & Büching, 2014). Although, in the modern period, we might trace the origins of the lab as an approach, attitude, or way of working much further back to the artist collectives of the early 20th century. Whilst Fab Labs originate from engineering and technological fabrication spaces and imply an emphasis on the space and technical facilities within this, the collective is bound by the common goal, manifesto, or methodological grounds for working. History abounds with a myriad of art collectives operating from wherever may be available, and so whilst the term 'lab' is a derivation from laboratory and therefore indicates a space rather than mode of thought, it is the latter which best describes the Creative Labs at the University of Leeds. It is an agreement, commitment, and process of collaborative action between the participants. The creative lab therefore acts as a kind of 'third-space' where new ideas can really flourish. The programme can directly trace its origins to the Culture Hack movement, founded by Rachel Coldicutt of Caper Ltd as well as drawing inspiration from FutureLab in Linz and Media Lab in Madrid. These initiatives offered up new modes of innovating and working outside institutional norms to create new collaborations and areas of research. It is worth noting the work of the Institute for Creativity, Arts, and Technology as their focus on how to join artists, designers and scientists 'in a living laboratory that fosters creativity and promotes reflection' adding how they 'are solving the complex problems of the world'. Such collaboration requires a high level of social, knowledge, and cultural propinquity due to it being dependent upon the 'convergence of interests' (Inshakov, 2013, p. 47).

The primary research aim is to understand how the participants of the University of Leeds Creative Labs Programme perceive their involvement and to propose a theory of creative collaboration from this.

METHODOLOGY

The Creative Labs programme at the University of Leeds was launched in 2012 as a mechanism to help university academics and creative partners innovate research and practice. Through the Leeds Creative Labs, the university provides funding, inspiration, opportunities and above all, the co-creative space to share ideas and experiences without deadlines and targets. A kind of 'engineered serendipity' in a 'third space' where inspiration can occur, and new ideas generate. Since the inaugural edition of the Leeds Creative Labs, the programme has given rise to 35 collaborations across nine editions. The Labs have incubated a diverse array of concepts and prototypes synthesised by an equally diverse range of talents and had a broad range of impacts. In 2015 an evaluation of the Creative Labs was commissioned in an attempt to build an understanding of what contributed to the success of the Labs and how this approach might be replicated in other contexts. Through this process, it was discovered that the Leeds Creative Labs sits amongst a landscape (if not a connected ecosystem) of similar programmes and models for innovating across the north of England and in Europe.

The research design was qualitative and inductively built from an iterative process of interviewing. A sampling frame of 21 participants who were identified as having been active and engaged with Creative Labs and of these 14 were able to take part in the schedule of semi-structured interviews. The interviews were all conducted online via video conferencing tools in 2020. The process of thematic qualitative analysis and data coding helped elaborate a resulting theoretical model through an iterative analysis of the interviews (a spiral approach – Auriacombe & Schurink, 2012). This facilitates a process of 'abstracting out beyond the codes and themes to the larger meaning of the data' (Creswell, 2013, p. 187). Furthermore, the application of this approach means that data collection and analysis necessarily take place simultaneously (Dawson, 2009, p. 120).

Thus, the main aim is to understand the experience of the participants in Creative Labs to improve the understanding of the project as well as the journey of each participant. The 14 participants represented five different 'editions' of the Creative Labs programme (2012, 2015, 2017, and 2018). Seven of these were from art practices and seven were collaborating academic researchers and each interviewee took part in just one edition (a single year) of the programme.

DATA SUMMARY

The following summaries represent some of the particular areas of interest that emerged from the much more extensive discussions with interviewees:

Interviewee 1 – Artist

Creativity as a social consensus.

Interviewee 1 joined the first edition of Creative Labs and the key theme emerging from the interview process was the value of collaboration in terms of responding and adapting to each other whilst connecting and playing with different ideas. The interviewee describes the need to maintain a level of 'playful openness' in order to find collaborative common ground: '*It is about being flexible and building creativity from consensus*'. They also outline the importance of the Lab Coordinator in 'curating conversations'.

Interviewee 2 – Academic

Changes how I talk, rather than how I do.

Interviewee 2 identified the opportunity to '*to do outreach in a new and interesting way*'. In this sense, they felt that they had developed a fresh perspective on how they might conceptualise and talk about their work in different ways and to different audiences. They describe the Creative Labs as a '*fun process*' which is often an overlooked aspect of creative collaboration and a necessary part of building confidence to take risks outside of one's comfort zone. The notion of fun returns to the importance of a 'playful' attitude as necessary for experimentation and exploratory collaboration.

Interviewee 3 and Interviewee 4 – Artists

Interviewees 3 and 4 were interviewed together. The experience for these participants was described in terms of being a 'learning journey'. Their experience was primarily from the commercial side of the cultural and creative industries and were seeking to collaborate with academics and learn more about research. The interviewees reflected on being exposed to a new environment that was challenging but brought benefits. Through building a closer understanding of knowledge domains previously far from their professional experience they felt more capable of allowing new influences to permeate their practice.

Interviewee 5 – Academic

Interviewee 5 describes their motivation for joining the Creative Labs programme initially as searching for new approaches to develop ideas for public engagement in the sciences via exposure to the new and accessible language. However, throughout the interview process they shift to describing the Creative Labs programme in much wider, personal development terms. Despite coming to the Creative Labs with a relatively narrow set of expectations they outlined the value to the participants in terms of supporting mental health and well-being through the act of 'trying something new' and 'finding an outlet for creativity'. Interviewee 5 highlights how underrated creativity is in science and that from their experience in the Creative Labs felt empowered to challenge these ideas. Furthermore, they acknowledged that making choices with partial information and in a timebound context may be extremely important to success and could define the creative process in science. Referring to the relationship created with the artist the experience was positive. They found concepts in common and 'enjoyed the experience of learning from each other'. Additionally, the challenge of boundary-crossing and having to describe ideas to those from different backgrounds provokes new ways of thinking as well as being open to new perspectives and approaches in collaboration. This is a particularly important conclusion when considering the value of the Creative Labs as a means to support entrepreneurs and related actors in joining formal creative clusters.

Interviewee 6 – Artist

The experience of the Creative Labs for this interviewee was one of a journey of discovery. Interviewee 6 is a photographer whose motivation to join the programme was to extend their potential for creative work into the documentation of science-based research. Through the opportunity for cross-disciplinary collaborative working, Interviewee 6 described that they built a better understanding of topics beyond their previous experience which led to new ideas. They were able to observe, ask, engage, connect, and confront 'different realms' which helped develop their personal and professional path. Interviewee 6 describes the 'imposed playfulness' of the Creative Labs as an important underpinning for the whole process.

Interviewee 7 – Artist

Interviewee 7 particularly valued the opportunity to exchange knowledge, not just with the partner they were matched with for the Creative Labs programme – but also with their respective wider teams. Going into a research space as an artist was described as feeling like they were stepping 'out of place' For this interviewee in particular the opportunity to feel uncertain about their surroundings and even a little uncomfortable fostered an openness to learn and enquire. Finding commonalities in this kind of situation was described by Interviewee 7 as particularly enriching for their practice, enabling a more nurturing experience.

Interviewee 8 – Artist

Interviewee 8 recalled their time with the Creative Labs as a 'very rare opportunity to spend time throwing ideas around' whilst creating fruitful relationships. They describe the programme as an enriching experience that enabled them to push their professional boundaries. The synergy with the collaborative team was described as invaluable, not only for embracing new ideas but also for learning how to let go of others. This is an interesting outcome in terms of understanding innovation and creative practice from an arts entrepreneur's perspective. Interviewee 8 highlights that they approached the process with respect, openness, and a willingness to be exposed to the expertise of others. They also articulate something that most of the interviewees describe in one form or another throughout the interview process and that is the notion of a 'state of flux' where communication, understanding, and even one's own professional confidence feel somewhat unsteady and uncertain in the initial stages of experimentation. Patience and empathy are important to foster in these conversations in order for participants to move through this initial stage of uncertainty.

Interviewee 9 – Academic

Interviewee 9 is an academic, musician, and writer. They describe the Creative Labs as an organic experience defined by three broad aspects: (1) hospitality as an experience without pressure; (2) broadening understanding through creative conversations; and (3) developing a new initiative: 'The Creative Lab had the power to host and did so by striking a fruitful balance between conditional and unconditional hospitality'. Interviewee 9 described the experience as not being restrictive and enabling them and the collaborative team to talk freely, sometimes in a disconnected manner, until their ideas began to converge around a common conceptual ground: 'What was great about it is that you didn't have to produce anything and that is so different to the whole academia'. This 'unconditional hospitality', expressed through the programme in terms of a lack of any formal outputs, meant that participants felt the opportunity to be creative without this experience being loaded with tangible innovation as an expected outcome. This lack of required outcomes from the programme offered a much greater opportunity to collaborate without fixed ideas or specific agendas. It is interesting to note that despite this, almost all collaborations throughout the years had tangible project outcomes and many continued collaborations. Interviewee 9 described the programme as 'genuinely transformative'.

Interviewee 10 – Academic

As an academic scientist, Interviewee 10 noted that: 'We [scientists] struggle to appreciate what arts can bring to our projects, apart from just dissemination of research findings' and described that their motivation to be part of the Creative Labs was more personal than professional. Interviewee 10 sought to build a better understanding of the arts and creativity rather than having a particular project or area of research in mind for the collaboration. They describe the experience as yielding a 'blue sky collaboration' which resulted in a portfolio full of ideas with long-term application.

Interviewee 11 – Academic

As with many of the participants, Interviewee 11 acknowledged the value of having an alternative space to work where they could share and collaborate in an unfamiliar setting. It provided an important opportunity to 'really be in another person's place and feel what it feels like to be doing that work' – they describe this as a powerful experience. The creative collaboration is identified by the interviewee as going beyond an unequal relationship and therefore aiming to create a real collaboration where artists and scientists might share their ideas and build concepts. A recurring theme from discussions with the creative practitioners was the notion that artists were often incorporated into projects through a one-way communication process, and that often it was just the creative output, rather than the ideas, processes, and disruptions that they may bring to a collaboration, that was traditionally expected. The creative labs programme challenged this process and seems to have been successful in helping to provide a much more equitable and communicative experience.

Interviewee 12 – Academic

Interviewee 12 was part of the first Creative Labs cohort and described this as a 'light-bulb moment'. The core benefit of the experience was described as the ability to work outside the restrictions of the academy whilst having access to a 'neutral' space. Interviewee 12 describes this as a transformative experience for them and their team in creating a much greater capacity to innovate and generate new ideas. They describe the importance of acknowledging your own lack of knowledge in specific areas and being: 'open about your ideas, but also be open about your ignorance'. The connections started as the team discovered crossover areas of interest, which created a valuable and long-term bond.

Interviewee 13 – Artist

Interviewee 13 outlined how the creative labs experience is continuing to influence and develop their artistic practice and recognises that the programme was a valuable means to help them become more open, absorptive, and discover new ideas. In the initial stages, the interviewee recalls meeting the programme with a mix of curiosity and anxiety. An initial period of socialising and conversation was important here to build connection and trust which, as has been described previously, was greatly enhanced by the removal of deliverables and expectations of outputs. Interviewee 13 describes that every conversation they had with their collaborative partner 'sparked loads of ideas' and they were able to feel confident and comfortable with their own creative process. The interviewee commented that artists are used to being commissioned or having to apply for funds, whereas in the research they had the space and freedom to find a project to further develop their practice without the normal constraints.

Interviewee 14 – Artist

Interviewee 14 is a partner with a theatre company and recognised that artists could be valuable throughout the academic research process, not just in terms of engaging dissemination at the completion of the project. The value of the creative labs experience was described by Interviewee 14 as being kickstarted at the point that a strong friendship bond had been created. At this stage, they felt motivated to challenge themselves to come up with a tangible output. However, initially the motivation was simply 'just to get to know each other and have a fun time together'. The interviewee recalls this opportunity as very refreshing and highlighted the opportunity to create an equal partnership where the voice of the artist was at the same level as that of the researcher. They describe that a genuine work with an artist requires an exchange of ideas that goes beyond creating a connection with a wider audience.

All participants referred to the need to experience 'fun' – this is often a very under-rated and under-researched area of creativity and play. Whilst play is increasingly acknowledged as a valuable means to spark innovation, we often encounter the term in an organisational and educational setting with the prefix 'serious'. One assumes that the term 'play' is considered more palatable if it is for a serious purpose. However, the research here demonstrates the importance that interviewees placed on playfulness and fun alongside their professional practice, and especially when it is not immediately tied to expected deliverables and outcomes.

DISCUSSION

From the interviews with academic and creative practitioners and entrepreneurs who represent collaborations taking place throughout eight years of the Creative Labs programme, the following model of creative collaboration is offered here (Fig. 8.1). Rather than describing a particular product, innovative service or organisational process all participants reflected on the transformational personal development that they had experienced. Therefore, the model describes the process of building the capacity to innovate with partners beyond a participant's usual experience. The ongoing projects and new networks that most of the interviewees described as having developed are a testament to a newfound ability to connect with a wider array of actors in the local creative economy. It is for this reason that the model does not necessarily describe a process of innovation, but moreover a learning journey. The journey includes three stages. For a better understanding, each stage will be explained separately:

Flux State or State of Uncertainty

The initial stage that most of the participants described is referred to here as a 'Flux State' or state of uncertainty. It is here that participants may experience the feeling of being out of their comfortable working practice. The language used in conversation may be unfamiliar to each partner. Participants described a feeling of being 'out of their depth' and 'Intrigued and slightly anxious about how the process of collaboration will be' (Interviewee 13). Uncertainty was an important part of this experience, even in terms of the space used for collaboration; however, the risk of perceived failure or reputational loss due to the prospect of not being able to make the collaboration work is mitigated by the lack of

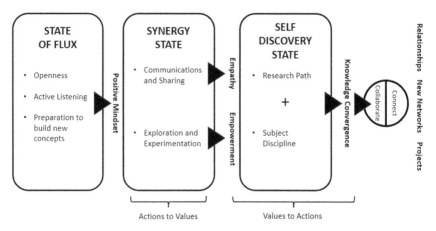

Fig. 8.1. Creative Labs Transformative Journey Model. *Source*: Authors' own.

expected deliverables from the programme. One of the participants described this as 'unconditional hospitality' which in turn helped them embrace the challenge.

> Be open about your ideas but also be open about your ignorance. (Interviewee 3)

> Be in the right frame of mind, experience the reality of the other could be life changing. Approach with respect, open and willing to hear the other's expertise as well as offer mine. (Interviewee 6)

A significant outcome of this research is therefore the importance of socialising and connection between collaborating participants. The concern and anxiety felt by some participants when attempting to collaborate with someone outside of their field of practice is exactly the kind of entry barrier which many microenterprises and arts freelancers face in a sector where paradoxically they are in the majority. Without the time or safe space afforded to them by a programme like this to develop trust as well as new knowledge and a shared cultural 'closeness', collaboration and clustering will always favour those with pre-existing propinquity.

This initial stage of flux and uncertainty is a necessary one. The context is important however, as it is not just about networking and talking to new contacts – it is the prospect of the conversation leading to a collaborative project which encourages the participants to reach out and find common ground. From the analysis of the interviews, it is clear that a key outcome of this stage is a positive mindset, which is needed to enter the next stage.

Synergy State

This stage reflects how the participants share their knowledge and are capable of finding a common ground between their professional experience and practice, both from a personal perspective, as well as a team perspective. It is here that previous actions, shared through conversation, help to form a set of common values. Later in the process these then inform plans for the collaborative action thereby moving from values to actions (i.e. Actions to Values to Actions). The notion of respect and equality was constantly repeated:

> There was a synergy between the team – common interests and ideas. Indeed, individuals that come together are the ones that push the boundaries. (Interviewee 7)

> Creative Labs create space to allow people to focus on developing, outside our egos. Adapting to each other, to being conscious they weren't part of a University, and they have more freedom. Therefore, factors like money, without thinking about the amount also add worth to the time you decide to give to the experience. Is that feeling of recognising my work, beyond its monetary value. (Interviewee 1)

All participants described the outcomes of this stage of collaboration as an increased level of communication and sharing. It is particularly worth noting the importance that arts entrepreneurs and freelancers placed on the experience of equity in idea development. This outcome is accompanied by a sense of exploration and experimentation into new areas previously untapped. These lead to a general sense of empathy with the project partner and empowerment to act.

Self-discovery State

The later stage is described as 'self-discovery' and is where all participants reflected not only on the project outcome, but also on their own development and change in practice. It was this personal transformation and capacity for boundary-crossing and creative experimentation that was seen to be the most valuable outcome from the experience. The main characteristic of the journey therefore is referred to as being 'transformative'. At an individual and collective level, it is evidenced in the way that participants change their understanding of interdisciplinary relationships – confirming their knowledge in certain cases as well as discovering new ways or approaches in others.

Most of the participants described continued and new projects with their partners, as well as expanding their networks. A newfound ability to connect outside of their typical practice was particularly evident in the discussions with artists and freelancers who now felt confident in collaborating outside of their traditional comfort zone.

CONCLUSIONS

Whilst microenterprises and freelancers make up a large proportion of the creative sector much innovation support, especially through formal creative clusters, is arguably focussed on a high growth profile. In this context, there is a concern that for many arts professions, the opportunities to collaborate in a wider creative economy, to harness new skills, technology and approaches, may be somewhat limited. This chapter explores a university Creative Lab programme as a potential way to bridge this divide. By offering the opportunity to develop creative collaborations in a playful and open manner, the academy may provide valuable support for smaller organisations struggling to find ways to connect into other disciplines or indeed make use of new technologies. In this initial research, it is important to theorise and capture how the process may be characterised.

The study has provided insights into how Creative Labs may be perceived and understood despite its flexible and open nature. It is hoped that the Transformational Journey model may act as a means to organise and anchor other such practical initiatives as well as acting as a starting point for further research.

A key research implication from this work is the role of propinquity, or conceptual and cultural closeness in creative collaboration. The Creative Labs Programme develops this closeness between participants as an antecedent to collaboration illustrating an important step in the development of nascent ecosystems in addition to potential collaborators simply being geographically proximities.

REFERENCES

Auriacombe C. J., & Schurink, E. (2012). Conceptualising qualitative research through a spiral of meaning-making. *Administratio Publica, 20*(3), 144–169.

Chung, C., Yang, L., & Cauldwell-French, E. (2018). Growing the UK's creative industries: What creative enterprises need to thrive and grow. Creative Industries Federation. https://www.creativeindustriesfederation.com/sites/default/files/2018-12/Creative%20Industries%20Federation%20-%20Growing%20the%20UK's%20Creative%20Industries.pdf

Creswell, J. (2013). *Qualitative inquiry & research design: Choosing among five approaches* (3rd Edn.). SAGE

Culkin, N. (2016). Entrepreneurial universities in the region: The force awakens? *International Journal of Entrepreneurial Behaviour & Research*, 22(1), 4–16.

Dawson, C. (2009). *Introduction to research methods: A practical guide for anyone undertaking a research project* (4th Edn.). How to Content. http://www.vlebooks.com/Vleweb/Product/Index/2036027?page=0

Delgado, M., Porter, M. E., & Stern, S. (2010). Clusters and entrepreneurship. *Journal of Economic Geography*, 10(4), 495–518.

Deloitte. (2021). *The future of the creative economy*. Deloitte. https://www2.deloitte.com/content/dam/Deloitte/uk/Documents/technology-media-telecommunications/deloitte-uk-future-creative-economy-report-final.pdf

Dobson, S., & McKendrick, J. (2018). Intrapreneurial spaces to entrepreneurial cities: Making sense of play and playfulness. *The International Journal of Entrepreneurship and Innovation*, 19(2), 75–80.

Dobson, S. & Suckley, L., (2015). 'A squash and a squeeze': Managing spatial relations in the office. *International Journal of Business Environment*, 7(2), 137–150.

Fost, D. (2008). *They're working on their own, just side by side*. New York Times.

Gandini, A. (2015). The rise of coworking spaces: A literature review. *Ephemera: Theory and Politics in Organization*, 15(1), 193–205.

Garcia, J. M., Klinger, J., & Stathoulopoulos, K. (2018). *Creative nation: How the creative industries are powering the UK's nations and regions*. NESTA. https://apo.org.au/sites/default/files/resource-files/2018-02/apo-nid134721.pdf

Gibson, C., (2010). Guest editorial—Creative geographies: Tales from the 'margins'. *Australian Geographer*, 41(1), 1–10.

Glaeser, E. L., Kerr, W. R., & Ponzetto, G. A. (2010). Clusters of Entrepreneurship. *Journal of Urban Economics*, 67(1), 150–168.

Hill, I., Manning, L., & Frost, R. (2021). Rural arts entrepreneurs' placemaking–how 'entrepreneurial placemaking' explains rural creative hub evolution during COVID-19 lockdown. *Local Economy*, 36(7–8), 627–649.

Inshakov, O. (2013). Collaboration as a form of knowledge-based economy organization. *Ekonomika Regiona*, 3(3), 45–52.

Kacperczyk, A. J. (2013). Social influence and entrepreneurship: The effect of university peers on entrepreneurial entry. *Organization Science*, 24(3), 664–683.

Mateos-Garcia, J., & Bakshi, H. (2016). *The geography of creativity in the UK*. Nesta.

Moreton, S. (2018). Contributing to the creative economy imaginary: Universities and the creative sector. *Cultural Trends*, 27(5), 327–338.

Petelczyc, C., Capezio, A., Wang, L., Restubog, S., & Aquino, K. (2018). Play at work: An integrative review and agenda for future research. *Journal of Management*, 44(1), 161–190.

Pratt, A. C. (2004). The cultural economy: A call for spatialized 'production of culture' perspectives. *International Journal of Cultural Studies*, 7(1), 117–128.

Rittel, H., & Webber, M. (1973). Dilemmas in a general theory of planning. *Policy Sciences*, 4(2), 155–169.

Schmidt, S., & Brinks, V. (2017). Open creative labs: Spatial settings at the intersection of communities and organizations. *Creativity and Innovation Management*, 26(3), 291–299.

Siepel, J., Camerani, R., Masucci, M., Ospina, J. V., Casadei, P., & Bloom, M. (2020). *Creative industries radar: Mapping the UK's creative clusters and microclusters*. Creative Industries Policy & Evidence Centre led by Nesta.

Velez, J., Siepel, J., Hill, I., & Rowe, F. (2022). *Mapping and examining the determinants of England's rural creative microclusters*. National Innovation Centre for Rural Enterprise (NICRE). Research Report No 7: May 2022. https://www.ncl.ac.uk/mediav8/nicre/files/NICRE%20Research%20Report%20No%207%20with%20Creative%20PEC%20May%202022%20Mapping%20and%20examining%20the%20determinants%20of%20England's%20rural%20creative%20microclusters.pdf

Walter-Herrmann, J., & Büching, C. (Eds.). (2014). *FabLab: Of machines, makers and inventors*. Transcript Verlag.

Whittington, K. B., Owen-Smith, J., & Powell, W. W. (2009). Networks, propinquity, and innovation in knowledge-intensive industries. *Administrative Science Quarterly*, *54*(1), 90–122.

CHAPTER 9

BUILDING ONLINE COMMUNITIES TO SUPPORT WOMEN CREATIVE ENTREPRENEURS DURING LOCKDOWN

Beki Gowing

University of the Arts London, UK

ABSTRACT

The COVID-19 pandemic and global lockdowns forced us all to spend more time online. This chapter compares in-person and online community building as a business support tool for women creative entrepreneurs. Four cycles of action research collected qualitative data and tested different iterations of a peer-coaching training programme, with two cycles held in person pre-pandemic and two held online peri-pandemic. Communities were created during the structured sessions and benefits are considered in the context of social capital generation. The affordability and accessibility of in-person and online support is also assessed. Results show online participants developed close bonds and rapport with their new community as quickly as participants at in-person sessions. These relationships were long-lasting, with several groups continuing to meet months after the study ended. The peer-coaching training approach provided a low-cost option for business support and the move to online increased accessibility. Putnam's theory of bridging social capital explains why community building between diverse individuals is useful for entrepreneurs, as it introduces new perspectives and expands connections. Participants found underlying commonalities in their personal values and entrepreneurial experiences, which helped them build these connections. This study presents a comparison between the in-person and online sessions and proposes that online structured peer-coaching sessions can provide business support to women creative entrepreneurs by helping them increase their social capital.

Keywords: COVID-19; community; social capital; women's entrepreneurship; creative enterprise

INTRODUCTION

In March 2020, I was partway through a research project exploring the impact of teaching peer-coaching techniques to a group of women business owners. Peer-coaching in general is an under-researched area and research into the impact of peer-coaching on social capital creation for entrepreneurs is extremely limited. I hoped to understand the role peer coaching could play in supporting women's creative entrepreneurs. Previous research has identified women entrepreneurs as at risk of isolation, low income, and burnout (Dumas, 2001; Kariv, 2013), in addition to the threats of mental health issues (Gross & Musgrave, 2017), exploitation (McRobbie, 2015) and lack of state support (McRobbie, 2016) experienced by many creative entrepreneurs. My past experience running a design studio and working as a business coach with creative SMEs mirrored many of these findings. I used voluntary-response sampling to recruit those who self-identified with this demographic. This included an intersection of freelancers, pre-launch founders and experienced business owners; people working within and aligned to creative industries; and those experiencing female societal pressures as outlined by Kariv (2013).

I initially ran in-person sessions offering iterations of a peer-coaching training programme. Two research cycles were completed: the first testing the structure and content of the sessions, and the second identifying the impacts of peer coaching and community building. With the arrival of the UK lockdown in the spring 2020, the third and eventual fourth iterations moved online. While navigating the extreme anxiety of the situation, the change in delivery created an interesting comparison – how would the online peer coaching and community building compare to the in-person sessions? And could online peer coaching offer an affordable and accessible approach to business support for women creative entrepreneurs? The impact of multiple lockdowns, social distancing, and changes in public behaviour has created additional issues for this demographic. Analysis is still emerging; Xu and Jia's work found that COVID-19 significantly decreased Chinese entrepreneurs' personal wellbeing (2022), and approximately 75% of UK entrepreneurs have reported a loss in trading (Ute, 2021). Entrepreneurs in the creative industries have suffered from the cancellation of live events, the closure of cultural venues, the narrow focus of government support packages, and additional mental health problems (Khlystova, 2022). The Office for National Statistics has released data highlighting the concerning repercussions of the COVID-19 pandemic on women's wellbeing, mental health, and their additional time spent on unpaid childcare and household work (2021). Therefore, any approach that can provide accessible and affordable business support for women creative entrepreneurs is highly desirable. Additionally, the pandemic has increased our reliance on digital technology (McKinsey, 2020), so it is sensible to explore the impact of online business support on entrepreneurs' social capital.

In this chapter, peer coaching is defined as a group of two or three participants supporting each other through dialogue. This format helps them each work through challenges and commit to a course of action. The group participants take turns to fulfil the role of coach and coachee (and the role of observer in groups of three), and they work in the same groups every session. The peer-coaching training programme in this study contains a series of sessions. Each session includes workshop-style taught content on a coaching or communication tool or theory; peer-coaching practice in groups of three; and whole-group discussions and reflections. The in-person and online sessions followed similar formats.

The study used an action research approach to run four sequential research cycles between October 2019 and August 2020 to 57 total participants. Each cycle ran an iteration of the peer-coaching training programme and collected qualitative data through participant interviews, surveys, session transcriptions, and personal field notes.

The findings suggest participants in the in-person and online sessions had similar experiences. All developed close relationships with the other members of their groups, and analysis suggests this form of community building built social capital. The structured format of the sessions supported their personal development as business leaders and helped them communicate. There was no noticeable difference in results between the in-person and online sessions. However, the online sessions delivered an additional benefit, as they could also be accessed by a wider and more diverse audience.

LITERATURE REVIEW

Women Creative Entrepreneurs

The original study explored the community support needed by enterprising women due to the societal impacts of gendered expectations. Gendered societal or familial expectations may dictate women's time available for personal development and the type of support they require (Dumas, 2001; Kariv, 2013; Sweetman & Pearson, 2018). Research by De Simone et al. shows the pandemic has increased the family and entrepreneurial demands made on women entrepreneurs. This increase further reduced their time available for personal development and the likelihood of their entrepreneurial success (2021). Dumas explains that business support tailored to skills acquisition, education, building self-confidence, accessing information, and challenging entrepreneurial gender stereotypes are most important for developing women entrepreneurs (2001). Kariv builds on this list, suggesting that tools to support professional networking, mental health, work/life balance, a propensity to internalise failure, and loneliness are also needed (2013). From personal experience, I recognise many of these issues and believe peer coaching and community building could be a partial solution. This belief led to the creation of the study.

Coaching and Peer-Coaching

Coaching can take many different forms and is widely used in various situations to support individuals and teams. Professional coaching uses dialogue to facilitate learning and encourage goal-focussed action. It is typically delivered one-to-one or with small teams by a professional and accredited coach. Research by Thomas, McDonagh and Canning demonstrates the value of professional coaching for supporting creative entrepreneurs (2014), although the financial investment needed to pay for professional coaching can be a barrier to access. Peer coaching is a low-cost approach reciprocally delivered by trained peers. It is widely and successfully used during nurse and teacher training (Badowski, 2019; Hohensee & Lewis, 2019). The evidence base for peer coaching is less rigorous than other coaching approaches. However, it is widely agreed to be low cost, easy to implement, and, when conducted appropriately, can reduce participant's stress levels, build self-confidence, develop interpersonal relationships, and create a sense of community (Badowski, 2019; Chen, 2017; Hagen et al., 2017; Parker et al., 2014; Prince et al., 2010). Unlike professional coaching, peer coaching also offers participants reciprocal and reflexive learning opportunities and the possibility of building peer support networks (Parker et al., 2014; Prince et al., 2010). Kutzhanova et al. propose peer coaching as a tool for developing entrepreneurial skills through group learning (2009). I agree with this perspective, but believe the benefits of peer coaching for entrepreneurs exceed skill development and can also build social capital. Therefore, I propose peer coaching can be a potential low-cost tool to provide business support and create social capital for women creative entrepreneurs.

Community Building and Social Capital

With women entrepreneurs identified as a group who need specific business support, and peer coaching identified as a potential tool for delivering this, I next sought to understand the value of networks and social capital for entrepreneurs. Evidence shows community building can provide entrepreneurs with emotional support (Kariv, 2013), access to finance (Todd, 2012), access to opportunities (Halpern, 2006), knowledge and resource sharing (Ebbers, 2014), feedback and ideation (St-Jean & Audet, 2012) and potential increased economic returns (Halpern, 2006). Kariv outlines how women especially receive pre- and post-startup benefits from supportive communities (2013). Communicating with others shares knowledge and develops our thinking by introducing us to new perspectives. If we consider communication as a 'process of sharing meaning through the exchange of information' (Castells, 2012, p. 5), we can appreciate the importance of community and networks in the social production of knowledge. Ideas on social capital developed by Portes (1998) and Putnam (2001) explore the benefits of altruism and generalised reciprocity that seem to align with peer coaching. For example, Putnam establishes the concept of bonding and bridging.

Bonding is when strong social ties between members of homogeneous groups are strengthened, while bridging is when weak social ties between members of heterogeneous groups are formed (2001). He explains how these bridging ties may encourage social inclusion. From a peer-coaching perspective, I expected the new perspectives and expanded connections fostered during a peer-coaching session could support entrepreneurs. Kariv (2013) explains, 'social capital is essential to the myriad resources and transactions that are critical in the early stages of the new venture process' (p. 203). As the business develops, the social capital provides access to resources and knowledge, which in turn, further increases business sustainability (Greve & Salaff, 2003). Even if we ignore the other benefits of peer coaching (reducing stress levels, etc.), it is a cost-effective high return on investment (Hagen et al., 2017) method of developing social capital for entrepreneurs.

Online Learning and Online Communities

The global lockdowns of 2020 significantly accelerated our adoption of digital technology (McKinsey, 2020) and encouraged an abundance of new activity in online learning and online communities. Many of us now use technology differently than we did in 2019, particularly in how we communicate and interact with others. As the sessions comprising my third and fourth research cycles moved online, an unexpected but interesting comparison between the in-person and online communities developed. Once a robust I.T. infrastructure is in place, online learning can offer 'accessibility, affordability [and] flexibility' (Dhawan, 2020, p. 6). It is particularly well suited to adult education as the sessions can be scheduled around other commitments. Participants can be drawn from a wide geographical area (James & Thériault, 2021), offering increased information sharing and networking benefits (Wong, 2021). From a peer-coaching perspective, a more geographically diverse cohort can be recruited online, offering additional opportunities for generating bridging social capital. The digital transformation ensures most UK entrepreneurs have the means and ability to utilise this online support (Nambisan, 2019). However, this is not true of all demographics. Access to technology and user ability should first be considered before assuming online support will broaden accessibility.

Meurer notes that surprising little is known about how online communities create support for entrepreneurs. Their research into online community business support for entrepreneurs during the COVID-19 pandemic outlines how entrepreneurs, when experiencing specific issues, used online message boards to resolve, reframe, reflect and refocus their problems (2022). Similarly, research by Jang and Choi explored the social capital generated by online message board users during the pandemic. They identify that sharing personal feelings and giving emotional support facilitates the formation of online communities. These can serve as a space providing emotional functions that are not met in other parts of user's lives (2020). This aligns with pre-pandemic research by Leovardis which makes similar findings when interviewing women entrepreneurs and 'mompreneurs' about online mother-entrepreneur support sites and social networks (2018). These studies differ from my work as interactions were generally reactive, user-instigated and text-based, with no external/facilitator influence.

In contrast, my work explores if using a proactive approach with structure, a more diverse user group, video-based interactions, and teaching peer-coaching techniques can still create an online community, generate social capital and provide business support.

When deciding to move the peer-coaching sessions online, I read Chen's successful 2017 online support group. They effectively built a virtual community, developed resilience, and reduced burnout among participants. There were similarities between our approach and research aims, which suggested online sessions could be successful. Rapport-building exercises during the in-person workshops were developed in response to Kariv's (2013) work on women effectively reading non-verbal cues and facial expressions (p. 458). Therefore, with the move to online, it seemed video conferencing would be a suitable medium, as it offers interactivity, immediacy, and more opportunities for visual communication.

METHODOLOGY

The original study into the benefits of peer coaching included a wider literature review and expert interviews, which informed the structure and contents of the sessions. A summary of the structure and contents is included here to aid understanding. Each session lasted approximately two hours and was delivered by an individual facilitator to a group of participants. During the first session, the participants were grouped into three. They worked in the same groups during the practice parts of each session. This group size allows participants to alternate between the roles of coach, coachee, and observer, creating a reflexive learning environment. Timings and activities changed over the study, but most sessions followed the structure outlined in Table 9.1.

Table 9.1. An Overview of the Structure Behind Most In-person and Online Sessions (280 words).

Approximate Timings	Activity
15 minutes	Welcome
	Session overview
	Group check-in
40 minutes	Introduction to a coaching or communication tool, model, or theory
	This part included taught content, group discussions, group exercises, and/or individual exercises, depending on the topic
50 minutes	Divide into groups of three for peer-coaching practice:
	- 5 minutes: Contracting with each other, agreeing on initial roles and the session format
	- 15 minutes in the first role (coach, coachee or observer)
	- 15 minutes in the second role
	- 15 minutes in the third role, so all participants have performed all roles
15 minutes	Return to the main group
	Group reflection
	Opportunity to ask questions

Research Philosophy, Design, and Data Collection

The study began with a hypothesis informed by personal experience: women creative entrepreneurs find peer coaching and community building beneficial. I felt action research to be a suitable approach, as it supports 'hands-on research' (Quigley, 1997, p. 38) and an iterative testing and development framework. Consequently, pragmatic philosophy is suited to action research, as it focusses on complex 'real-world research' (Duram, 2010) and allows a choice of research methods unimpeded by theoretical constraints. Pragmatism does not seek an overarching 'truth', instead, studying human experience to understand the best solution for a given situation. This philosophy was well suited to the disruptive events of March 2020 that occurred in the middle of the study. Action research outlines a cyclical process where cycles of practical research are planned, conducted, analysed, and reflected on. In line with most other action research studies, I used multiple data sources to enable triangulation (Sagor, 2000). The study's small sample size limits the usefulness of quantitative data, so qualitative data was collected through participant questionnaires, interviews, session transcripts, and personal field notes. All participant data was anonymised, with personal identifiers separated from (coded) personal data.

- The first research cycle was delivered as three weekly in-person peer-coaching sessions to eight participants. Participants were creative founders and postgraduate students at Goldsmiths, University of London. This initial cycle tested the structure and content of the peer-coaching sessions and the impact on participants' sense of rapport with the group. Data was collected from participant baseline and evaluation questionnaires, follow-up semi-structured interviews with three participants, and field notes.
- The second research cycle was delivered as three weekly in-person peer-coaching sessions to 22 creative founders. This cycle tested the structure and content with a larger audience and identified what a third and more in-depth study should explore. Data collection methods included participant baseline and evaluation questionnaires, research field notes, and a participant semi-structured interview.
- The third research cycle moved online and delivered five weekly peer-coaching sessions to 17 participants. All participants were UK-based creative freelancers and entrepreneurs, recruited through social media and professional networks. The results of this cycle are compared against the earlier in-person sessions to understand if the same approach could work effectively online. Three participants were interviewed, and all participants completed weekly questionnaires, participated in a follow-up focus group, and completed a follow-up questionnaire three months after the programme ended.
- The final research cycle delivered a stand-alone two-hour online peer-coaching session to 10 participants. This cycle explored the bridging social capital potential of online peer coaching. Therefore, I recruited participants from a wider range of geographic locations, ethnicities, and educational backgrounds. Participants provided feedback through baseline and evaluation questionnaires.

Data Analysis

Each research cycle produced qualitative data, which was analysed to uncover the story it reveals (Sagor, 2000) and to determine if further research cycles were necessary. After the peer-coaching sessions had finished, each cycle included a reflection stage. During this stage, the data was collated and analysed using a three-level coding approach. First, a data-driven, inductive approach was used to read and annotate the data, creating potential codes and identifying meaning. Second, the literature review and the cycle's aims and objectives generated codes. These were used during a second deductive theory-driven reading. Third, codes and data were read together, enabling the identification and interpretation of wider patterns and context. As Quigley (1997) recommends, I discussed the findings and analysis with peers. This iterative approach meant the analysis informed the next research cycle and helped identify the study completion after four research cycles.

FINDINGS AND DISCUSSION
A Structured Approach to Community Building

Unlike the organic, open community described by Jang and Choi (2020) and Meurer (2022), this study created closed communities that were supported with structured sessions and taught content. My past experiences at networking events taught me that trust and honesty are difficult to forge in a room of strangers, particularly when those strangers are also running businesses and may be in competition. Lencioni describes this issue in his work on building teams, explaining how trust is the essential first step beyond which a group of people is unlikely to create anything meaningful (2002). The lack of trust was a concern, so the first session of each cycle included rapport-building exercises and active listening practice. Other topics covered in the sessions include reflective writing, goal setting, the GROW coaching questions model (Alexander, 2006), and understanding personal values. Participant quotes include, 'This coaching has helped me to help myself and others unpick things so they're not so scary', 'It's made me think about myself way more, be more reflective about how, what, and why I do. It's made me think about how to support others to find their own answers', 'I found it really inspiring to talk to other creatives in this sort of way', and 'You sit down with people you don't know, and by actively listening you realise the person in front of you is going through exactly the same stuff'. These comments highlight the reciprocal nature of peer coaching (Parker et al., 2014) and suggest significant benefits are attained through structured conversations with others. These findings build on Thomas' work (2014) to suggest creative entrepreneurs not only benefit from professional coaching but also peer coaching. Participants described their continued use of communication tools such as active listening and using open questions outside of the training sessions. One described how she adapted an exercise into a game for her children. These tools easily became embedded in the entrepreneurs' lives, impacting their wider community in addition to the communities built by the study. Despite my concerns, competition did not arise as a barrier to trust. Participants remarked that listening to others and showing empathy helped them notice their similarities. In turn, this developed their self-awareness and encouraged individuals to show themselves the same compassion they showed other members of their group. Therefore, a structure that offers a form of communication training (such as peer-coaching techniques), structured conversations (such as peer-coaching practice), and a space for reflection and asking questions (such as a follow-up group discussion) is a potential way to build a community of entrepreneurs.

Comparison Between Building In-person and Online Communities

Despite never meeting in person, the participants of the online research cycles reported quickly building long-lasting cohesive communities. My approach to measuring and analysing group cohesiveness developed over the study, as this is easier to observe in person. Field notes from the first two research cycles record intimate body language such as leaning in, mimicry, smiling, and sustained eye contact increasing as the sessions progressed. Collective habits such as sitting in the same positions and speaking with the same people also developed, suggesting developing rapport. Comments on the evaluation questionnaires echoed my field notes. These behaviours were harder to observe online, so results rely on participant comments. One participant in the third cycle remarked, 'It's amazing that despite three strangers coming together and talking..., how quickly we were really open with one another. I was surprised, especially through a screen'. Other participants in both online research cycles made similar comments. This feedback suggests the shift to online delivery did not impact community building, although the influence of lockdown and COVID-19 placed significant additional pressures on participants. This result aligns with pre- and peri-pandemic research on the success of digital communities (Chen, 2017; Jang & Choi, 2020; Meurer, 2022). Despite the abrupt change to online, the third research cycle was the most extensive. Participants completed follow-up questionnaires after each session and again three months after the training ended to understand the longevity of any impacts. These later surveys revealed that three of the seven peer-coaching groups continued to meet regularly online. They described the online community as an 'anchor' and a 'lifeline' during the UK lockdown. Deep collaborative relationships formed during both online research cycles, and two years later, some are still in place and bearing creative fruit. However, unlike the in-person groups, participants of the third and fourth research cycles only spoke to others during the structured practice sessions and whole group discussions. This encouraged online participants to form strong bonds with others in their practice group but not with the wider group. In contrast, in-person participants could also speak during unstructured times, such as before and after sessions and during breaks. This suggests online sessions can build small communities and long-lasting business and creative relationships, but the rapport between larger communities may be harder to establish.

Accessibility and Affordability

I hoped to understand if online peer coaching could offer an accessible and affordable approach to business support. Peer coaching is already regarded as an economically viable coaching approach (Hagen et al., 2017) and the move to online significantly increased accessibility. The removal of limits on room size and geographic location allowed more participants to attend. The third research cycle saw a wider spread of ages and experience levels than before, possibly due to not paying transport or refreshment costs (James & Thériault, 2021) and the flexibility to fit sessions around their other commitments (Dhawan, 2020). However, online accessibility relies on equal access to the internet. Unexpectedly, online sessions were as labour intensive as in-person sessions. The organisation and administration for the third research cycle was significant, as I first had to plan and create an effective online learning environment (Maltby & Mackie, 2016). Internet connectivity and reliability was a problem for everyone, causing occasional disruptions. These issues should be considered, and mitigation plans developed, before the study is repeated or scaled. Affordability did not change with the move to online, as compared to professional coaching, the sessions were already low-cost to deliver. The online costs of a Zoom subscription, website hosting, and a facilitator's time, are balanced by the in-person costs of room hire, printing, and a comparable amount of the facilitator's time. Overall, the study suggests in-person and online peer coaching is an affordable approach to building communities and social capital for entrepreneurial women. Online peer coaching can also offer increased accessibility without forfeiting quality, providing the chosen population can reliably access the internet.

Group Diversity

Despite the diversity in geography, ethnicity, age, and educational background, participants identified similarities in their personal values and entrepreneurial experiences. The in-person nature of the first two research cycles meant participants shared many similarities, while the online third and fourth cycles encouraged participant diversity. Putnam's theory of bridging social capital (2001) explains why community building between diverse individuals is useful for entrepreneurs, as it introduces new perspectives and expands connections. This was seen in participant comments, such as, 'If there is a safe environment created and a mutual understanding, I don't think it matters how similar or different the person is since we are going for the same goal of helping each other out' and 'We started spotting similarities between ourselves, even if we might be quite different'. The participants found underlying commonalities in the things that mattered to them and their experiences of being women creative entrepreneurs. These commonalities were enough to bridge their differences and develop rapport. The literature shows this type of community building creates social capital, which is beneficial for entrepreneurs at all stages of business (Greve & Salaff, 2003; Kariv, 2013). Notably, all four research cycles experienced a high drop-out rate. Across all four research cycles, between 10% and 50% of participants withdrew from the study (participant numbers stated in the methodology are those who completed the sessions). Therefore, this approach is not suitable for everyone and the benefits stated were only experienced by those who chose to continue attending. Further research is needed to understand the mechanisms and motivators affecting this population's participation. Overall, findings show the peer coaching sessions created social capital for the women creative entrepreneurs regardless of group diversity, because participants seek out similarities and focus on common goals. Additionally, when the group was diverse, it facilitated the generation of bridging social capital, which offered additional networking and development opportunities for entrepreneurs.

CONCLUSION

The communities created using structured sessions and taught content during four action research cycles, delivered significant benefits for the participants. The activities practised during peer coaching sessions, such as active listening, practising self-reflection, and sharing knowledge, began a reciprocal and reflexive process which helped form community bonds, support personal development, and build social capital. The in-person and online sessions held during this study delivered similar results, and both formats had low delivery costs. However, online sessions that used video conferencing software could reach a wider and more diverse audience, while achieving similar impacts. This suggests that online peer coaching and community-building sessions are as beneficial as in-person sessions. Additionally, the online approach can offer affordable and accessible business support to women creative entrepreneurs.

Research limitations include the small sample sizes and the specific external situation created by the early stages of the COVID-19 pandemic. The comparison is between online sessions and an earlier in-person, pre-pandemic version of the study, instead of a control group. Participants who described the sessions as a 'lifeline' may have experienced high anxiety levels and missed their regular in-person community support due to lockdown restrictions. If repeated again, Zoom fatigue (Bailenson, 2021) and a return to 'normal' life could alter the results of the study. Further research could repeat and improve this study, potentially running concurrent online and offline sessions with larger sample sizes. It could also explore motivations for participants leaving or remaining in online business communities, if certain personality types are better suited to peer-coaching support, and how to use the online peer-coaching format to encourage community building among a larger community.

REFERENCES

Alexander, G. (2006). Behavioural coaching—the GROW model. In J. Passmore (Ed.). *Excellence in coaching: The industry guide* (pp. 83–93). Kogan Page.
Badowski, D. (2019). Peer coaching integrated in simulation: Improving intraprofessional teamwork, *Journal of Professional Nursing*, 35(4), 325–328. https://doi.org/10.1016/j.profnurs.2018.11.001
Bailenson, J. N. (2021). Nonverbal overload: A theoretical argument for the causes of zoom fatigue. *Technology, Mind, and Behavior*, 2(1). https://doi.org/10.1037/tmb0000030

Castells, M. (2012). *Networks of outrage and hope: Social Movements in the Internet Age*. Polity Press.
Chen, B. (2017). The professional working group—How to create and use a process group to build community, prevent burnout, and make work-life sustainable (FR417). In *The annual assembly of the American academy of hospice and palliative medicine and the hospice and palliative nurses association* (p. 2).
De Simone, S., Pileri, J., Rapp-Ricciardi, M., & Barbieri, B. (2021). Gender and entrepreneurship in pandemic time: What demands and what resources? An exploratory study. *Frontiers in Psychology*, *12*, 668875. https://doi.org/10.3389/fpsyg.2021.668875
Dhawan, S. (2020). Online learning: A panacea in the time of COVID-19 crisi. *Journal of Educational Technology Systems*, *49*(1), 5–22. https://doi.org/10.1177/0047239520934018
Dumas, C. (2001). Micro enterprise training for low-income women: The case of the community entrepreneurs programme. *The Journal of Entrepreneurship*, *10*(1), 17–42. https://doi.org/10.1177/097135570101000102
Duram, L. (2010). Pragmatic study. In N. Salkind (Eds.), *Encyclopedia of research design*. SAGE Publications, Inc. https://doi.org/10.4135/9781412961288.n326
Ebbers, J. J. (2014). Networking behavior and contracting relationships among entrepreneurs in business incubators. *Entrepreneurship Theory and Practice*, *38*(5), 1159–1181. https://doi.org/10.1111/etap.12032
Greve, A., & Salaff, J. W. (2003). Social networks and entrepreneurship, *Entrepreneurship Theory and Practice*, *28*(1), 1–22. https://doi.org/10.1111/1540-8520.00029
Gross, S. A., & Musgrave, G. (2016). Can music make you sick? Music and depression. *A study into the incidence of musicians' mental health. Part 1–pilot survey report. Help Musicians Music Tank*. Music Tank.
Hagen, M. S., Bialek, T. K., & Peterson, S. L. (2017). The nature of peer coaching: Definitions, goals, processes and outcomes. *European Journal of Training and Development*, *41*(6), 540–558.
Halpern, D. (2006). *Social capital* [Reprint]. Polity Press.
Hohensee, C., & Lewis, W. E. (2019). Building bridges: A cross-disciplinary peer-coaching self-study. *Studying Teacher Education*, *15*(2), 98–117. https://doi.org/10.1080/17425964.2018.1555525
James, N., & Thériault, V. (2021). Reimagining community and belonging amid COVID-19. *Studies in the Education of Adults*, *53*(1), 1–3. https://doi.org/10.1080/02660830.2021.1889092
Jang, I. C., & Choi, L. J. (2020). Staying connected during COVID-19: The social and communicative role of an ethnic online community of Chinese international students in South Korea. *Multilingua*, *39*(5), 541–552. https://doi.org/10.1515/multi-2020-0097
Kariv, D. (2013). *Female entrepreneurship and the new venture creation: An international overview*. Routledge.
Khlystova, O., Kalyuzhnova, Y., & Belitski, M. (2022). The impact of the COVID-19 pandemic on the creative industries: A literature review and future research agenda. *Journal of Business Research*, *139*, 1192–1210. https://doi.org/10.1016/j.jbusres.2021.09.062
Kutzhanova, N., Lyons, T., & Lichtenstein, G. (2009). Skill-based development of entrepreneurs and the role of personal and peer group coaching in enterprise development. *Economic Development Quarterly – ECON DEV Q*, *23*(3), 193–210. https://doi.org/10.1177/0891242409336547
Leovardis, C., Bahna, A., & Cismaru, D. M. (2018). Between motherhood and entrepreneurship: Insights on women entrepreneurs in the creative industries. *Challenging the Status Quo in Management and Economics*, 1383–1404.
Lencioni, P. (2002). *The five dysfunctions of a team: A leadership fable* (1st ed.). Jossey-Bass.
Maltby, A., & Mackie, S. (2009). Virtual learning environments – help or hindrance for the 'disengaged' student? *ALT-J*, *17*(1), 49–62. https://doi.org/10.1080/09687760802657577
McKinsey & Company. (2020). How COVID-19 has pushed companies over the technology tipping point—and transformed business forever. McKinsey.com. https://www.mckinsey.com/business-functions/strategy-and-corporate-finance/our-insights/how-covid-19-has-pushed-companies-over-the-technology-tipping-point-and-transformed-business-forever
McRobbie, A. (2015). Notes on the perfect: Competitive femininity in neoliberal times. *Australian feminist studies*, *30*(83), 3–20.

McRobbie, A. (2016). Towards a sociology of fashion micro-enterprises: Methods for creative economy research. *Sociology, 50*(5), 934–948.

Meurer, M. M., Waldkirch, M., Schou, P. K., Bucher, E. L., & Burmeister-Lamp, K. (2022). 'Digital affordances: How entrepreneurs access support in online communities during the COVID-19 pandemic', *Small Business Economics, 58*(2), 637–663. https://doi.org/10.1007/s11187-021-00540-2

Nambisan, S., Wright, M., & Feldman, M. (2019). The digital transformation of innovation and entrepreneurship: Progress, challenges and key themes, *Research Policy, 48*(8), 103773. https://doi.org/10.1016/j.respol.2019.03.018

Office for National Statistics. (2021). *Coronavirus and the different effects on men and women in the UK, March 2020 to February 2021.* ONS.gov.uk. https://www.ons.gov.uk/peoplepopulationandcommunity/healthandsocialcare/conditionsanddiseases/articles/coronaviruscovid19andthedifferenteffectsonmenandwomenintheukmarch2020tofebruary2021/2021-03-10

Parker, P., Kram, K. E., & Hall, D. T. (2014). Peer coaching: An untapped resource for development. *Organizational Dynamics, 43*(2), 122–129. https://doi.org/10.1016/j.orgdyn.2014.03.006

Portes, A. (1998). Social capital: Its origins and applications in modern sociology. *Annual Review of Sociology, 24*(1), 1–24.

Prince, T., Snowden, E., & Matthews, B. (2010). Utilising peer coaching as a tool to improve student-teacher confidence and support the development of classroom practice. *Literacy Information and Computer Education Journal, 1*(1), 45–51. https://doi.org/10.20533/licej.2040.2589.2010.0007

Putnam, R. (2001). Social capital: Measurement and consequences, *Isuma: Canadian Journal of Policy Research, 2*(1), 41–51.

Quigley, B. A. (Ed.). (1997). Creating practical knowledge through action research: Posing problems, solving problems, and improving daily practice. *New directions for adult and Continuing Education* (p. 73). Jossey-Bass.

Sagor, R. (2000). *Guiding school improvement with action research.* Association for Supervision and Curriculum Development.

St-Jean, E., & Audet, J. (2012). The role of mentoring in the learning development of the novice entrepreneur. *International Entrepreneurship and Management Journal, 8*(1), 119–140. https://doi.org/10.1007/s11365-009-0130-7

Sweetman, C., & Pearson, R. (Eds.). (2018). Gender, business and enterprise. *Working in gender & development.* Practical Action Publishing Ltd.

Thomas, J., McDonagh, D., & Canning, L. (2014). Developing the arts entrepreneur: The 'Learning Cloud', *The Design Journal, 17*(3), 425–443. https://doi.org/10.2752/175630614X13982745783046

Todd, R. (2012). Young urban Aboriginal women entrepreneurs: Social capital, complex transitions and community support, *British Journal of Canadian Studies, 25*(1), 1–19.

Ute, S., Zbierowski, P., Pérez-Luño, A., Klausen, A. M., Efendic, A. S. (2021). Entrepreneurship during the Covid-19 pandemic: A global study of entrepreneurs' challenges, resilience, and well-being. *King's Business School: KBS Covid-19 Research Impact Papers, No. 4.* https://www.kcl.ac.uk/business/assets/pdf/research-papers/global-report-entrepreneurship-during-the-covid-19-pandemic-a-global-study-of-entrepreneurs'-challenges-resilience-and-well-being.pdf

Wong, A., Ho, S., Olusanya, O., Antonini, M. V., & Lyness, D. (2021). The use of social media and online communications in times of pandemic COVID-19. *Journal of the Intensive Care Society, 22*(3), 255–260. https://doi.org/10.1177/1751143720966280

Xu, Z., & Jia, H. (2022). The influence of COVID-19 on entrepreneur's psychological well-being. *Frontiers in Psychology, 12*, 823542.

CHAPTER 10

THE 'CREATIVE VILLAGE': A CREATIVE ENTREPRENEURSHIP FRAMEWORK FOR CATALYSING AFRICA'S CREATIVE AND CULTURAL INDUSTRIES

Adeyinka Adewale[a], Jean-Pierre Choulet[a], Chike Maduegbuna[b], Barry Van Zyl[a] and Stephen Budd[c]

[a]Henley Business School, UK
[b]Afrinolly Creative Hub, Nigeria
[c]Stephen Budd Music Ltd, UK

ABSTRACT

This chapter explores a practical way of realising Africa's creative and cultural industries (CCIs) potential as a new frontier for development. It answers the question of how can young African creatives be nurtured to build creative enterprises? Using insights from extant literature identifying some of the key contextual challenges, we developed and deployed a prototype innovative platform called the 'Creative Village' to address these challenges in a practical way at one of Africa's biggest Music reality TV shows in Nigeria. A qualitative multistakeholder data collection approach called the Ecosystem Insights

Approach (EIA) was adopted to explore these challenges and the appropriateness of the proposed Creative Village solution.

Findings identify some key constraints that creatives face such as weak structures and infrastructure, weak artist education, low levels of investment, and the underdevelopment of the music value chain. We conclude that the creative entrepreneurship framework called the 'Creative Village' and its key features is a viable way of jumpstarting and catalysing the already vibrant yet undertapped CCI in Africa, but this platform must be built on five philosophical pillars: An inclusive platform for individual talents regardless of their gender, location or disability to find expression; developing a holistic, professional creative entrepreneur who understands their craft and the business of their craft; creating a platform that allows for different dimensions of authenticity to thrive; a platform that unifies different players in the Nigeria music ecosystem through the right partnerships; a platform that enhances local markets and connects musicians to regional and international market.

Keywords: Ecosystem; creative village; media; music enterprise; African entrepreneurship

INTRODUCTION

Despite an over-reliance on oil and other extractives, Africa's greatest advantage has always been its human capital. The median age in Africa's vast and increasing population will be nineteen by 2030 (Myers, 2016; International Monetary Fund, 2019; CIA World Fact Book, 2020). This signals a robust youthful continent and suggests a massive talent pool of creative energy as the next frontier of the continent's development (Dredge, 2019b). The COVID-19 pandemic as well as other global geopolitical trends has accelerated this agenda. As the virus shock has made all sectors volatile, with declines in both oil and non-oil sector GDP in most parts of the continent, African states are forced to look to other revenue generating possibilities. Key sectors such as agriculture, technology, tourism and the creative industries (film, fashion and music) have underpinned a lot of sustainable recovery agendas for many African states (Hruby & Annan, 2020).

What is clear is that Africa's creative industries have the potential to serve as profitable investment areas yet many African nations struggle to leverage the potential of the CCIs (Adedeji, 2016). As Lobato (2010) suggests, a recurring theme in the research of cultural industry in Africa and other developing regions is 'the understanding of how these countries can effectively leverage their cultural assets and integrate them into global economic networks, thus providing new sources of revenue, employment and growth' (p. 338). Consequently, the focus of relevant stakeholders is on the development of case studies and policy advice that can assist in realising this objective. Although the CCI literature in Africa has explored the key challenges and the business prospects of the sector, especially in job creation (e.g. Milićević et al., 2013; Snowball et al., 2017), very few have presented a practical case study addressing some of the well-known key concerns. It is within this gap that we intend to contribute to the literature.

This chapter therefore presents a case study to answer the question: How can young African creatives be nurtured to build the creative enterprises that will build Africa's economy? In answering this question, we sought to understand the most significant entrepreneurial challenges the African context poses to young creatives attempting to build sustainable careers in the industry as well as to explore viable ways of transforming them into creative entrepreneurs who understand their craft and the business of their craft.

THE POLICY CONTEXT OF AFRICA'S CREATIVE AND CULTURAL INDUSTRIES

The African Union (AU) themed year 2021 is the year of the arts, culture and heritage in alignment with Aspiration 5 of the Agenda 2063 (DeGhetto et al., 2016; Ndizera & Muzee, 2018). Aspiration five states 'An Africa with a strong cultural identity, common heritage, shared values and ethics' (African Union, 2022). The goal of this aspiration according to the AU is to enable an African cultural renaissance 'inculcating the spirit of Pan Africanism; tapping Africa's rich heritage and culture to ensure that the creative arts are major contributors to Africa's growth and transformation; and restoring and preserving Africa's cultural heritage, including its languages' (African Union, 2022). The purpose of this declaration was to enable member states of the AU and Regional Economic Communities (RECs), working with key stakeholders in both the private and public sector, to collaboratively actualise policies and programmes towards establishing a more robust and sustainable creative industries sector (AU Echo, 2021). This is also meant to increase advocacy for the adoption of the Charter for African Cultural Renaissance (which to date has only been ratified by 14 of the 55 member states) and the Plan of Action on Cultural and Creative Industries in Africa which aims to build a thriving cultural ecosystem.

Besides this Pan-African policy, which is yet to be fully adopted by key member states, individual countries and some RECs also have their own cultural policies. For instance, Nigeria has had a cultural policy since 1988 (with almost the same objectives as the newer policies being enacted (Joshua & Omotoso, 2016). Yet, as Ndizera and Muzee (2018) argued although Agenda 2063 has been created with the right vision and the right approach (bottom-up), in its implementation it will encounter similar setbacks which have prevented previous long-term plans from being successful. According to them, these include 'limited finances, lack of ownership, lack of political will, diverse and sometimes conflicting interests, and lack of ideological backup to sustain the vision' (p. 142). Thus, unless adequate measures are put in place to overcome these challenges, Agenda 2063 may be added to the pile of numerous other planning documents which were never implemented or perhaps as young creatives on the continent interpret it – a tale of many broken promises. This unfortunately has been the African story on policies. The implementation and sustenance of often well-written policies are the biggest hurdle the continent needs to overcome, and this is true for the development of CCIs as well.

CHALLENGES AND POTENTIAL OF AFRICAN COUNTRIES CCIS: REFLECTIONS ON NIGERIA

The extant literature on CCIs in Africa has extensively discussed many of the key challenges and potential of the industry. Broad themes emerging from the literature that have focussed on key challenges of CCIs in Africa have identified issues around defining the scope of CCIs, policy challenges, ineffective value chains, uncoordinated stakeholder interventions in the industry and so on (Fry et al.., 2018; Nzere, 2018; Osasona, 2021). Similarly focus on the potential of African CCIs has often been discussed around their capacity for innovation, wealth creation towards poverty reduction, job creation towards eradicating unemployment, instilling cultural values as well as keeping the African cultural identity intact (see Joshua & Omotoso, 2016; Lobato, 2010; Maiwada et al., 2012; Snowball et al., 2017 as prime examples).

The consensus of these different literature is that the contribution of Africa's CCI to the global market is very minimal. Despite this, Nigeria's Nollywood is globally acclaimed as the second largest film producer in the world, which releases well over 1000 titles a year without assistance from the government, NGOs or international film festivals (Lobato, 2010). Similarly, Nigeria is known as the 'The musical Heartbeat of Africa' best known for its distinctive Afrobeat sound, which combines jazz, traditional Ghanaian and Nigerian music to give a unique style (Rotinwa, 2020) with a combined ability of generating a forecasted US$10.8 billion in 2023 in Nigeria's Entertainment and Media (E&M) market alone (PricewaterhouseCoopers, 2020a). Similarly, in fashion, the desire for African fabrics has resulted in cross-over designs with major global designers now incorporating African print in their best-selling ranges.

Music export from Africa continues to generate conversations and growing interest across the world with the rise of the 'Afropop' genre and the most recent Grammy wins by young African talents, all of which have shown strong promise. Netflix's strong African content is a further testament to the potential the film sector has on the continent (Dredge, 2019a, 2019b). The same can be said of African fashion that has remained increasingly popular and profitable on the global scene. In other words, Africa's creative and cultural industries (CCIs) have opened the continent to global opportunities through the impact of its music, film, and fashion. According to PwC's Entertainment & Media Outlook 2019–2023 report, total recorded music revenue in Nigeria was $32m in 2019, or $0.15 per head (PricewaterhouseCoopers, 2020b). That is far lower than the per-capita totals in China, Turkey and Russia; markets renowned for being unwilling to spend money on music (Nigeria's GDP per capita was just $5,900 in 2017, less than a third that of China). At the same time, music income is on the increase, and PwC predict that Nigeria would be the world's fastest-growing E&M market over the coming five years thanks to the boom in mobile internet consumption. Africa's music industry is set for sustained growth thanks to the adoption of streaming. Whilst recorded music continues to decline, music streaming revenue is estimated to increase by 40% over the next two years in Nigeria resulting in revenues of $17.5 million by 2023 (MusicAlly, 2020).

Yet, the literature on the challenges of the Nigerian music industry identifies why the market has not become the juggernaut it should be on paper. Yoel Kenan of Africori cites: 'a lack of education' in the African music industry, adding: 'we've got great new entrepreneurs, managers, labels and artists who don't always have the experience' (Gilbert, 2020). In other words, a lot of creatives in Africa know their craft but are vastly uneducated on the business of their craft and are therefore unable to build sustainable enterprises from their crafts. Besides this, there is also an underperforming publishing environment where copyright infringements are considered the order of the day (Gilbert, 2020). Building on the lack of copyright infrastructure, the International Confederation of Societies of Authors and Composers (CISAC, 2019) found that whilst Europe brings in more than half of music collections worldwide, Africa's contribution was 0.8%, in comparison to the Asia-Pacific (15.7%) and Latin American (5.4%) regions.

Monetisation is also a significant challenge with consumers often unwilling to pay for music, and many artists unwilling to charge for it. Film and music are largely financed through the informal economy (Ernst&Young, 2015) as the formal creative industry has long suffered from a lack of access to capital, due to traditional risk-averse banking and the inability to meet collateral requirements. PricewaterhouseCoopers (PwC) reports that digital infrastructure is poor and that whilst mobile internet access is available almost everywhere in Nigeria, quality and reliability vary enormously. Paul Okeugo (Chocolate City Group) says, 'There are also challenges around enabling payments from people who don't have credit cards and also piracy' (MusicAlly, 2020). On a more practical level poor infrastructure (epileptic power supply, bad roads, limited rehearsal facilities and equipment rental companies) also pose significant challenges for music production as it increases the time and cost to create content (U.S. Department of Commerce, 2020).

As the African music business continues to grow, so does the need for disruptive innovation and new ways of doing things, and bypassing traditional infrastructures and adopting a 'pull' model as opposed to the usual 'push' approach. (Christenson & Ojomo, 2019). In advancing this agenda, despite many promises by governments in the form of policies, very little is being done to actualise this shift. The wide-scale reforms necessary across the areas of monetary policy, trade policy and the regulatory business environment have not been as progressive as expected. This has left Artists, music producers, record labels and other creative stakeholders with limited choice but to take it upon themselves to keep building what could one day be a multi-billion dollar CCI.

In summary, the extant literature reviewed identified some of the key challenges and potential of CCIs in Africa. We built an intervention around some of these challenges as an empirical case study and as a contribution to the literature on how these challenges can be resolved in Africa. How we designed this intervention, collected and analysed data will be the focus of subsequent sections.

METHODOLOGY

Our Solution

The study set out to answer the question: How can young African creatives be nurtured to build the creative enterprises that will build Africa's economy? In addressing our research question, we built our understanding of some of the key issues plaguing CCIs in Africa from the extant literature as discussed in the previous section. We categorised the challenges from the previous section into three: poor education, ineffective monetisation and weak value chains. Our proposition was that African creatives who will build the enterprises that will build Africa's economy must be:

1. Creatives who understand the business of their craft.
2. Creatives who can build businesses with sustainable and scalable business models.
3. Creatives who are connected to the local, regional and global ecosystem for improved market access and value chain enhancement.

Our proposed solution to these needs is called the *Creative Village'* – an innovative virtual platform designed and deployed to systematise talent discovery, education and market linkage processes. The *Creative Village* concept embeds talent discovery + education + incubation + acceleration + market connection platform.

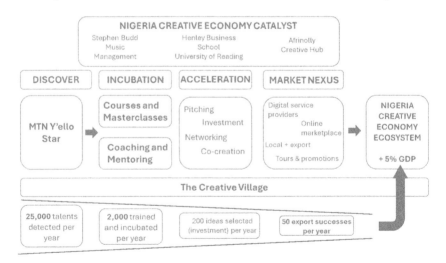

Fig. 10.1. A Diagrammatic Representation of the 'Creative Village.'
Source: Authors' own.

Research Design

To test the *Creative Village*, a prototype platform was built and fully deployed for one of Nigeria's biggest music reality TV shows – MTN Yello Star music talent competition. MTN Yello Star Music Reality Show is a new MTN Nigeria project that encapsulates a music reality show and youth empowerment initiative. It was launched in 2020 and the first edition was successfully concluded on 13 December 2020. The project was designed to search for, discover, nurture, expose and launch music talents (youths) in Nigeria. Discovered talents were assembled in an incubation hub where their skills and talents are honed through masterclasses, coaching, mentoring and practical sessions by renowned lecturers, and distinguished music artists. Through the technical partner, Afrinolly Creative Hub, MTN Yello Star have partnerships with Henley Business School UK for Creative Entrepreneurship, Berklee College of Music USA for Music Training and Music Business; and Yusef Malik (six times Grammy Award winner) for mentorship.

This competition therefore provided the perfect project to deploy and test our prototype of the *Creative Village* platform and to infuse other key features of the concept especially the incubation (e.g. music and business education) and some elements of acceleration (e.g. mentoring with industry experts) and market linkage (e.g. exposure to being heard by leading producers and record label owners) into the music reality TV show.

The components of the digital platform prototype include:

- Call-To-Entry (including database and content management system).
- Online Audition (no expenses for physical auditions).
- Online Certified Masterclasses from Henley UK and Berklee Music College USA.
- Online engagement with Industry Experts for mentoring and Peer-to-Peer Forums.
- Content Provision (performance shows and lifestyle content).

As the prototyping was going on, real-time data collection was happening simultaneously.

We adopted a multistakeholder research (Winn & Keller, 2001) approach we called 'Ecosystem Insights Approach' (EIA) to conduct user feedback and market feasibility of the *Creative Village* concept. The EIA investigates the feasibility of the proposed innovation by keeping the intended end-user at its core (to gain a deeper understanding of their pains and needs) whilst gathering insights from other stakeholders within the music industry ecosystem to understand how the needs of the end-users align or misalign with gaps in the industry. The blend of these two perspectives helped our evaluation of the idea of the *Creative Village* and its feasibility as a catalyst for Nigeria' creative economy and by extension Africa. The rationale for this approach is that the Nigerian music industry landscape is so complex that seeing the challenge through the lens of the end-users alone is not sufficient in ensuring the intended broader impact of our proposed innovation. This further helps us engage in quality data triangulation.

Data Collection and Analysis

We collected data from two major sources:

1. **End-User Focus Groups:** Focus Groups are group discussions organised to explore a specific set of issues such as people's views and experiences of something (Colucci, 2007; Kitzinger, 1994). By asking a series of questions and allowing participants to engage in rich discussions around these questions, we captured qualitative data from fourteen end-users who were also the highly talented contestants in the MTN Yello Star music competition auditioned and selected through the *Creative Village* platform prototype. Open-ended questions were asked and insights collated around core needs and challenges as young creative talents in Nigeria, expectations for the future, and overall experience with key features of the Creative Village platform (Auditioning, masterclasses, mentoring, etc). This enabled us to capture powerful personal stories of the real challenges young creatives face was crucial at this phase of our engagement with the end-users.
2. **In-depth stakeholder interviews:** In-depth stakeholder interviews were designed to gather insights into the state of the Nigerian music industry especially the key challenges, gaps and opportunities for improving the industry. Seven key industry stakeholders were identified and interviewed who together share decades of experience doing business in the Nigerian music scene and have a track record of working with young creative talents from Nigeria. These stakeholders spanned key aspects of the Nigerian music industry value chain. To ensure the excessive local biases are checked, two UK-based stakeholders with vested pan African interests and one US-based Nigerian artiste, songwriter and instrumentalist were also interviewed to bring some balance to the opinions of Nigeria-based stakeholders. These stakeholders were agents, record label owners, producers, talent managers, music lawyers, marketers, and experienced musicians.

Data was analysed using Thematic Analysis (TA) (Joffe, 2012). TA 'is a method for systematically identifying, organising, and offering insight into patterns of meaning (themes) across a data set' (Braun & Clarke 2012, p. 57). We followed a six stages process for the data analysis. We started by familiarising ourselves with the data, generated initial codes, searched for themes, reviewed potential themes, and finally named the themes (Clarke et al., 2015).

FINDINGS

The key themes emerging from the data are presented in two sections. First, we present a detailed description of the key CCI challenges from the perspectives of both the young creatives and the industry stakeholders. The submissions confirmed the challenges found in the literature but provided a more practical analysis of these issues. Secondly, key themes arising from the experiences of the end users of the creative village platform were presented in the form of key principles

The 'Creative Village'

that could make platforms like the Creative Village become the types of solutions that will nurture the creative entrepreneurs that will build the businesses that will build Africa.

Challenges of African CCIs

A summary of key themes and codes emerging from the data is presented in Fig. 10.2. Three key themes emerging under the broad umbrella of challenges include: Weak infrastructure, Underdeveloped value chain as well as Artiste and consumer education.

Weak Structures and Infrastructure

A first submission on a critical note was the weak structures that have typified the Nigerian and African creative industry. The essential structures that allow for the generation of appropriate economic activities from creative talents are largely missing and where present inadequate to support the large talent pool. The stakeholders and artists argued some of these key elements would include inadequate

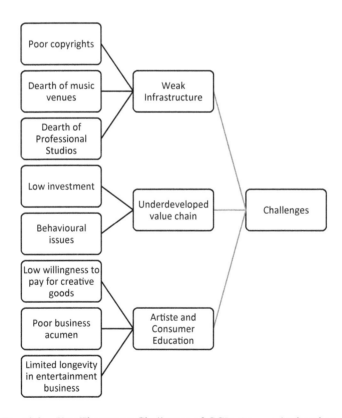

Fig. 10.2. Key Themes on Challenges of CCIs. *Source*: Authors' own.

infrastructure, insufficient legal protection and copyright management and low levels of investment overall. The infrastructure challenge included a shortage of music venues, professional studios and others such as operationalising local and foreign touring. The inadequacy of these basic infrastructures implies the quality of output is often affected and is linked to the limited chances of attaining commercial success.

As one of the industry stakeholders said

> What is the level of our infrastructure? So, we are actually in a pretty terrible state, if we want to be sincere with ourselves. 99% of the studios that exist are, owned studios. Even the record labels don't have professional studios. So, it brings the question of the quality of the output. – Participant 1

Likewise, there have been significant ongoing challenges with establishing effective royalty management systems and legal structures that can guarantee copyright infringements are adequately compensated. It is not the availability of the right laws that is the issue but their enforcement and length of time in following through on court cases. With the royalty collection and management system, the organisations involved have faced significant internal and external crises that have crippled their activities, thereby hindering a major potential revenue stream for local artistes within the country.

Artiste and Consumer Education

Education was identified as a deficient yet significant need in the industry. The education theme that emerged from the stakeholder interview had two strands. Music education for artistes and consumer education. There is a dearth of 'hard' and 'soft' music education for artistes including technical music skills such as vocal training, instruments training, and the music business education component which is also almost non-existent in a structured format. Without these, a lot of talented but musically uneducated talents are emerging resulting in significant long-term issues. Examples of musicians being duped by their managers because they had very little understanding of their business models and revenue streams or the prevalent issue of signing contracts that put artistes at a disadvantage were some of the consequences of weak music education systems.

> Education in the sense that it's going to cover all the many lackings that the industry currently has now – the education and musicianship education and sound engineering, education and all the all the valuable skills that we've lost ... just for people to be informed. – Participant 2

On the other hand also is the need to educate consumers out of seeing creative talent and their outputs as items to consume freely. This is a significant issue as the willingness to pay for creative products by the masses is quite low and has also fed into the culture of piracy. The strong sense of entitlement by consumers to free creative output is almost cultural yet incorrect. A shift in consumer behaviour and attitude towards appreciating the creative talent of artistes enough to pay for their creativity can therefore only be achieved through deliberate education. This implies helping consumers understand that what it means to be a true fan includes willingness of pay for artistes' products and investing in their craft through proper patronage. This trend was also identified as being responsible for stifling creativity amongst artistes such that there is a widespread belief that only certain types of music sung in certain ways sell in certain circles.

Underdevelopment of the Music Industry Value Chain

The underdevelopment of the entire music industry's value chain is another critical factor. In the Nigerian music industry today, there are misconceptions about the role of each point of the value chain. Most artistes are one-man, one-stop shops that try to do everything or keep their activities tightly controlled within a close circle. For example, it is difficult to make a living being a song writer hence most song writers end up wanting to perform their own songs but may not necessarily be good singers.

> You cannot speak of an industry that does not cater for the value chain. So, you can have a few successful artists, I mean a handful ... maybe ten. Ten people can never make an industry, so I wouldn't say we don't have an industry I will say we have weak structures ... it is difficult, very difficult be successful or to have a sustainable career. – Participant 3

Likewise, artistes who utilise song writers think it weakens their credibility as creatives because their songs are not self-written or self-composed. Also, the fact that the revenue structure within the industry relies a lot on shows means those who are meant to be specialists along the value chain vie to be the visible person on the microphone so that they can attract the gigs that will make them money. This has been further compounded by the poor royalty collection systems/infrastructure within the industry which limits earning potential. Hence, existing financial institutions do not consider artistes as investable due to the wider industry constraints that limit the ability of artistes to build sustainable business models in support of their ventures.

The Creative Village Experience

Data from the focus group interview on the experience of the artists on the *Creative Village* platform (see Fig. 10.3) and its key features generated the following key themes as elements that are necessary for young creatives to build sustainable creative ventures: Inclusion, Authenticity, Education, Access and Connectivity.

Inclusion

The notion of inclusion was divided into gender, location and disability. The industry may not be as inclusive for women as it could be and is skewed in favour of male artistes. Closing the gender gap through dedicated investment in female acts underpinned this submission. Similarly, having any chance of success is often associated with being in certain major cities thereby excluding talents from other parts of the country in as much as people living with disabilities, yet talented have often found it difficult travelling to major competitions for auditions. The Creative Village enabled more participants from diverse locations in Nigeria, women and people living with disability to get involved. This was linked to the social challenges

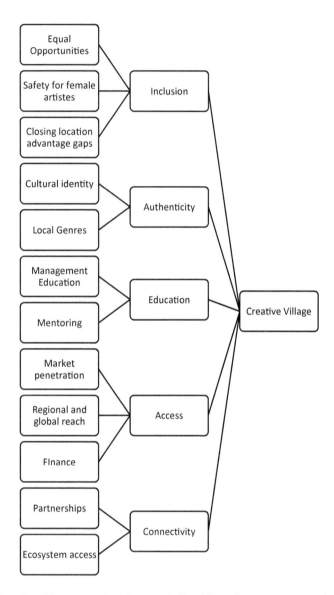

Fig. 10.3. Key Themes on the '*Creative Village*' Experience. *Source*: Authors' own.

female artistes face with accessing industry opportunities, especially the objectifying of female talents and associated sexual exploitation tendencies raises the palpable fear of not being treated at par with male acts for their talents.

> So I would try my best to put more women in the industry, so that the ones that are there don't have to try and kill themselves to remain there. – Participant 4

Likewise, the challenge of talent discovery underpinned the latter point which prompted the recommendation for investment in adequate discovery platforms similar to the *Creative Village*. The overreliance on music talent hunt competitions is not sustainable and the reference made to the adequacy of discovery platforms suggests some sort of systematisation of talent discovery processes beyond talent competitions.

Authenticity

A second theme emerging from the Creative Village experience was the concept of authenticity. Participants felt that the platform enabled them to remain true to their artistic and cultural identity which is essential to global success. As some of the participants argued, in a market where 'Americanisation' sells, having local music genres and encouraging young creatives to be true to their craft was a key advantage since the true essence of CCIs is in their authenticity which gives each culture its uniqueness and value. As one of the participants alluded:

> Our local music genres have a lot of value and being able to infuse them into the work we do is a part of the creative freedom this kind of platform provides. – Participant 5

Education

A third theme was education. Upon seeing the impact of the masterclasses delivered jointly by Henley Business School (covering the business of music) and Berklee College of Music (focussing on technical music skills), the young creatives felt the limited access to music and music business education is a significant hurdle. They acknowledged that as the Nigerian music landscape is already competitive, running on talent alone can be limiting and the place of skill and a better understanding of how the industry works limits how opportunities are spotted, evaluated and harnessed. As some of the participants suggested:

> Being a part of the Henley Business School Masterclass has been a paradigm shift for me and has activated a lot in me. It has shown me how to understand the structures of the industry by showing me opportunities in the industry – Participant 6

> I've learned not to leave my music to chance. I have to be deliberate with my music and should treat my music like any other product as it deserves to be pushed to the market. I've also learned from Henley how to push my music thank you. – Participant 7

Remarkably, education was also associated with improving the overall quality of artistry which in turn improves attractiveness to investors willing to invest in talent development structures as well as in individual artists. This notion begins to position each artist as a kind of 'start-up' that can attract investment to start, stabilise and scale their craft.

Access

Artistes and young creatives have the key challenges they collectively agree to face: Access to platforms and the right opportunities as well as access to funding. The transition of aspiring artistes into commercially viable acts is usually hindered by limited access to finance. The deployment of finance according to the end-users is more towards marketing and promotion on relevant platforms and not necessarily with production costs which though could be challenging is mitigated by the abundance of low-cost producers in the industry. This for the end-users was also linked with increasing chances of discovery by the right stakeholders if their talents are on display at a well-known, purpose-built venue to which access is easier.

> Like create a platform where musicians that are not well known, can actually come back, put their best foot forward. Over time, they actually start making big bucks. – Participant 7

> I will first start with a platform like Freedom Park of Bagobiri. So it's a platform where artists have opportunities for gigs and networking, performance and also developing our theatre arts. – Participant 8

This factor was interpreted on one hand as finding the right platform to connect meaningfully with other acts, and key players in the value chain including record labels. The *Creative Village* provided a weekly platform through the competition for these young creatives to produce music and to get connected to local, regional and global markets thereby improving access which hitherto may have been out of reach.

Connectivity

The connectivity to a wider ecosystem was also mentioned as a key element the *Creative Village* enabled. With the proliferation of upcoming artists pushing content on social media, building a strong marketing strategy backed by the wider ecosystem was identified as crucial. Participants argue that the importance of being a part of an ecosystem is that it could foster the right kinds of partnerships that can become win-win for all parties involved. Also, the issue of isolation artists face, where they create content alone, market alone and doing everything like a one-man shop could be mitigated by enabling connection to the ecosystem. As one of the participants suggested:

> I know popular artiste who deployed N30million (£45,000) towards the production and marketing of a single track. That money did not come form him alone and he is not on a record label. He leveraged partnerships within the ecosystem to produce that track. – Participant 9

Contributions

Indications from the two data points suggested there are obvious systemic issues within the Nigerian and indeed African CCIs, yet the potential of CCIs to become a major contributor to the national GDP of African countries is quite evident and promising. What seems clear, especially in the wake of the COVID-19 pandemic and the virtual delivery of the pilot programmes shows the African market is ready for this innovation and the youth whose lifestyle revolves around content consumption on the internet are willing and ready to seize opportunities that are presented to them. The key components of the *Creative Village* as shown earlier in Fig. 10.1 indeed meet the key gaps in the market and have the potential to transform young creatives into creative entrepreneurs building sustainable businesses that will build Africa.

This practical case study of the *Creative Village* as a purpose-built platform, deployed and studied for its impact is a major contribution to the literature on African CCIs as it offers practical and empirically backed solutions to the key challenges many prior studies have found. This advances policy beyond words into clear actions with measurable impact which can be scaled for further sustainable impact. Another key contribution is that this study has drawn its insights from multiple stakeholders placing the young creatives at the centre of the agenda. This methodological approach to understanding African CCIs is crucial for policy formation and implementation and allows for breaking the silos amongst ecosystem players.

CONCLUSION

In conclusion, this study suggests that the availability of the right platform that is inclusive and systematises talent discovery, incubation, acceleration and connection to the market is an important first step in harnessing the potential of African CCIs. The *Creative Village* presents a quick win in that, it will immediately provide the much-needed opportunities to teeming aspiring creatives to get their discovery and professional development journeys started at low cost. This approach provides a much-needed head start in getting these creatives ready for the ongoing revolutions within the industry for the regional and global opportunities that are emerging and will soon place a demand on their talents. What data has indicated quite clearly is that the *Creative Village* platform and indeed any intervention introduced at this stage of the African creative industry development must be built on at least five philosophical pillars:

- An inclusive platform for individual talents, regardless of their gender, location or disability to find expression.
- Developing a holistic, professional creative entrepreneur who understands their craft and the business of their craft.
- Creating a platform that allows for different dimensions of authenticity to thrive for example, cultural authenticity that will revive local music genres.
- A platform that has unifies different players in the Africa creative ecosystem through the right partnerships.
- A platform that enhances local markets and connects musicians to regional and international markets.

REFERENCES

Adedeji, W. (2016). The Nigerian music industry: Challenges, prospects and possibilities. *International Journal of Recent Research in Social Sciences and Humanities*, 3(1), 261–271.

African Union. (2022). *Our aspirations for the Africa we want*. Retrieved August 12, 2022, from https://au.int/agenda2063/aspirations

AU Echo. (2021). *AU Echo 2021 edition- theme `Year of the arts, culture and heritage'*. One Million by 2021 Initiative. Retrieved April 3, 2021, from http://1millionby2021.au.int/news/

Braun, V., & Clarke, V. (2012). *Thematic analysis*. American Psychological Association.

Christensen, C. M., Ojomo, E., & Dillon, K. (2019). *The prosperity paradox: How innovation can lift nations out of poverty*. HarperCollins.

Central Intelligence Agency World Fact Book (2020). *Nigeria*. Retrieved July 8, 2020, from https://www.cia.gov/the-world-factbook/countries/nigeria/

CIASC. (2019). *Global collections report 2019*. CIASC. Retrieved December 6, 2018, from https://www.cisac.org/CISAC-University/Library/Annual-%20Reports/2019-annual-report

Clarke, V., Braun, V., & Hayfield, N. (2015). Thematic analysis. *Qualitative psychology: A practical guide to research methods*, *222*, 248.

Colucci, E. (2007). 'Focus groups can be fun': The use of activity-oriented questions in focus group discussions. *Qualitative Health Research*, *17*(10), 1422–1433.

DeGhetto, K., Gray, J. R., & Kiggundu, M. N. (2016). The African Union's agenda 2063: Aspirations, challenges, and opportunities for management research. *Africa Journal of Management*, *2*(1), 93–116.

Dredge, S. (2019a). *African music: 'We're here to stay, and you're going to know about it!'* Music Ally. Retrieved February 7, 2021, from https://musically.com/2019/01/23/africa-music-here-to-stay/

Dredge, S. (2019b). *African streaming service Boomplay now has 75m users*. Music Ally. Retrieved February 7, 2021, from https://musically.com/2020/06/03/african-streaming-service-boomplay-now-has-75m-users/

Ernst&Young. (2015). *Cultural times: The first global map of cultural and creative industries*. EY. Retrieved August 10, 2022, from https://unesdoc.unesco.org/ark:/48223/pf0000235710

Fry, C., Flatter, G. C., Maxted, S., & Murray, F. (2018). *Nigeria's 'New Oil': Fuelling the growth of the music industry in Lagos through entrepreneurship*. MIT Innovation Initiative, MIT Legatos Centre. https://reap.mit.edu/assets/Case_Study_Nigeria.pdf

Gilbert, B. (2020). *This must be the place*. Synchtank. https://www.synchtank.com/author/ben-gilbert/

Hruby, A., & Annan, R. (2020). *Coronavirus: Now is the time to invest in Africa's creative industries*. The Africa Report.com. Retrieved July 20, 2022, from https://www.theafricareport.com/31417/coronavirus-now-is-the-time-to-invest-in-africas-creative-industries/

International Monetary Fund. (2019). *World economic outlook, growth slowdown, precarious recovery*. Retrieved January 26, 2019, from https://www.imf.org/en/

International Trade Administration U.S. Department of Commerce. (2020). *Nigeria – Country commercial guide*. Retrieved March 10, 2020, from https://www.trade.gov/country-commercial-guides/nigeria-media-andentertainment-industry-nollywood-and-nigerian-music

Joffe, H. (2012). Thematic analysis. In D. Harper & A. Thompson (Eds.), *Qualitative research methods in mental health and psychotherapy: A guide for students and practitioners* (pp. 203–223). Wiley-Blackwell.

Joshua, O. B., & Omotoso, O. (2016). Cultural and creative industries as approaches for reducing youth unemployment in Nigeria. *Social Science Research*, *3*(1), 140–162.

Kitzinger, J. (1994). The methodology of focus groups: The importance of interaction between research participants. *Sociology of health & illness*, *16*(1), 103–121.

Lobato, R. (2010). Creative industries and informal economies: Lessons from Nollywood. *International Journal of Cultural Studies*, *13*(4), 337–354.

Maiwada, S., Dutsenwai, S. A., & Waziri, M. Y. (2012). Cultural industries and wealth creation: The case of traditional textile industry in Nigeria. *American International Journal of Contemporary Research*, *2*(5), 159–165.

Milićević, V., Ilić, B., & Sofronijević, A. (2013). Business aspects of creative industries from a global perspective. *Management*, *66*, 5–14.

MusicAlly. (2020). *Country profile – Nigeria 2022 – Music Ally*. MusicAlly. Retrieved June 1, 2020, from https://musically.com/2022/06/20/country-profile-nigeria-2022/

Myers, J. (2016). *The world's 10 youngest populations are all in Africa*. World Economic Forum. Retrieved March 9, 2022, from https://www.weforum.org/agenda/2016/05/the-world-s-10-youngest-countries-are-all-in-africa/

Ndizera, V., & Muzee, H. (2018). A critical review of Agenda 2063: Business as usual?*African Journal of Political Science and International Relations*, *12*(8), 142–154.

Nzere, S. (2018). *The Nigerian music industry: Making the music pay through intellectual property* (pp. 1–26). UNESCO Infusion Lawyers. Retrieved September 10, 2021, from https://infusionlawyers.com/wp-content/uploads/2018/01/The-Nigerian-Music-Industry_-Making-the-Music-Pay-through-Intellectual-Property-by-Solomon-Nzere.pdf

Osasona, O. J. (2021). *Contributions of cultural industries to Nigeria economy*. Retrieved April 1, 2021, from https://en.unesco.org/creativity/sites/creativity/files/qpr/contributions_of_cultural_industries_by_osasonaolutimi_james.pdf

PricewaterhouseCoopers (2020a). *Nigeria economic alert*. PwC. Retrieved August 5, 2022, from https://www.pwc.com/ng/en/publications/economy-alert.html

PricewaterhouseCoopers. (2020b). *Africa entertainment and media outlook 2019–2023*. PwC. Retrieved January 18, 2022, from https://www.pwc.co.za/en/publications/entertainment-and-media-outlook.html

Rotinwa, A. (2020). Nigeria's Afrobeats superstars take on the world. *Financial Times*. Retrieved January 16, 2022, from https://www.ft.com/content/60084cef-9c34-4d12-8407-ea7007f0054e

Snowball, J., Collins, A., & Tarentaal, D. (2017). Transformation and job creation in the cultural and creative industries in South Africa. *Cultural trends*, 26(4), 295–309.

Winn, M. I., & Keller, L. R. (2001). A modeling methodology for multiobjective multistakeholder decisions: Implications for research. *Journal of Management Inquiry*, 10(2), 166–181.

COGNITIVE ASPECTS OF DOING
CCI ENTREPRENEURSHIP

CHAPTER 11

EXPLORATION OF ENTREPRENEURSHIP EDUCATION AND INNOVATIVE TALENT TRAINING MODEL: NEW NORMAL PERSPECTIVE*

Lei Jian Qiang[a], Oo Yu Hock[b] and Osaro Aigbogun[a]

[a]*Binary University of Management and Entrepreneurship, Malaysia*
[b]*Asia e-University (AeU), Malaysia*

ABSTRACT

The COVID-19 pandemic has influenced entrepreneurial behaviour, including creative industries that have been negatively impacted due to the loss of patrons constrained by movement restrictions. This crisis has led to the failure of many small and medium-sized enterprises (SMEs) and an increase in unemployment. These challenges led to the rapid development of e-commerce and created new business models and firms, which has promoted the development of the economy. Increased marketing channels have become an emergent trend. Facing this challenge, talent development is the most critical factor for scientific and technological innovation, and innovation-driven entrepreneurship is essential in building such talent. The cultivation of innovative talents has become a critical mission of Chinese national education policies. This study analyses the effects of entrepreneurship education (EE) on innovative talent

---

*Extracts in this chapter have been taken from Lei et al. (2021).

training models using a mixed-method methodology. The study identifies two dimensions of EE, namely institutional environment (IE) and supporting infrastructure (SI), having a significant direct effect on student's innovation capability. The results highlighted learning institutions should combine innovation-driven entrepreneurial ecosystem cultivation with EE programmes, while strengthening support of IE and infrastructure that enhances the student's innovation practice ability with both human and social capital. Furthermore, practice-oriented innovative EE should be encouraged to enhance innovation capability in the new economic environment.

Keywords: Ecosystem; entrepreneurship education; innovative talent; internet entrepreneurship; new economy; social capital

INTRODUCTION

Since 2020, the COVID-19 pandemic has had a significant impact on the economic and social life of various countries (World Bank, 2020). The pandemic affected Guangxi province in China in multiple ways. Guangxi is a southern Chinese autonomous region that borders Vietnam. The range of effects of the pandemic on this province includes weakening investment, creating long-term economic trauma, unemployment, human capital damage, school education loss, and global trade and supply chain disruptions.

A slowdown in economic productivity since the global financial crisis and the combined effects of COVID-19 has had a profound impact on progress towards meeting the socio-economic development goals (Pazarbasioglu, 2020). The impact of the pandemic on specific industries during the pandemic has varied. Construction of new infrastructure, including new 5G base stations, intercity high-speed rail and urban rail transit, new energy vehicle charging, big data centres, artificial intelligence, involving many industries led by the new development concept. Such a concept is driven by technological innovation, based on information networks, for high-quality development needs, providing digital transformation, intelligent upgrades and integration of innovation infrastructure systems. Under the normal prevention and control of the epidemic, the new infrastructure plays a prominent role in supporting the realisation of sustainable development goals.

Since 1999, China began to expand its higher education sector with student numbers increasing more than eight times, from 1 million in 1998 to 8.7 million in 2020. According to the National Bureau of Statistics of China, the unemployment rate remained around 5% from 2014 to 2018. Under the surge of the global pandemic, China's State Council announced that the urban survey unemployment rate in 2020 has risen to 6%. The number of college and university graduates reached 9 million in 2021. Thus, entrepreneurship education (EE) is expected to make a large contribution to creating an impetus for the economy and increasing community income (Sani et al., 2018).

In 2002, university EE was officially launched in China, because entrepreneurship is an important means of fostering economic development and relieving employment pressure. EE has gradually been popularised in colleges and universities. Since then, the Chinese government proposed a 'mass entrepreneurship' and 'mass innovation' development strategy at the Davos Economic Forum in 2014. Moreover, Liu (2016) stated the innovation and EE of college students has become a strategic problem of great importance to the country, society and universities, and its development and effectiveness are directly related to the strategic measures of the construction of an innovative country. Given the importance of EE to cultivate innovative entrepreneurship talents and increasing social productivity, there is an important significance in studying the relationship between the stakeholders and innovation activities. Thus, the innovation research applying the Triple Helix Model of Innovation has found three main stakeholders in the entrepreneurship ecosystem, which are crucial: The government, the university, and the industry (Etzkowitz & Leydesdorff, 1995). The main purpose of this study is to evaluate the influence of EE on the innovative talent training model in China.

CONTEXT AND LITERATURE REVIEW

Chinese Entrepreneurship Education Performance

The EE literature review has been undertaken considering entrepreneurial ability, entrepreneurial culture, innovative spirit, and entrepreneurial intention (Bazan, 2020; Lorz, 2013; Nabi et al., 2017; Pittaway & Cope, 2006; Sirelkhatim & Gangi, 2015). The previous literature found the innovation field was typically focussed on national innovation, innovative cities, and enterprise innovation levels, however, insufficient attention is paid to demonstrating the influence of EE factors affecting students' innovation capability (Sánchez, 2013). This is seen in EE from the perspective of the new economy. Wang and Kim (2017) applied We-media decomposition to analyse the problems of developing college students' entrepreneurial innovation education and developing the conceptual model of inculcating innovation ability. The findings suggest that innovation spirit, innovative thinking, entrepreneurial activity, and entrepreneurial capacity have a positive effect on entrepreneurial innovation ability.

Entrepreneurship Education and Other Contributing Factors

EE is a creative endeavour and as such the establishment of enterprises is not its central goal. Its goal is to cultivate learners' innovation, entrepreneurial spirit, ability, and literacy (Wu et al., 2018). Scott (1995) stressed the institutional environment (IE), that institution theory can make society stable and have cognitive, normative, and regulatory restraint mechanisms and activities. Scott proposed three kinds of restriction behaviours: regulation, normalisation, and cognition. Similarly, Baumol (1993) suggested the IE of a country/region comprises local rules/conditions, in which local individuals or organisations have legitimacy and support only when they operate. Gnyawali and Fogel (1994) believed that supporting infrastructure (SI) consists of physical, institutional, and organisational structures that support economic activities such as entrepreneurship. However, Van de Ven (1989) stressed the perspective of the social system arguing that the three functions of the social system provide the infrastructure essential to the emergence of industries. Harris (1995) argued that peer input (PI) refers to peer consultations, which often means interactive work products during the development of an evolving institution, providing open communication of data, insights, and ideas. Moreover, peer relationships have a double impact on innovation ability. Nanda and Sørensenan (2006) proposed a hypothesis that an individual's colleagues may influence their transition to entrepreneurship by observing how diversity in a person's peers' previous careers relates to their own tendency to become entrepreneurs.

Entrepreneurship Education and Innovation Capability among Undergraduates

The theory of innovation capability interaction suggests innovation is an individual's behaviour in a particular situation prior to experience. Personal factors and environmental factors influence innovative behaviour before producing innovative results (Woodman & Schoenfeldt, 1990). Furthermore, Chen (2018) suggested that innovation-driven EE has the most original innovative elements and the typical education mode of innovative talent training. The difference between these three modes is the content of original innovative elements. Zhong (2021) noted entrepreneurs need to acquire theoretical knowledge through EE. In addition, entrepreneurial capital is important for entrepreneurs. Therefore, the deepening development of students with the background of the new media network era requires the support of universities. To establish and improve a perfect network EE system, the network skills need to be cultivated and strengthened, and then high-quality network EE will be realised.

METHODOLOGY

In order to collect as much adequate information as possible and ensure a high degree of rigour, this study conducted a mixed method. In this research, a survey design containing a quantitative approach is employed using a structured questionnaire as the main source of the research instrument (Perri & Bellamy, 2012).

Population and Sampling Technique

Probabilistic sampling is a simple random sampling, which means that each element in the group of interest has an equal and independent chance of being selected (Saunders et al., 2009). Therefore, the total population of senior (of fourth year) undergraduates in the three selected Chinese universities in Guangxi, China, is 15,365 students. Moreover, this study uses cluster sampling to determine the location of the data collection by dividing the geographic dispersion of the universities. Ochoa (2017) reveals that the use of cluster sampling has advantages in research, as it is effective for geographically dispersed populations of raw data collection and needs to be divided by locations. Yamane (1967) provides a simplified formula to calculate sample sizes. Thus, of a total of 400 participants, 50.99% of them were students majoring in business management, 22.08% in humanities and art, 14.35% in information technology and 12.58% were in trade major. A pilot study was conducted on 50 respondents before the survey and the questionnaire was completed, with 40 questions.

The Development of Instruments

Instruments in this study were modified based on the relevant literature of previous scholars (Scott, 2008; Timmons, 1998; Van de Ven, 1989). There are six tools used for evaluated EE: (1) Curriculum System Construction (CSC); (2) Qualified Faculty Assessment (QFA); (3) Institutional Environmental Assessment (IEA); (4) Supporting Infrastructure Assessment (SIA); (5) Innovative Capability Assessment (ICA); and (6) Peer Input Assessment (PIA). The validity and reliability of the study questionnaire were assessed by the sensitivity of the predictors of entrepreneurial education through pre-test and post-test. Sekaran and Bougie (2010) argue that it reduces problems caused by wording and bias. Response options for all items range from 1= height disagree to 5= height consent (1= height disagree, 2= disagree, 3= neutral, 4= consent, and 5= height consent). This study used Smart PLS3.0 to run the SEM (structural equation model) to evaluate the research model by a quantitative method.

Measurement Model

The first phase of PLS evaluates the goodness of the measurement model by both convergent and discriminant validity. In this research framework, there are three exogenous variables: entrepreneurship education programme (EEP), IE, support infrastructure and innovation capability, which is an endogenous variable. Fig. 11.1 illustrates the confirmatory factor result $R^2 = 0.821$, R square notes the fitting degree of the model equation in regression analysis. Lu and Dosher (2000) stated that greater than 0.6 indicates fitting is good. SRMR is the difference between the observed correlation and the predicted correlation. Values less than 0.10 (in the conservative sense) are considered a good fit (Hair et al., 2014), and the PLS bootstrapping procedure provides the SRMR criterion. So, the cut-off of 0.08 seems satisfactory for the PLS path model as suggested by Hu and Bentler (1998). The results exhibit that the SRMR value is 0.042, less than the critical value of 0.08. Therefore, it is shown that there was a good fit for the current research model.

The detection method of measuring variables is generally to see that the Cronbach's Alpha value of three EE variables and innovation capability variables cannot be significantly improved after deleting any other item, which complies with the optimal reliability standard proposed by Zhang et al. (2016). Table 11.1 shows all Cronbach's Alpha values in this study were greater than 0.9, indicating good reliability.

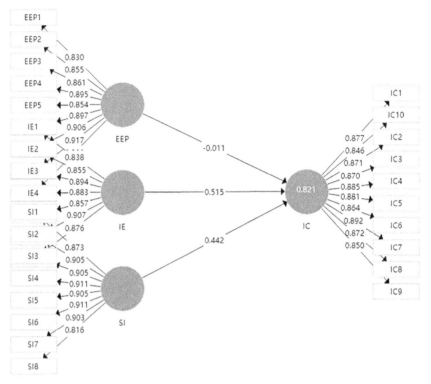

Fig. 11.1. The Measurement Model of Exogenous variables and Endogenous variables: Entrepreneurship Education Programme (EEP), Institutional Environment (IE), Supporting Infrastructure (SI), and Innovative Capability (IC). *Source:* Authors' own.

Furthermore, because the current model contained reflective scale measurement, the convergent validity was assessed by examining the indicator loading, average variance explained (AVE) and composite reliability (CR). Ashill et al. (2005) note when the AVE is greater than 0.50, the variance shared with the construction and its measure is greater than the error. The AVE of each potential variable is above 0.50. However, the scope of AVE is 0.774 (EEP) and 0.762 (IE), 0.795 (support infrastructure), and finally 0.759 (innovation capacity). Table 11.1 shows that the CR for each variable is more than 0.70 based on the findings by Hair et al. (2011), which indicates that the variables used are fully reliable. The minimum value for CR was 0.957 (IE) and the maximum was 0.969 (including EEP, support infrastructure, and innovation capacity).

The results (in Table 11.2) show the squared root of AVE for each construct is evidently higher than the correlation for each construct indicating adequate discriminant validity for the constructs proposed in this research. Overall, the measurement model demonstrated adequate convergent validity and discriminant validity.

Table 11.1. Construct Reliability and Validity.

Constructs	Cronbach's Alpha	CR	AVE
Entrepreneurship Education Programme (EEP)	0.963	0.969	0.774
Institutional Environment (IE)	0.948	0.957	0.762
Supporting Infrastructure (SI)	0.963	0.969	0.795
Innovative Capability	0.965	0.969	0.759

Source: Authors' own.

Table 11.2. Fornell-Larcker Criterion.

	EEP	IC	IE	SI
EEP	0.880			
IC	0.766	0.871		
IE	0.811	0.873	0.873	
SI	0.814	0.860	0.830	0.892

Source: Authors' own.

FINDINGS

All 400 participants were senior undergraduate students including 301 female respondents and 99 males, the inequality was the result of the universities and majors selected. The quantitative data of the survey were transferred from the Excel spreadsheet to the SPSS20 data analysis system at the end of the data collection period. There were numerous items covering this study, so the research was carried out with descriptive statistical analysis to explore each variable, using the data analysis from each item's mean, standard deviation, and variance. Although PLS is a nonparametric approach, which does not require a normal distribution of data, it is still important to make sure that the data is close to having a normal distribution (Hassan et al., 2014). To assess non-normality, skewness and kurtosis values were obtained (Hair et al., 2011). Therefore, the results indicated that the skewness and kurtosis of most items ranged between -1 and $+1$, which suggested that the non-normality of data is not an issue in this research.

Structural Model

This study evaluated the path relationship (structural model) in four steps, including collinearity issues, R^2 levels, and t values of standard beta, for guided 5000 resampling in accordance with Hair et al. (2014). The analysis results and data of the model adaptation are shown in Fig. 11.2. The R^2 and adjustment R square show the fitting degree of the model equation in regression analysis; in reference to this, Lu and Dosher (2000) noted that when the result is greater than 0.6 indicates, the fitting is good. The innovation capability is demonstrated by a large effect (0.821) with independent variables in this study.

A multivariate linear regression was used to test the hypotheses and the two different effects of adjusting variables. To analyse the mechanism of EE on innovation capability, we analysed the direct effect of EE on innovation capability.

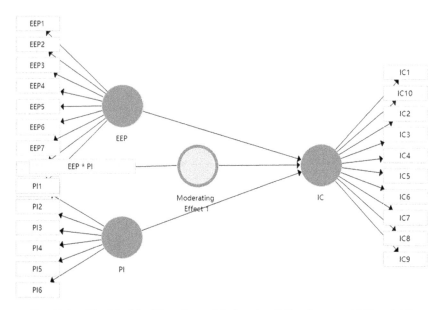

Fig. 11.2. The Model of Peer Input Moderating Effect Between EEP and IC.
Source: Authors' own.

Table 11.3. The Results of Structural Model.

Hypothesis	Direct Relationship	Beta	*t*-values	*p*-values	Decision
H1	EEP → IC	−0.011	0.167	0.867	Not Supported
H2	IE → IC	0.515	7.663**	0.000	Supported
H3	SI → IC	0.442	4.725**	0.000	Supported

Source: Authors' own.
*$p<0.05$; **$p<0.01$; EEP = entrepreneurship education programme, IE = institutional environment, SI = supporting infrastructure, IC = innovation capability; *t*-value > 1.96

Here, the EEP, IE, and SI are used as an independent variable, innovation capability as a dependent variable, and gender, major, family financial background, and entrepreneurial experience as control variables for the multiple regression analysis. The results are shown in Table 11.3, the relationship between EEP and innovation capability is not positively significant ($\beta = -.011$, $p > 0.05$), but the influence of the other two independent variables on the innovation capability of the dependent variable, IE ($\beta = 0.515$, $p < 0.01$) and SI ($\beta = 0.442$, $p < 0.01$) has significant, positive effects on innovation capability. All the VIF (EEP = 3.589, IE = 3.859, SI = 3.941) in the model are less than five and the tolerance is greater than 0.1, which indicates that there are no serious collinearity problems (Zhang et al, 2016). Overall, the hypothesis testing does not support H1, but support hypothesis H2 and H3. This result is consistent with that of Walter and

Heinrichs (2015), who claim that EE stimulates entrepreneurs' activities and that entrepreneurship incubates in entrepreneurial-friendly IEs.

Moderator Effect Model

To further demonstrate the role of PI in moderating the relationship between EEP and innovation capability, this study used Smart PLS to draw a model diagram of the moderating effect, see Fig. 11.2, and the Bootstrap method 2000 times to detect the significance of moderator. The results highlight the interaction of PI and EE programme ($\beta = 0.062$, $p=0.354$), so given the fact that the p-value is greater than 0.01, the moderating impact is not significant. Meanwhile, the same inter-variable interaction effect detection method is used to verify whether the other two hypotheses are supported.

Regarding the verification of PI in regulating the relationship between IE and innovation capability, the results show the p-value for the interaction between the PI and the IE is 0.322 ($p>0.01$), the moderating impact is not significant. However, Uzzi and Dunlap (2005) state that compared with those who focus on gaining personal benefits from social networks and connections, individual actors find themselves in it, attributing social capital to an increased set of information and skills acquired by individual activities and the enhancement of their capabilities.

To demonstrate the role of PI in regulating the relationship between SI and innovation capability, the results show that the p-value of interaction between PI and SI is 0.177 ($p>0.01$), so the moderating impact is not significant.

DISCUSSION

This study examines the influence of EE on innovation capability among undergraduates in China. Moreover, the findings illustrate how PI moderating variables affect the relationship between the acquisition of EE and social capital (IE, support facilities) in EE and the capability of entrepreneurial innovation. However, as Table 11.4 notes the three assumptions of H4, H5 and H6 do not demonstrate any significant effect. The results mirror Heger et al. (2015) who stated that, given the importance of entrepreneurship, public and private organisations are interested in the topic of mechanisms or infrastructure to support entrepreneurship. During the qualitative interview process with students and teachers, they were asked what human capital could be acquired through

Table 11.4. The Results of Moderator Effect Model.

Hypothesis	Moderating Effect (PI)	Beta	t-values	p-values	Decision
H4	EEP → IC	0.062	0.928	0.354	Not Supported
H5	IE → IC	0.061	0.991	0.322	Not Supported
H6	SI → IC	−0.038	1.352	0.177	Not Supported

Source: Authors' own.
*$p<0.05$; **$p<0.01$; EEP = entrepreneurship education programme, IE = institutional environment, SI = supporting infrastructure, IC = innovation capability, PI = peer input; t-value > 1.96

university EE? Most teachers responded in a positive manner, but the students gave an uncertain response. When asked to share their views on how social capital affects student's innovation capability, several themes emerged. Both teacher and student participants gave a positive answer regarding social capital. While asked to share their views on how the peer effect affects students' innovative entrepreneurial behaviour, two themes emerged. Both teacher and student participants gave positive responses regarding PI.

The reason why the results showed an insignificant direct effect of EEPs on innovation capability, even in the presence of peer pressure, is because there is an assumed and also proven research studies regarding the relationship between innovation influence and entrepreneurial development, including the importance of innovation impact study on new global business enterprises. The latter is an outcome of the direct and indirect contribution of the education curriculum that incorporated innovation as an integral part of its course or program. EE is, therefore, an extended stand-alone subject or programme on its own merits. Moreover, we might query why the quantitative results do not mirror the results from the qualitative data. This is because the opinions of respondents from the triangulation of data are from a diversity or variegated perspectives based on the respondents' perceptual preferences (Creswell, 2003).

CONCLUSIONS

To summarise, EE projects do not have a significant, positive impact on innovation ability, and the IE and SI have a significant, positive impact on students' innovation ability. Furthermore, the findings reveal the social capital obtained from the IE and SI in entrepreneurial practice play an important role in promoting innovation capacity. The findings confirmed that the current education system and curriculum are not yet mature because teachers lack experience and knowledge, current teaching models are not appropriate, constraining the country's demand for innovative talents (Zhang et al, 2020). Moreover, PI can assist students who lack entrepreneurial experience and inform networking solutions that inspire and influence students' entrepreneurial intentions through their own successful experiences and role models (Hendriks, 1999).

Several responses indicated that the construction of EE is a process that requires the long-term investment and support of the government and universities. To obtain the human capital of innovative talents, the government and administrators need to create a sustainable entrepreneurial culture and ecosystem. Thus, the government and universities should not only invest funds in the construction of EE, but also increase the improvement of the entrepreneurship policy framework and support with teacher training and design of the practical teaching model. Equally important, support for the incubation facility platform and the transformation of technological achievements should be considered.

In 2020, the Coronavirus epidemic created global upheaval, and the global health crisis met existing business models that were no longer valid. For example, the catering and retail sectors have been negatively impacted, although online education and e-commerce have been significantly redeveloped. Due to the limitations caused by the pandemic, online questionnaires and interviews were used in this study from May 2020 to August 2020. During the pandemic, many schools in China have switched to online education models or blended learning. However, EE is a practical course which requires an experiential dimension. Due to the challenges of the pandemic, entrepreneurship teachers need to be familiar with the new media entrepreneurship model.

Additionally, Zhang et al. (2020), suggested that the current education system and online resources are not mature, teachers lack experience and knowledge, and teaching models are not robust, constraining the country's demand for innovative talents. Thus, future research work should investigate whether the new media resources have a significant influence on improving the capability of student entrepreneurs' innovation and entrepreneurship under the new normal economic environment. In particular, increasing the understanding of new media e-commerce platforms and technologies may help innovative talent training and access entrepreneurial financing opportunities.

REFERENCES

Ashill, P. R., Fulker, J. L., & Hackett, K. C. (2005). A review of recent developments in flow control. *Aeronautical Journal*, *109*(1095), 205–232.

Baumol, W. J. (1993). Health care, education and the cost disease: A looming crisis for public choice. *Public Choice*, *77*(1), 17–28.

Bazan, C. (2020). A systematic literature review of the influence of the university's environment and support system on the precursors of social entrepreneurial intention of students. *Journal of Innovation and Entrepreneurship*, *9*(4), 20–28.

Christensen, C. M., Bartman, T., & Van Bever, D. (2016). The hard truth about business model innovation. *MIT Sloan Management Review*, *58*(1), 31–40.

Cope, J., & Watts, G. (2000). Learning by doing–an exploration of experience, critical incidents and reflection in entrepreneurial learning. *International Journal of Entrepreneurial Behavior & Research*, *6*(3), 104–124.

Creswell, J. W. (2003). *Research design: Qualitative, quantitative and mixed methods approaches* (2nd Edn.). Sage.

De Jong, J., & Den Hartog, D. (2010). Measuring innovative work behaviour. *Creativity and Innovation Management*, *19*(1), 23–36.

Etzkowitz, H., & Leydesdorff, L. (1995). The triple helix: University-industry-government relations: A laboratory for knowledge based economic development. *EASST Review*, *14*(1), 14–19.

Fayolle, A. (Ed.). (2007). *Handbook of research in entrepreneurship education: A general perspective* (Vol. 1). Edward Elgar Publishing.

Fetters, M., Greene, P. G., & Rice, M. P. (Eds.). (2010). *The development of university-based entrepreneurship ecosystems: Global practices*. Edward Elgar Publishing.

Gatewood, E. J., Shaver, K. G., & Gartner, W. B. (1995). A longitudinal study of cognitive factors influencing start-up behaviors and success at venture creation. *Journal of Business Venturing*, *10*(5), 371–391.

Gnyawali, D. R., & Fogel, D. S. (1994). Environments for entrepreneurship development: Key dimensions and research implications. *Entrepreneurship Theory and Practice*, *18*, 43–62.

Hair, F., Sarstedt, M., Hopkins, L., & Kuppelwieser, V. (2014). Partial least squares structural equation modeling (PLS-SEM): An emerging tool in business research, *European Business Review*, *26*(2), 106–121.

Hair, J. F., Ringle, C. M., & Sarstedt, M. (2011). PLS-SEM: Indeed a silver bullet. *Journal of Marketing Theory and Practice*, *19*(2), 139–151.

Harris, J. R. (1995). Where is the child's environment? A group socialization theory of development. *Psychological Review, 102*, 458–489.

Hassan, A. S., Elsherpieny, E. A., & Haroun, N. M. (2014). Application of generalized probability weighted moments for skew normal distribution. *Asian Journal of Applied Sciences, 2*(1), 73–99.

Heger, D., Audretsch, D. B., & Veith, T. (2015). Infrastructure and entrepreneurship. *Small Business Economics, 44*(2), 219–230.

Hendriks, P. (1999). Why share knowledge? The influence of ICT on the motivation for knowledge sharing. *Knowledge and Process Management, 6*(2), 91–100.

Henry, C., Hill, F., & Leitch, C. (2005). Entrepreneurship education and training: Can entrepreneurship be taught? Part I. *Education + Training, 47*(2), 98–111.

Honig, B. (2001). Learning strategies and resources for entrepreneurs and intrapreneurs. *Entrepreneurship Theory and Practice, 26*(1), 21–34.

Hu, L., & Bentler, P. M. (1998). Fit indices in covariance structure modeling: Sensitivity to under parameterization model misspecification. *Psychological Methods, 3*, 424–453.

Hua, Z., Yang, J., & Coulibaly, S. (2006). Integration TRIZ with problem-solving tools: A literature review from 1995 to 2006. *International Journal of Business Innovation and Research, 1*(1–2), 111–128.

Ismail, M. (2005). Creative climate and learning organization factors: Their contribution towards innovation. *Leadership & Organization Development Journal, 26*(8), 639–654.

Kraaijenbrink, J., Bos, G., & Groen, A. (2009). What do students think of the entrepreneurial support given by their universities? *International Journal of Entrepreneurship and Small Business, 9*(1), 110–125.

Lei, J., Hock, O. Y., & Karim, A. M. (2021). Exploration of entrepreneurship education and innovative talent training model: New economic perspective. *International Journal of Academic Research in Business and Social Sciences, 11*(11), 1366–1382.

Leitch, C., Hazlett, S. A., & Pittaway, L. (2012). Entrepreneurship education and context. *Entrepreneurship & Regional Development, 24*(9–10), 733–740.

Liu, X. F. (2016). Enabling rapid network innovation for heterogeneous vehicular communication. *IEEE Network, 30*(4), 10–15.

Lorz, M. (2013). Entrepreneurship education: A systematic review of the methods in impact studies. *Journal of Enterprising Culture, 21*(2), 123–151.

Lu, Y., & Tang, M. F. (2014). Does Chinese university entrepreneurship education fit students' needs? *Journal of Entrepreneurship in Emerging Economies*, Emerald Group Publishing.

Lu, Z. L., & Dosher, B. A. (2000). Mechanisms of perceptual attention in precuring of location. *The Vision Research, 40*(10–12), 1269–1292.

Martin, B. C., McNally, J. J., & Kay, M. J. (2013). Examining the formation of human capital in entrepreneurship: A meta-analysis of entrepreneurship education outcomes. *Journal of Business Venturing, 28*(2), 211–224.

Maxwell, J. A. (2005). Conceptual framework: What do you think is going on? *In Qualitative research design: An interactive approach* (3rd Edn.). Sage.

Nabi, G., Liñán, F., Fayolle, A., Krueger, N., & Walmsley, A. (2017). The impact of entrepreneurship education in higher education: A systematic review and research agenda. *Academy of Management Learning & Education, 16*(2), 277–299.

Pazarbasioglu, C. (2020). Unprecedented damaged by Covid-19 requires unprecedented policy response. *Future Development, 26*(3), 118–127.

Pittaway, L. A., Gazzard, J., Shore, A., & Williamson, T. (2015). Student clubs: Experiences in entrepreneurial learning. *Entrepreneurship & Regional Development, 27*(3–4), 127–153.

Pittaway, L., & Cope, J. (2006). Entrepreneurship education: A systematic review of the evidence. *International Small Business Journal, 25*(5), 479–510.

Preeti, P. (2020). Impact of Covid-19 pandemic on education system. *International Journal of Advanced Science and Technology, 29*(9), 3812–3814.

Rae, D. (2002). A narrative study of entrepreneurial learning in independently owned media businesses. *International Journal of Entrepreneurship and Innovation, 3*(1), 53–59.

Sanchez, J. C. (2013). The impact of an entrepreneurship education program on entrepreneurial competencies and intention. *Journal of Small Business Management, 51*(3), 447–465.

Sani, A., Ekowati, V. M., Wekke, I. S., & Idris, I. (2018). Respective contribution of entrepreneurial leadership through organizational citizenship behaviour in creating employee's performance, *Academy of Entrepreneurship Journal, 24*(4), 1–11.

Scott, W. R. (2008). *Institutions and organizations: Ideas and interests*. Sage Publications.

Sirelkhatim, F., & Gangi, Y. (2015). Entrepreneurship education: A systematic literature review of curricula contents and teaching methods. *Cogent Business & Management, 2*(1), 105–203.

Solomon, G. (2007). An examination of entrepreneurship education in the United States. *Journal of Small Business and Enterprise Development, 14*(2), 168–182.

Uzzi, B., & Dunlap, S. (2005). How to build your network? *Harvard Business Review,83*(12), 53.

Van de Ven, A. H. (1989). Using paradox to build management and organization theories. *Academic of Management Review, 14*(4), 562–578.

Walter, G. S., & Heinrichs, S. (2015). Who becomes an entrepreneur? A 30-years-review of individual-level research. *Journal of Small Business and Enterprise Development, 28*(1), 15–23.

Wang, Z., & Kim, G. H. (2017). Can social media marketing improve customer relationship capabilities and firm performance? Dynamic capability perspective. *Journal of Interactive Marketing,39*(1), 15–26.

Wu, Y. J., Yuan, C. H., & Pan, C. I. (2018). Entrepreneurship education: An experimental study with information and communication technology. *Sustainability,10*(3), 691.

Zhang, C. H., Li, D., & Wang, S. Y. (2016). Implementing smart factory of Industrie 4.0: An outlook. *International Journal of Distributed Sensor Networks,12*(1), 31–59.

Zhang, W., Lu, L., Shi, X. X., & Zhang, Q. P. (2020). Managing open innovation from a knowledge flow perspective: The roles of embeddedness and network inertia in collaboration networks. *European Journal of Innovation Management, 59*(1), 19–28.

CHAPTER 12

NEUROENTREPRENEURSHIP: PIERCE THE VEIL OF CREATIVITY IN WORKPLACES

Rajat Sharma and Rita Devi

School of Commerce & Management Studies, Central University of Himachal Pradesh, India

ABSTRACT

Entrepreneurship is not limited to managing and creating a business; other diverse domains have been explored by various scholars. The concept has been defined and explored in various aspects including cultural entrepreneurship (Gupta & Anandaram, 2022) ethnic, feminist, institutional, and various others. To obtain further insights into entrepreneurship, Krueger and Welpe (2014) sought to collaborate on the cognitive and emotional aspects and termed it neuro-entrepreneurship. Literature trends on neuro-entrepreneurship are generally confined to opportunity recognition, risk-taking measures, and decision patterns. It is too early to reach any conclusion as no empirical research has been undertaken on the topic yet. Neuroscience techniques such as fMRI and Magneto-encephalography (MEG) are trying to reveal the hidden phenomenon behind the decision-making process in entrepreneurs. The COVID-19 pandemic forced entrepreneurs to face a new reality: That is not only the crisis in physical resources but also caused a disrupted mental state. Entrepreneurs are seeking new ways to get back on track and potentially neuroscience will assist them. This chapter discusses the background literature on neuro-entrepreneurship and an overview of the rationales of neuro-entrepreneurship in organisational settings. It explains the cognitive and emotional dimensions of the brain controlling decision-making in entrepreneurs. This chapter establishes a connection between decision-making and creativity at the workplace with the help of neuroscience techniques of entrepreneurs and future directions towards achieving a creative entrepreneurial system by amalgamating neuroscience techniques and decision-making for improving entrepreneurial activities.

Keywords: Neuro-entrepreneurship; decision making; creativity; neuroscience techniques; creative entrepreneurial system

INTRODUCTION

Entrepreneurship has occupied various fields initially emerging from economics (1870–1940), then adopted into the social sciences from 1940 to 1970, and thereafter dominated by the field of management from 1970 onwards (Landström & Lohrke, 2010; Pérez-Centeno, 2018). During 1940–1950, various social science scholars considered entrepreneurship an empirical phenomenon, and by the end of the 1960s, psychologists entered into the field to explore the role of traits and personality in entrepreneurship. Entrepreneurship and intrapreneurship are identical terms, but there is a difference. Intrapreneurship refers to organisations that change the visionary structure and implement entrepreneurial ideas; the former is about the initiative, innovation, and decision-making to take risks regarding economic activities. Intrapreneurship may be considered as a second stage of entrepreneurship. Intrapreneurs are specialists to transform the organisation into a creative and innovative structure through the proper use of knowledge and training (Cadar & Badulescu, 2015). The credit goes to Pinchot and Pinchot (1978) for introducing the terms intrapreneurs and intrapreneurship (Pinchot, 2010) and defining them as an activity or business practice to encourage, motivate, and credit the entrepreneurial personality in an organisation to innovate quickly. Management science has demonstrated that for an organisation to be successful, a balance should be maintained between radical innovation (exploration) and maintaining or improving the existing process (exploitation). These two are the major factors on which the decision-making of employees working in an organisation is dependent (Laureiro-Martinez et al., 2014). However, existing research in this field remains confined to the physical aspects, cognitive and behavioural dimensions were not considered.

Certain evidence demonstrates brain functions and changes in the brain chemicals during the decision-making process of an entrepreneur help them to become more creative and innovative. Only in recent times has research started to unfold brain functions in terms of entrepreneurship. Entrepreneurship domains such as cognition, institution (Mitchell et al., 2007), knowledge (Shane, 2003), and mindsets (De Holan, 2014) are now some of the favourite topics of researchers (De Holan, 2014). An extension has been made to the attributes of behaviour instead of what they are thinking, how they are thinking, and why they are thinking by decoding the brain stems with the help of neuroscience techniques (De Holan, 2014). The interdisciplinary approach enables researchers to explore brain function and a path for aligning entrepreneurship with that of neuroscience.

Consumer research, financial research, and even organisational behaviour have a slight impact on neuroscience techniques, and now cognitive neuroscience has emerged in the entrepreneurship domain (Girişken & Çakar, 2021; Massaro, 2020). A step-by-step approach followed by researchers started by amalgamating neuroscience techniques with entrepreneurship and then enters the concepts of innovation and creativity in the second (Girişken & Çakar, 2021; Krueger, 2017).

NEUROENTREPRENEURSHIP

Ireland et al. (2003) describe the entrepreneurial mindset as 'the ability to sense, act and mobilise under certainty'. Neuroscience techniques, no doubt, are the most efficient techniques for defining brain structures, especially in interdisciplinary research (Girişken & Çakar, 2021; De Holan, 2014). To further explore entrepreneurship concepts there are two potential methods, firstly via cognitive point, where entrepreneurship concepts revolve around entrepreneurial mindset and heuristic theories; and secondly through behavioural aspects where scientists study the decision-making abilities of entrepreneurs (Korpysa, 2020). Neuroscience is the key to opening the complex phenomenon of cognition and affective process in decision-making in entrepreneurs. Various advanced techniques from magneto-encephalography (MEG) to electro-dermal activity (EDA), simplify the complex activity underneath the brain. Structural and functional are the two techniques, where the former gives clear and steady images of the anatomical structure of the brain; whereas, physiological processes beneath the neural activity can be traced by functional technique. So, functional magnetic resonance imaging (fMRI) and MEG are the major functional imaging techniques used and applied to the field of entrepreneurship. Therefore, with clear temporal and high spatial resolutions, these technologies enable researchers to find the answers to questions located deep in the brain (Carter & Shieh, 2015). The research began in 1990 when various concepts of neuroscience and cognitive psychology were merged to measure entrepreneurial intention. Bird (1988) explains that entrepreneurship intention starts with beliefs, wants, needs, and habits in a person in two parameters: (1) alignment – that guides the process of entrepreneurial intention that aligns towards a single direction or purpose. Alignment actually, narrows down many inner voices that reflect different and complex values, needs, memories, and wishes and (2) attunement – related to information processing that one receives. Attunement primarily requires vigilance, extroversion, mindedness, and the ability to learn from mistakes (Bird, 1988).

CONTEXT AND THEORETICAL FRAMING

Lawrence et al. (2008) successfully compared serial entrepreneurs with that managers and gave a new dimension to academics 'cold cognition' and 'hot cognition'. Cold cognition demonstrates rational thinking and hot cognition refers to emotional thinking. Notably both the aspects are generated in two different lobes of the frontal cortex in the brain. This study allowed the researchers to understand the theory of entrepreneurship with the help of neuroscience techniques (Krueger et al., 2011; Lawrence et al., 2008). Moreover, Zald et al. (2008) undertook multiple experiments on dopamine receptors in entrepreneurs and concluded that entrepreneurs have several dopamine receptors than the general population which allowed them to make accurate and error-free decisions at challenging times. More dopamine receptors made entrepreneurs able to understand the situation more effectively and risk-taking opportunities (Krueger & Day, 2010). Shane (2003) argues that entrepreneurs and non-entrepreneurs are having different decision-making processes but the study was not supported by empirical evidence (Krueger & Day, 2010; Shane, 2003). These studies by various researchers made the field active to answer questions like does cortical activation in the brain have some role to play in entrepreneurial decision-making (Perez-Centeno, 2018; Sharma et al., 2021; Welpe et al., 2012), How the brain regions of an entrepreneur are involved in the process of decision-making and reward opportunities (Srivastava et al., 2019; Sharma et al., 2021), and is there any connection between creativity, recognition, and evaluation for improved decision-making (Foo, 2011; Sharma et al., 2021; Zahra et al., 2005)?

Various neuroscience techniques are there to answer the questions asked above and can also explore more dimensions related to entrepreneurs (Massaro, 2020; Sharma et al., 2021). Electroencephalogram (EEG), fMRI, computed tomography (CT), and position emission tomography (PET) are some of the neuroscience techniques that are effective in unfolding brain dimensions (Mitchell et al., 2007; Sharma et al., 2021).

THE RATIONALE IN ORGANISATIONAL SETTINGS

Cognitive and emotional brain dimensions: Decision-making is one of the most important aspects in an organisational setting, especially for an entrepreneur. Cognition and emotion always back the decision-making process. Therefore, it is necessary to go through the brain functions that customise cognition and emotional aspects in an entrepreneur that lead them to take a particular decision. For an entrepreneur, environmental scanning is important and generally, there are three dimensions related to entrepreneurial alertness: *scanning and searching; association and connection, and evaluation and judgement* (Tang et al., 2012). The fundamental component is scanning and searching because it makes an entrepreneur aware of opportunities, situations, and evaluation of resources available (Tang, 2016). It helps entrepreneurs to develop the cognitive framework to interpret and organise information for entrepreneurial decisions (Mitchell et al., 2007; Sassetti et al., 2021; Tang, 2016). Superior cognitive processes are the brain functions that make an entrepreneur interact with the world. Perception, decision-making, motor skills, language skills, and social skills all are the dimensions related to the cognitive abilities of an entrepreneur.

Cognition is the mind maps and sense-making process that guides the actions of an individual. These are scripts adopted from the field of cognitive psychology and have been studied in organisations' practice for decades

(Fiol & Huff, 1992; Hodgkinson et al., 1999). These are some of the powerful 'see' things differently and guide their actions. Kelly (1955) developed *Personal Construct Theory* related to mind maps in organisational psychology as tools for finding explanations for creativity and decision-making in organisational settings. The theory is an abstraction and symbolisation of events and things that guide managers' and entrepreneurs' intake in several decisions related to creativity (Brännback & Carsrud, 2009). There are assumptions behind mental prototypes that connect opportunity and sustainability with that of entrepreneurs and it was noted that the mental prototypes of entrepreneurs are diverse from those of other individuals (Krueger et al., 2011; Welsh & Krueger, 2009). The collaborative research of neuroscience and entrepreneurship opened the window for researchers to explore the hidden dimensions beneath the brain system, especially where neural activity is prominent in obtaining results related to neurophysiology antecedents to emotions, cognitions, and decision-making in an individual. MRI and other techniques have shown more activation in the frontal polar cortex (associated with decision-making) in entrepreneurs than in managers (Gielnik et al., 2020).

Activation in the orbitofrontal cortex (OFC) made entrepreneurs aware of distinguishing the difference between broad (talent, intelligence) *vs* narrow (cleanliness, tidiness) aspects. In broad inferences, entrepreneurs rely on goal-relevant heuristics based on talent and intelligence; but in narrow inferences, entrepreneurs focussed less on heuristic traits (Hughes & Zaki, 2015). Decision-making in entrepreneurs always has a connection with reasoning and cognitive components. Various studies have demonstrated that prefrontal areas exhibit domain independence in relational reasoning and posterior occipital deals with domain independence reasoning (Krawczyk, 2010). As for cognition, emotions also play a vital role in shaping the decision-making of an entrepreneur. There are different types of emotions that help entrepreneurs select the correct options among the alternatives. There are primarily eight major emotional themes that affect decision-making. Integral emotions are the type of emotions that are caused by the decision itself and always run parallel to decisions. Incidental emotions are based on past incidents and affect the decisions of an entrepreneur. Emotional valence are pleasant or unpleasant social dimensions that affect the decision-making process (Lerner et al., 2015).

CREATIVITY AND NEUROSCIENCE TECHNIQUES

The techniques of cognitive neuroscience made considerable progress in the field of creativity by mapping brain networks. The constant interaction between default networks and executive control networks in posterior inferior parietal brain regions enhances creativity in tasks. Creativity emerges from three brain functions: imagination (default mode), Salience and last are Executive actions (Beaty et al., 2020). Beaty et al. (2020) explained theoretically the process of cognition and creativity. The process starts with goal-directed memory retrieval that is solely associated with the information stored in memory. The second step is to differentiate that information through divergent thinking and the last is a self-generated response based on internal processes.

Now the research is focussed on measuring brain activity especially cognitive neuroscience with the help of neuroscience techniques. The domain of cognitive neuroscience studies the impact and implementation of opportunity recognition on an individual task. The impulses and neural activation in the cerebral hemisphere are the source, and both the right and left hemispheres to play their part. The left hemisphere is associated with the accumulation of knowledge that enables an individual to behave according to the situation and the right hemisphere, associated with the search and discovery of innovation (Charles, 2013; Kesra & Mateusz, 2018). With the help of these neuroscience techniques, the literature pattern shifted to explore more brain dimensions related to cognition and creativity. Now brain neural networks have been studied with the help of EEG electroencephalogram to look into human behaviour, attitudes, and entrepreneurial activity (Mateusz et al., 2019). fMRI functional magnetic resonance imaging is an advanced technique than EEG exploring the neural details and identifying the impulses generated during opportunity recognition and decision making (Korpysa, 2020). Neuroscience techniques are trying to fill the gap between the theory of entrepreneurial cognition and practical aspects. The trends help researchers to understand the opportunity threats, and recognise strategies for decision-making concerning entrepreneurial frameworks (Korpysa, 2020).

Creativity is based on how quickly an entrepreneur can generate novel and useful ideas. Schumpeter (1942) proposed that entrepreneurs are more creative than others in an economic system and thereafter numerous studies have been conducted that examined the relationship between entrepreneurship and creativity. It is not possible to locate the origin of creativity in a single brain region. As for neuroentrepreneurship, creativity is associated with the frontal cortex which is also responsible for working memory. Another part associated is the hippocampus which connects creativity with past experiences. The hippocampus connects all the information of the past in a new and original way by allowing the generation of new ideas. Creativity acts as an internal motivator for entrepreneurs (Abraham & Windmann, 2007; Milano et al., 2021). Creativity in an organisational setting is mainly composed of two aspects: (1) work that is novel (original and unexpected) and (2) appropriate (useful, adaptive, and task constraints) (Sternberg & Lubart, 1999). The research-related to creativity is typically related to social, psychological, and cognitive historical domains and the brain mechanism behind all these has not been previously explored (Dietrich, 2004; Ward et al., 1999). Neural activity in the brain connects various information-processing systems simultaneously to decode the emotional and cognitive information in the dorsolateral prefrontal cortex (Dietrich, 2004). The neocortex is the main functional division of the brain that has a ventral fissure and connects three lobes to posterior cortices-temporal, occipital, and parietal; and these three lobes are associated with a long memory. The prefrontal cortex exhibits super control over emotions and cognitive behaviours. The frontal lobe is associated with cognitive flexibility and freedom. Cognitive flexibility and freedom further generate creativity in the brain by adopting new rules with the help of convergent and divergent thinking (Deitrich, 2004). With the help of EEG and fMRI neuroscience techniques, researchers concluded which brain part processes which brain function is involved in entrepreneurial creativity and decision-making.

Ortiz-Terán et al. (2013) studied EEG and concluded that brain hemispheres are what makes entrepreneurs make fast and accurate decisions. Ortiz-Terán et al. (2013) suggest that entrepreneurs are more effective when controlling feelings and responding to external stimuli than others, resulting in enhanced opportunity judgement. Laureiro-Martínez et al. (2014) used the fMRI technique and concluded that frontal polar cortex (FPC) is more powerful in entrepreneurs which makes them active for upcoming opportunities and higher managerial efficiency. Laureiro-Martínez et al. (2014) concluded that entrepreneur's neural impulses are responsible for making more accurate decisions than managers. Neural impulses also control the utilisation of better entrepreneurial opportunities.

Bernoster et al. (2018) employed EEG and explored entrepreneurial attitudes that are formed due to neuroplasticity, control, intentions, norms, and the entrepreneurial orientation of an individual. Shane and Nicolaou's (2019) fMRI explained the entrepreneur's passion for entrepreneurship and the entrepreneur's ability to invest time and money are the two variables and a positive correlation is seen between these two, and this is because of neural impulses occurring in the brain of the entrepreneur; Entrepreneurs' passion and the capacity to take risky decisions are directly proportional to each other.

Lahti et al. (2019) used fMRI to explore the neural stimuli which generally minimise the impact of negative emotions in entrepreneurs, and also minimise the anxiety and fear. As parents care for their children, the same feeling gets generated in the minds of entrepreneurs related to their venture (Korpysa, 2020). Kolb (1984) distinguished the functional areas of the brain and brain functions concerning the learning domain in an entrepreneur. All the lobes of the brain get covered and also mentioned which lobe is associated with which function and learning domain as shown in the table.

Functional area of the brain	Primary function	Learning domain	Kolb's learning cycle
Temporal lobe	Feeling	Affective learning	Concrete experience
Occipital lobe	Watching	Visual learning	Reflective observation
Parietal lobe	Doing	Physical learning	Active experimentation
Frontal lobe	Thinking	Cognitive learning	Abstract conceptualisation

Sources: Kolb (1984) and Dietrich (2004).

In addition, Moore et al. (2009) demonstrated that a higher divergent-thinking score – most creativity tests are effectively tested for divergent thinking. One possible explanation for this finding is that a reduced size leads to a more efficient brain organisation. Based on the above, we conjecture that one could predict a smaller corpus callosum size in ratio to total white matter volume in entrepreneurs compared to non-entrepreneurs, due to the established links between creativity and entrepreneurship. Neuroscience holds that white matter is primarily responsible for creativity in entrepreneurs. White matter connects the right and left hemispheres of the corpus callosum.

DISCUSSION AND CONCLUSION

This chapter provides insight into the contribution of neuro-entrepreneurship particularly in the areas of creativity and creative decision making and focusses on establishing a connection between decision-making and creativity at the workplace with the help of neuroscience techniques in entrepreneurs. The amalgamation of neuroscience techniques with entrepreneurship gave us the passcode to access the brain functioning of entrepreneurs. While research in the field of neuro-entrepreneurship has increased it still lacks further empirical support to justify claims of correlation and causation. Based on the literature, it has been found that various neuroscience techniques like EEG, fMRI, CT, and PET are highly effective in unfolding brain dimensions (Sharma et al., 2021) and also facilitate further understanding of the theory of entrepreneurship. The collaborative research of neuroscience and entrepreneurship opened the window for researchers to explore the hidden dimensions beneath the brain system, especially where neural activity is prominent in getting clearer results related to neurophysiology antecedents to emotions, cognitions, and, decision-making in an individual. Neuroscience techniques (EEG, PET, and fMRI) reveal various brain functions and chemicals that are involved in entrepreneurial decision-making and creativity. Scientifically, the research is active and the results are clear but it lacks support from social science research studies. The two elements namely: in the flesh (i.e. frontal cortex of the brain) and chemical receptor (dopamine) direct the entire story. The frontal cortex is the centre of origin of cognition which in turn activates the memory and decision-making function. Based on evidence from the literature, this part is more active in the brain of entrepreneurs and aids them to predict the situation and move effectively. Through detailed analysis of the literature on neuroscience techniques, entrepreneurship, and creativity, it can be concluded that creativity and entrepreneurship are interlinked by several brain functions. EEG, PET, and fMRI indicated that the brain functions involved are the same that get activated in creativity and entrepreneurship. The hippocampus gets activated in the prefrontal cortex which leads an entrepreneur to have a creative idea. The role of dopamine and serotonin is prominent in entrepreneurs for creativity. With the help of neuroscience techniques, it can be drawn that the receptors of dopamine and serotonin are much more in entrepreneurs than non-entrepreneurs. The parietal occipital lobe and dorsum stratum are the origin centres of these two hormones called creative thinking and success hormones.

Although, the knowledge about the functioning of the human brain and its association with entrepreneurship, creativity, and decision-making is still curtailed and in progress. To sum up, researchers are continuing to carry out studies that widen their knowledge of the brain's nature and processes related to it. However, despite the limitations stemming from limited research on neuro-entrepreneurship and the intricacy of studies on the functioning of the human brain, cognitive neuroscience techniques should be more frequently used to examine their role in an organisational setting. Regardless of this limitation, it seems evident that the advances in cognitive neuroscience should be a mandatory standpoint for research on the behaviour of entrepreneurs. Due to the results of cognitive neuroscience research, the theory of entrepreneurship is being enriched with issues related to cognitive and emotional decision-making, creativity, and its association with neuroscience techniques which results in improved insight, especially in an organisational setting.

REFERENCES

Abraham, A., & Windmann, S. (2007). Creative cognition: The diverse operations and the prospect of applying a cognitive neuroscience perspective. *Methods, 42*(1), 38–48. https://doi.org/10.1016/j.ymeth.2006.12.007

Beaty, R. E., Seli, P., & Schacter, D. L. (2020). Network neuroscience of creative cognition: Mapping cognitive mechanisms and individual differences in the creative brain. *Current Opinion in Behavioral Sciences, 27*, 22–30. https://doi.org/10.1016/j.cobeha.2018.08.013

Bernoster, I., Rietveld, C., Thurik, R., & Torrès, O. (2018). Overconfidence, optimism and entrepreneurship. *Sustainability, 10*, 2233. https://doi.org/10.3390/su10072233

Bird, B. (1988). Implementing entrepreneurial ideas: The case for intention. *Academy of Management Review, 13*(3), 442–453.

Brännback, M., & Carsrud, A. (2009). Cognitive maps in entrepreneurship: Researching sense making and action. *Understanding the Entrepreneurial Mind, 1*, 75–96. https://doi.org/10.1007/978-1-4419-0443-0

Cadar, O., & Badulescu, D. (2015). Entrepreneur, entrepreneurship and intrapreneurship: A literature review. *The Annals of the University of Oradea, Economic Sciences* (pp. 658–664). Munich Personal RePEc Archive. https://www.researchgate.net/publication/289125304

Carter, M., & Shieh, J. (2015). *Guide to research techniques in neuroscience*. Elsevier Books.

Charles, G. (2013). The co-operative, transformative organization of human action and knowledge. *Journal of Pragmatics, 46*(1), 8–23.

Dietrich, A. (2004). The cognitive neuroscience of creativity. *Psychonomic Bulletin & Review, 11*(6), 1011–1026.

Fiol, C. M., & Huff, A. S. (1992). Maps for managers: Where are we? Where do we go from here? *Journal of Management Studies, 29*(3), 267–285.

Foo, M. D. (2011). Emotions and entrepreneurial opportunity evaluation. *Entrepreneurship: Theory and Practice, 35*(2), 375–393. https://doi.org/10.1111/j.1540-6520.2009.00357.x

Gielnik, M. M., Cardon, M. S., & Frese, M. (Eds.). (2020). *The psychology of entrepreneurship: New perspectives* (1st ed.). Routledge. https://doi.org/10.4324/9781003137573

Girişken, A., & Çakar, T. (2021). What is neuroentrepreneurship? The theoretical framework, critical evaluation, and research program Nörogirişimcilik Nedir? *Teorik Çerçeve, Kritik Değerlendirme ve Ar aştırma Programı, 17*(36), 2975–2991. https://doi.org/10.26466/opus.840936

Gupta, A., & Anandaram, S. (2022). Catalysing cultural entrepreneurship in India. *Observer Research Foundation*, (544). 1–25. https://www.orfonline.org/research/catalysing-cultural-entrepreneurship-in-india/

Hodgkinson, P., Bown, N. J., Maule, A. J., Glaister, K. W., & Pearman, A. D. (1999). Breaking the frame: An analysis of strategic cognition and decision making under uncertainty. *Strategic Management Journal, 20*, 977–985.

De Holan, P. M. (2014). Management inquiry it's all in your head: Why we need. *Journal of Management Inquiry, 23*, 93–97. https://doi.org/10.1177/1056492613485913

Hughes, B. L., & Zaki, J. (2015). The neuroscience of motivated cognition. *Trends in Cognitive Sciences*, *19*(2), 62–64. https://doi.org/10.1016/j.tics.2014.12.006

Ireland R. D., Hitt M. A., & Sirmon D. G. (2003). A model of strategic entrepreneurship: The construct and its dimensions. *Journal of Management*, *29*, 963–990.

Kaffka, G., & Krueger, N. (n.d.). The entrepreneurial 'mindset ': Entrepreneurial intentions from the entrepreneurial event to neuroentrepreneurship. *Foundational Research in entrepreneurship studies* (1st ed., pp. 203–224). Palgrave Macmillan. https://doi.org/10.1007/978-3-319-73528-3

Kelly, G. A. (1955). *The psychology of personal constructs. Clinical diagnosis and psychotherapy*. W. W. Norton.

Kesra, N., & Mateusz, P. (2018). Cognitive neuroscience techniques in supporting decision making and the analysis of social campaign. *Proceedings of the international conference on accounting, business, economics and politics* (pp. 1–12). Tishk International University.

Kolb, D. A. (1984). *Experiential learning: Experience as the source of learning and development*. Prentice-Hall.

Korpysa, J. (2020). Neuroentrepreneurship a new paradigm in the management science. *Procedia Computer Science*, *176*, 2605–2614. https://doi.org/10.1016/j.procs.2020.09.309

Krawczyk, D. C. (2010). The cognition and neuroscience of relational reasoning. *Brain Research*, *1428*, 13–23. https://doi.org/10.1016/j.brainres.2010.11.080

Krueger, N. (2017) *Entrepreneurial intentions are dead: Long live entrepreneurial intentions, revisiting the entrepreneurial mind*. Springer International Publishing.

Krueger, N. F., & Day, M. (2010). *Looking forward, looking backward: From entrepreneurial cognition to neuroentrepreneurship*. Springer. https://doi.org/10.1007/978-1-4419-1191-9

Krueger, B. N., Hansen, D. J., Michl, T., Welsh, D. H. B., & Thinking, D. H. B. (2011). Advances in entrepreneurship, firm emergence and growth. In *Social and sustainable entrepreneurship* (Vol. 13, pp. 275–309). Emerald Group Publishing Limited. https://doi.org/10.1108/S1074-7540(2011)0000013014

Krueger, N., & Welpe, I. (2014). Neuroentrepreneurship: What can entrepreneurship learn from neuroscience. *Annals of Entrepreneurship Education and Pedagogy*, *2014*, 60–90.

Lahti, T., Halko, M. L., Karagozoglu, N., & Wincent, J. (2019). Why and how do founding entrepreneurs bond with their ventures? Neural correlates of entrepreneurial and parental bonding. *Journal of Business Venturing*, *34*(2), 368–388.

Landström, H., & Lohrke, F. (2010). *Historical foundations of entrepreneurship research*. Edward Elgar Publishing.

Laureiro-Martínez, D., Canessa, N., Brusoni, S., Zollo, M., Hare, T., Alemanno, F., & Cappa, S. F. (2014). Frontopolar cortex and decision-making efficiency: Comparing brain activity of experts with different professional background during an exploration-exploitation task. *Frontiers in Human Neuroscience*, *7*, 927.

Lawrence, A., Clark, L., Labuzetta, J., Sahakian, B., & Vyakarnum, S. (2008). The innovative brain. *Nature*, *456*(7219), 168–169.

Lerner, J. S., Li, Y., Valdesolo, P., & Kassam, K. S. (2015). Emotion and decision making. *Annual Review of Psychology*, *66*, 799–823. https://doi.org/10.1146/annurev-psych-010213-115043

Massaro, S. (2020). The organizational neuroscience of emotions. *The Cambridge handbook of workplace affect* (pp. 15–36). Cambridge University Press. https://doi.org/10.1017/978110 8573887.003

Mateusz, P., Singh, U., & Kesra, N. (2019). Application of EEG metrics in the decision-making process. *Experimental and quantitative methods in contemporary economics* (*Springer Proceedings in Business and Economics*, pp. 187–199). Springer.

Milano, B. A., Kimmelmann, J., Mussgnug, M., Espinoza, M. S., Waidelich, M., & Kirner, E. (2021). *Personality traits of entrepreneurs – A neuroscientific approach*. Hochschule Furtwangen University Imm.

Mitchell, R. K., Busenitz, L. W., Bird, B., Marie Gaglio, C., McMullen, J. S., Morse, E. A., & Smith, J. B. (2007). The central question in entrepreneurial cognition research 2007. *Entrepreneurship Theory and Practice*, *31*(1), 1–27.

Moore, D. W., Bhadelia, R. A., Billings, R. L., Fulwiler, C., Heilman, K. M., Rood, K., Gansler, D. A. (2009). Hemispheric connectivity and the visual–spatial divergent-thinking component of creativity. *Brain and Cognition*, *70*(3), 267–272. https://doi.org/10.1016/j.bandc.2009.02.011

Ortiz-Terán, E., Turrero, A., Santos, J. M., Bryant, P. T., Ortiz, T. (2013). Brain cortical organization in entrepreneurs during a visual Stroop decision task. *Neuroscience and Neuroeconomics*, *2*, 33–49.

Pinchot, E. S., & Pinchot, G., III. (1978). *Intrapreneur.com – Intra-corporate entrepreneuring.* http://www.intrapreneur.com/MainPages/History/IntraCorp

Pinchot, G. (2010). *The Pinchot perspective. In search of a future worth living.* http://www.pinchot.com/2010/01/back-to-intrapreneuring.html

Pérez-Centeno, V. (2018). *Brain-driven entrepreneurship research: Expanded review and research agenda towards entrepreneurial enhancement* [Working Paper No. 02/18, Institut für Mittelstandsforschung (IfM)].

Sassetti, S., Cavaliere, V., & Lombardi, S. (2021). The rhythm of effective entrepreneurs' decision-making process. The pathways of alertness scanning and search and cognitive style. A mediation model. *International Entrepreneurship and Management Journal*, *18*, 555–578. https://doi.org/10.1007/s11365-021-00759-1

Schumpeter, J. (1942). *Capitalism, socialism and democracy*. Harper & Brothers.

Shane, S. (2003). *A general theory of entrepreneurship: The individual-opportunity nexus*.

Shane, S., & Nicolaou, N. (2019). Common genetic effects on risk-taking preferences and choices. *Journal of Risk and Uncertainty*, *59*, 261–279. https://doi.org/10.1007/s11166-019-09316-2

Sharma, G. D., Paul, J., Srivastava, M., Yadav, A., Sarker, T., & Bansal, S. (2021). Neuroentrepreneurship: An integrative review and research agenda. *Entrepreneurship & Regional Development*, *33*(9–10), 1–31. https://doi.org/10.1080/08985626.2021.1966106

Srivastava, M., Sharma, G. D., & Srivastava, A. K. (2019). Human brain and financial behavior: A neurofinance perspective. *International Journal of Ethics and Systems*, *35*(4), 485–503. https://doi.org/10.1108/IJOES-02-2019-0036

Sternberg, R. J., & Lubart, T. I. (1999). The concept of creativity: Prospects and paradigms. In *Handbook of creativity* (pp. 3–15). Cambridge University Press.

Tang, J. (2016). Linking personal turbulence and creative behavior: The influence of scanning and search in the entrepreneurial process. *Journal of Business Research*, *69*(3), 1167–1174.

Tang, J., Kacmar, K. M. M., & Busenitz, L. (2012). Entrepreneurial alertness in the pursuit of new opportunities. *Journal of Business Venturing*, *27*(1), 77–94.

Ward, T. B., Smith, S. M., & Finke, R. A. (1999). Creative cognition. In *Handbook of creativity* (pp. 189–212). Cambridge University Press.

Welpe, I. M., Spörrle, M., Grichnik, D., Michl, T., & Audretsch, D. B. (2012). Emotions and opportunities: The interplay of opportunity evaluation, fear, joy, and anger as antecedent of entrepreneurial exploitation. *Entrepreneurship Theory and Practice*, *36*(1), 69–96. https://doi.org/10.1111/j.1540-6520.2011.00481.x

Welsh, D. H., & Krueger, N. (2009). Social? Sustainable? Entrepreneurship? A first look at mental prototyping of "social" entrepreneurship (summary). *Frontiers of Entrepreneurship Research*, *29*(21), 5.

Zahra, S. A., Korri, J. S., & Yu, J. (2005). Cognition and international entrepreneurship: Implications for research on international opportunity recognition and exploitation. *International Business Review*, *14*(2), 129–146. https://doi.org/10.1016/j.ibusrev.2004.04.005

Zald, D. H., Cowan, R. L., Riccardi, P., Baldwin, R. M., Ansari, M. S., Li, R., Shelby, E. S., Smith, C. E., McHugo, M., & Kessler, R. M. (2008). Midbrain dopamine receptor availability is inversely associated with novelty-seeking traits in humans. *Journal of Neuroscience*, *28*(53), 14372–14378. https://doi.org/10.1523/JNEUROSCI.2423-08.2008

SOCIAL SPACES AND PLACEMAKING FOR CCI ENTREPRENEURS

CHAPTER 13

COMMUNITY AND CREATIVE ENTREPRENEURSHIP: THE DYNAMIC RELATIONSHIP BETWEEN SOCIAL WORKSPACES AND CREATIVE ENTREPRENEURS

Annette Naudin

Birmingham City University, UK

ABSTRACT

There is a common misconception that entrepreneurship in the cultural and creative industries can be characterised by the tension between artistic aspirations and the economic sustainability of the enterprise. The image of a bohemian artist, associated with Paris of the twentieth century, remains a significant aspect of the contemporary creative worker's identity. Yet, a more nuanced understanding of creative entrepreneurship situates creative practices in a relational environment and allows us to analyse diverse non-economic values and motivations. Through qualitative research, this chapter explores the distinctive practices of a small group of cultural and creative industry entrepreneurs based in studios in a post-industrial heritage building. Framed by the impact of COVID-19, this research situates entrepreneurs within social communities: a milieu for developing their creative entrepreneurial identities. The research suggests that workspaces and personal values play a significant role in shaping entrepreneurial practices, and that these are entangled with a sense of responsibility to locality and community.

Keywords: Community; collaboration; values; mutual support; creative entrepreneurship; artists

This chapter explores a community-based workspace for cultural and creative industry (thereafter CCI) micro-entrepreneurs, located in an economically deprived urban context, in the United Kingdom. The research investigates the nature and significance of socially embedded entrepreneurial development (McKeever et al., 2014) for creative individuals whose identity and work practices are motivated by a diverse set of values. The precarious nature of cultural and creative micro-entrepreneurship (thereafter referred to as 'creative entrepreneurship and creative entrepreneurs'), and the complexities associated with constructing a creative or artistic identify are fragile and continuously re-defined (Taylor & Littleton, 2012). Furthermore, as Banks and O'Connor (2020) argue, the pandemic further exacerbated the inequalities and the insecurities already evident in the CCIs workforce. This chapter explores these challenges in a relational context, by analysing creative entrepreneurs in their workplace. As we (slowly) emerge from the pandemic, there is a need to pause and reconsider the value of the CCI sectors beyond their economic contribution. The creative entrepreneurs in this study navigate creative, environmental, and social values as part of the economic sustainability of their enterprise, providing alternative ways of conceptualising entrepreneurship (McRobbie, 2011). The disruption caused by COVID-19, is an opportune moment to reflect on these values and to explore them as a moment in time. Underpinned by critical debates from interdisciplinary perspectives, this chapter is concerned with social relations in community spaces (Pratt et al., 2019) as a means of understanding creative entrepreneurship. The significance of community found in 'creative hubs' and clusters of creative workers (Florida, 2002) is not new and has been popular with policymakers seeking to regenerate post-industrial cities. But what is the significance of the dynamic between workspace, community and entrepreneurship in the CCIs? Given the negative impact of the pandemic on the CCI sector (Comunian & England, 2020), has this redefined the nature of creative entrepreneurship? Does a study of creative entrepreneurs in social spaces inform a new understanding of entrepreneurship?

To explore these questions, the chapter focusses on qualitative empirical data from social media content and interviews with creative entrepreneurs based in studio spaces, in an industrial heritage building in the United Kingdom. The participants include micro-entrepreneurs working in different sub-sectors of the CCIs, such as photography, metalwork, art, and ceramics. The method includes interviews with the Chief Executive who manages the building and observations through visits to individual studios, coworking areas, cafes and the exhibition space. This study identifies three themes which help to conceptualise the relationship between creative entrepreneurs and the spaces in which they work: Firstly, community and the significance of place; secondly, motivation and shared values; and finally, developing an enterprise. The findings and discussion offer a relatively positive characterisation of creative entrepreneurship, although, as Bandinelli and Gandini (2019) state, shared workspaces produce fertile ground for 'collaborative individualism', suggesting an instrumental use of community and support. As a place of work, the building houses these contradictions, demonstrating the complexities of contemporary entrepreneurship.

CONTEXT AND FRAMING

Entrepreneurship in the CCI has been a feature of modern British culture for several years, typified by sub-culture scenes, DIY cultures, and often associated with a night-time economy (McRobbie, 2007; O'Brien, 2014). A connection to bohemian lifestyles can be seen in the activist, sometimes radical and alternative approaches to cultural and creative work. Until New Labour's much-criticised 'Cool Britannia' (O'Brien, 2014), entrepreneurial modes of work fuelled an alternative creative economy, but it was rarely perceived as an exemplar of entrepreneurship. In many ways, it had more in common with other hidden economies, such as what Webb et al. (2009) describe as socially acceptable illegal practices (Napster for example). Similarly, Carter (2018) argues that fan economies, despite being neglected due to the sense that they fall between 'amateur' and 'professional' practices, can result in acts of enterprise.

While these practices are not unique to the United Kingdom, it is the British New Labour government of the early 2000s which made the economic case for the CCI and which became interested in their entrepreneurial practices. According to Ross (2008), the nature of cultural work did not receive much attention until the emergence of CCI policies, during New Labour's period in government. From then on, the over-celebration and negative impact of flexible modes of work, typified by creative entrepreneurs, became a source for critical debate by scholars such as Angela McRobbie, Rosalind Gill and Andy Pratt, to name but a few. We are now familiar with an idealised version of CCI work (Gill et al., 2019), represented as creatively fulfilling work and infused with mythical notions of a bohemian lifestyle. In contrast, the realities of establishing and sustaining a career or a micro-enterprise in the CCIs, can be described as a precarious endeavour and likely to only generate a modest income (Banks, 2007; Oakley, 2014). The dichotomy presented by these contrasting viewpoints has been brought into sharp focus during the COVID-19 pandemic, highlighting the underlying inequalities and the insecurities of CCI work (Banks & O'Connor, 2020). Even in countries such as the United Kingdom, which benefits from substantial public investment in the CCIs, lockdowns and the cancellation of events have had a very negative impact. In the United Kingdom, this follows years of austerity measures in the form of government cuts to the arts and wider CCIs, leaving the sector in a vulnerable position (Bakare, 2020). Despite this challenging landscape, some CCI micro-enterprises have managed to keep their heads above water, adapting to new circumstances and rethinking the nature of their enterprise. Creative entrepreneurs are responding to changing economic conditions and developing socially engaged enterprises. Specifically, in this context, and in response to the ongoing insecurities in CCIs, there is evidence of collaboration, 'mutual aid' (de Peuter & Cohen, 2015) and a sense of responsibility to the locality. There is the potential for mutual support and solidarity among creative entrepreneurs, provided by alternative, affordable community workspaces (Sandoval & Littler, 2019). This chapter explores the significance of community-based workspaces and socially embedded enterprises (McKeever et al., 2014) as an environment for re-thinking creative entrepreneurship.

CREATIVE ENTREPRENEURSHIP

As with most industries, creative entrepreneurs share some attributes, although it should be noted that these are not fixed and there are multiple perspectives for researching creative and entrepreneurial motivations (Horvath & Dechamp, 2021). Scholars who have explored changes in work, argue that a change in terminology, from 'cultural worker' to 'cultural entrepreneur' can be understood as indicative of a shift towards accepting a neoliberal model of work (Ellmeier, 2003). This is depicted as the negative impact of self-employment and the inequalities in the creative workforce, documented by scholars such as Rosalind Gill (2002) (also see Gill & Pratt, 2008; McRobbie, 2002). Despite this, micro-enterprises in the CCIs persist and continue to re-invent models of entrepreneurial work to suit their creative practices. This is described by Beaven (2012) as a pragmatic response, simply to continue their creative practice, even if they are unwillingly pushed into creative entrepreneurship (Oakley, 2014). By gaining deeper insights into entrepreneurial contexts and motivations, we challenge myths and dominant ideas (Jones & Spicer, 2009; Shane, 2007). Entrepreneurs do not exist in a vacuum but rather, they react to historically and socially located environments through a relational process, informed by the communities found in that milieu (Chell & Karataş-Özkan, 2010; Naudin, 2018).

COLLABORATION, COMMUNITY, AND CREATIVE ENTREPRENEURSHIP

In *the Independents*, Leadbeater and Oakley (1999) identify the relationship between creative work, micro-enterprises and their locality. The outcome is significant in two ways: firstly, the authors note that creative entrepreneurs (or *Independents*), support each other through casual, informal networks; and secondly, that their creative work has a significant impact locally, in regenerating parts of cities and contributing to a sense of place. The impact on creative workers is that proximity to others provides a supportive environment, the possibility for exchanging ideas and supports the process of becoming a creative entrepreneur. Furthermore, there are opportunities for cultivating an identity, based on a sense of belonging (Eikhof & Haunschild, 2006) and informed by a community of practice. The clustering of enterprises in hubs and coworking spaces has become commonplace, and these environments offer opportunities for the development of distinctive cultures as well as models of mutual support (Long & Naudin, 2019). Shared creative spaces reinforce informal networks, sometimes described as the root of many inequalities in the sector (Lee, 2011). Indeed, there is a dichotomy in the literature between an analysis of the role of networks as leading to inequalities in the CCIs (see Brook et al., 2018; Gill, 2002), in contrast to an acknowledgement that networks offer support, solidarity and a sense of community (Patel, 2020). More supportive networks are found in sub-sectors of the CCIs (Scott, 2012) and when creative entrepreneurs are deeply rooted in their locality (Banks, 2007; Naudin, 2018). For instance, Scott (2012) highlights the strong social bonds between DIY and music producers, describing that it is possible to observe both instrumental and communitarian motivations for mutual support, although as de Peuter and Cohen (2017) point out, mutual aid does not offer the kind of social support provided by unions or social welfare. Nevertheless, there are examples of solidarity and the potential for addressing some inequalities in aspects of creative entrepreneurship. In contrast to forms of neoliberal individualism, sometimes associated with popular representations of entrepreneurs, this chapter considers progressive motives for creative entrepreneurship by paying attention to the environment in which cultural work is produced (Luckman, 2012).

METHODOLOGY

The research draws on methods from media and cultural studies to investigate the lived experiences of creative entrepreneurship in a relational environment. The lived experience enables the researcher to investigate the creative entrepreneur's story: A reflexive narrative which offers possibilities for theorising experience, in a space in which identities are shaped and constructed (Gray, 2002).

Through observation and textual analysis of the material collected, the research reveals the ways in which individual agents, play an active role in shaping and imagining their world (Holland et al., 2003). The method for this research draws on the work of Chell and Karataş-Özkan (2010) who explore the entrepreneur's embedded position within social structures. Their approach is underpinned by Pierre Bourdieu's (1986) conceptual tools, which help us understand the interplay between individual agency and social spaces. As Chell and Karataş-Özkan's (2010) explain, the creative entrepreneur's 'experience is influenced by the social space – the socio-cultural – but not reduced to it' (p. 91). This methodology invites researchers to be immersed in the social settings, enabling close observation of the social dynamics at play (Johannisson, 2011). As Newth (2018) argues, the value of immersing oneself as a researcher is to gain a deeper understanding of the organisation or individuals. As a local resident, I have visited the space, attended events, used facilities such as the café and co-working space, and observed its development over a period of time. Bearing in mind this embedded experience, critical distance is achieved through the researcher's engagement with the literature.

The method combines qualitative empirical data through four interviews alongside social media content and personal experience of the space, people and locality. The participants are based in studio spaces, in a converted industrial heritage building, in a major UK city. The online material was collected from relevant websites and social media including company websites and Instagram accounts. A qualitative mixed-method approach was used, including three semi-structured interviews with creative micro-entrepreneurs who work in different sub-sectors of the CCIs, along with the Chief Executive Officer (CEO) of the building, which for this research will be known as Make. A qualitative textual analysis was used to examine and interpret the interview and social media data. Drawing on cultural studies research practices (Gray, 2002), this approach provides a critical understanding of the creative entrepreneurs' experience within specific contexts. The participants are identified in the chapter as Alex (photographer), Liz (metal worker creating small-scale products), Anabelle (art and ceramics) and Joanna is the CEO of Make.

Make is located at the heart of a multicultural community, in one of the most deprived areas of the city. As a heritage building, the space is full of post-industrial character, but it has not been fully refurbished and could be described as a messy working environment, mainly made up of studios, open and underdeveloped spaces, and a coworking area. I refer to the workspace as Make, to acknowledge its historical connection to making and industrial processes. For ethical reasons, interviewees, social media account details have been anonymised, the city is not named and key terms such as the title of an exhibition have been altered. The community is broadly described as 'creative', but this extends beyond the CCIs to include bike repairs, floral designs, furniture restoration, yoga and sound therapy. Data from relevant social media accounts was gathered over a period of three months, alongside observations at the venue which were noted in a reflective diary. This approach has provided insights in the form of individual narratives from participants (Pickering, 2008), alongside an understanding of both physical and online environments. The creative entrepreneurs work flexible hours but generally attempt to be full-time, either working by themselves or working collaboratively. Most of their income comes from selling their products or services and they describe themselves as professional rather than amateur creative workers. Their income is derived from a mix of funded projects, educational activities and commercial work. The building is managed by a charitable organisation which was set up, approximately 10 years ago and it has received very little public funding other than for a selection of small projects.

FINDINGS AND DISCUSSION

Community and the Significance of Place

Workspaces such as Make enable creative entrepreneurs to express social values through their desire to participate and contribute to a geographically located community of practice. The dominant working culture originates from a commitment to a socially engaged vision for individuals and for collective work. This is evidenced through projects, and it is articulated as a philosophical position by studio partners, but it is also in promotional communication (such as Instagram posts).

Echoing Bank's (2007) study, community and the significance of place can be categorised in three ways: Personal relationships between creative entrepreneurs; the community within Make; and finally, the geographical locality within the city. Working relations, networks and opportunities for collaboration create conditions which go some way to address the precariousness of creative entrepreneurship. As the CEO, Joanna, explains:

> We do try to choose studio partners that are creative, specially makers that are willing to spend some of their time and energy interacting with the community and creating a social impact.

As CEO, Joanna organises events for various local organisations (women's organisations, organisations who work with children with disabilities and the women's enterprise hub) to ensure they can find out more about Make. Joanna's aspiration is to integrate Make, studio partners and local people in shared activities.

> Some studio partners for example did a carpentry thing and then there are a few times when co-workers wanted to collaborate with the bike project ... [And]in the meetings room the other day I saw some people I would never think would collaborate, so that was interesting! (Joanna, March 2022)

Joanna is aware of the limitations of the engagement with local communities, and she sees this as a work in progress. She shares examples of how they are beginning to make progress while acknowledging that Make needs to do much more.

> At the moment, most people who interact with the public don't necessarily interact with the local mostly Muslim community and that's something we are hoping to address.... But we have got to the stage where we have general members of the local community come in and engage. (Joanna, March 2022)

And for a few of the studio partners, the local community is not relevant or of interest. Liz explains that she runs workshops with schools and engages with the Jewish community but that's not the immediate locality, for her 'there's no significance to the location' (Liz, February 2022).

A more formal engagement is the consortium between five local community organisations who receive local authority funds to promote a regular event for the general public, known as Open Studio. One of the studio partners, Anabelle, expresses this in her Instagram post:

> It's been so fabulous to be involved with Open Studio, a funded cultural initiative, connecting communities .... (Anabelle, Instagram 2022)

The motivation for these collaborations and bringing communities together seems far removed from the 'collaborative individualism' Bandinelli and Gandini (2019) discuss. Instead, the participants in this study appear to gain the kind of social and cultural capital which can be a significant form of mutual support (Long & Naudin, 2019; Scott, 2012) rather than purely instrumental. The impact of collaborations and engaging with others is part of their creative entrepreneurship, but these actions can be hidden or under the radar, limiting our understanding of their significance to entrepreneurship or the wider community.

The social impact described here tends to be motivated by the creative entrepreneurs' interest in community engagement. In comparison, this differs from other creative workspaces such as those described by Morgan and Woodriff (2019) which seem to focus on collaborations for entrepreneurial development.

MOTIVATION AND SHARED VALUES

This research does not seek to disprove the idea that artistic expression or creative autonomy can be a motivating factor, but at Make, social support also acts as an important value. As Taylor and Littleton (2012) have demonstrated, artistic identities and motivations are not fixed. Individual cultural and social values are enacted collectively in coworking communities, shaping each other's approach to their entrepreneurial practice. Shared values are expressed through the nature of the products and services offered, such as workshops with local schools and women's groups. As Alex explains, this is not always evident, it is implicit.

> Underpinning ... there's an implicit .... The people who invest their time in sharing an art form, in a not very commercial way, there is implicitly the value you put on doing something creative is, I'd say, a communitarian or progressive .... (Alex, March 2022)

It also suggests that a creative entrepreneur, with different values might not fit in. As Morgan and Woodriff (2019) find in their study of coworking spaces in Sydney, there is evidence that individuals need to 'fit in' or 'gel' (p. 35). In comparison to others, Liz is more commercially orientated, and she is looking for a creative community but for her, this is more about sustaining her business.

> My motivation is getting my work out there and people seeing my work and recognising it. (Liz, February 2022)

In comparison, Alex expresses his commitment to Make and his sense of responsibility beyond his personal enterprise by explaining his choice to establish his photography enterprise at Make.

> Its run by a charity which has social, environmental, progressive aims ... it's one of the reasons why I've stayed here because I kinda have a sense of the vision behind it .... (Alex, March 2022)

In other words, the sustainability of his creative enterprise is intertwined with values which shape the culture of the place. Alex commits to Make, contributing and shaping a set of values through his engagement with projects which also fund his enterprise but he is always balancing different goals.

> We have added environmental impact to that ... and so a large part of the social impact is people who run a class or an event or an opportunity. For example, the sewing room, the pottery, the mix art project that are open to the community. Some of them regularly seek to work with disadvantaged communities. (Alex, March 2022)

In practice, this means that Alex goes out of his way to develop collaborative projects which are evaluated through their social impact as a key aspect of his enterprise. This encourages ways of working that are: creative, social and entrepreneurial. And as Anabel demonstrates, this is evidenced in small day-to-day acts, which she describes alongside an image of a milk jug, on Instagram.

> This beauty is heading for @XXXX because despite being a thriving community of potters, they don't have a milk jug! (Anabelle, Instagram 2022)

Having retrained to be a potter, after a career as a teacher, Anabelle takes much inspiration from her religious beliefs rooted in Quaker ethics in business. Starting her creative enterprise just before the COVID-19 pandemic suggests she had already made a life-changing decision, however, it is during the pandemic that she consolidated her friendship and connections with several studio partners who, like her, were (on and off) able to work in their individual studio during the pandemic.

Creative entrepreneurs in this study are concerned to develop an enterprise model which suits a wide set of values and ethical positions which echoes a long tradition of ethical community workspaces (Morgan & Woodriff, 2019). A workplace which embodies these values can be a refuge for some creative entrepreneurs: validating their personal ethical positions but also enhancing the nature of their creative entrepreneurship.

DEVELOPING AN ENTERPRISE

The pragmatic decision to set up as an enterprise (Beaven, 2012) affords creative workers the opportunity to experiment and re-invent entrepreneurship to suit their circumstances and values. In that sense, entrepreneurship is a process which takes place over a period of time rather than a fixed activity. Joanna explains that she is only too aware that establishing an enterprise is not something which happens overnight, and she states:

> We have shared spaces to make it more affordable for makers. We do have a policy which anyone can see but there is quite a bit of, I guess discretion, as to how we perceive whether a person needs a discount .... But we offer a long-term discount with people who are having a social impact and are able to share their data with us because that then contributes towards our own charitable status. (Joanna, March 2022)

There is an experimental, trial-and-error approach, which allows creative entrepreneurs to test ideas, develop skills or diversify. Collaborating helps to manage risks and enables studio partners to share knowledge and create opportunities for new markets. As Alex says, the impact is artistic, social and it offers new business opportunities.

> One of the reasons I was excited about it was because, as well as the community and public facing element, as artists, you know, it allows us to collaborate. And I feel that we all work a bit parallel and that gives us the chance to put our heads together a bit, which has a social aspect as well .... (Alex, March 2022)

Joanna explains that during lockdowns, she became aware that some creative enterprises would find it a challenge and she had to be flexible while being mindful that she also needs to manage Make as a sustainable enterprise. The COVID-19 pandemic heightened the need to understand and explore different entrepreneurial challenges for creative entrepreneurs (Comunian & England, 2020).

> During the pandemic we said to people, talk to us if you can't afford the rent. We have offered reductions during hardships. (Joanna, March 2022)

As a result of COVID-19, studio partners inspired each other to diversify, and several were successful. Anabelle, made good use of collaborations with another more established studio partner, also working in ceramics, and instead of competing they shared work and learned from each other. Liz, whose enterprise had been a balance between in-person workshops and selling products, took her work online. To her surprise, this worked well, and she has continued to send out craft boxes for online workshops throughout the country, reaching a wider market for her work. This was important for Liz because she is not confident about the sustainability of her creative enterprise and although her goal is to be a successful business, she finds it a challenge.

> I see myself as running a business. It started off as doing art classes for kids, but it has moved on. It is a business. A creative entrepreneur … I have to pay my rent and I like to be independent at home. (Liz, March 2022)

If anything, the pandemic has made Liz even more determined and clearer in terms of professional goals. Alex's goals are very different, but he also comes across as hopeful and more determined, after the lockdowns, stating: 'this is the community I work in, I've felt that more strongly coming out of COVID-19' (Alex, March 2022). As many have said, the COVID-19 pandemic has sharpened people's thinking and, in this case, helped creative entrepreneurs identify their priorities.

Nevertheless, running a creative enterprise is a balancing act. It is a continuous process which Alex negotiates with himself and with others as he seeks to establish his enterprise alongside an aspiration to create social impact.

> I'm not a commercial artist … the ethical compromises entailed in taking funding from specific sources, for example, the National Lottery funds might be questionable? But I've kind of forgotten about that a long time ago because my entire career I've written successful bids and that's a dominant way in this country. Art in a commercial context is different kinds of compromises. (Alex, March 2022)

As Joanna explains, she is aware that many social enterprises have become more established and they have a certain 'slickness', in contrast to her ambition for Make.

> I think we're doing something quite different from other places and people do comment on that. There isn't anything near them that does what we do. But we also want to be innovative in the way we do business in general. I sometimes get frustrated at how slick some projects are and are inapproachable. I want us to do something more down to earth and for people to see how we are doing it. Also, in terms of the building itself, rather than demolish it, we want to enhance what was there before. It does make it more difficult but also more affordable and accessible. Embracing the imperfection … but also as we 'green' the building, it would be great to tell that story too. (Joanna, March 2022)

In this context, entrepreneurship is framed by the idea of imagining different models but being transparent about developments and about the messiness of that process. The idea of embracing 'imperfection' captures the entrepreneurial practices depicted in this chapter. The individuals interviewed for this research aim to create sustainable enterprises, but their version of entrepreneurial success blends different priorities, which are partly inspired by their social environment.

CONCLUSION

In this chapter, creative entrepreneurship is characterised by collective and personal values in the milieu in which creative entrepreneurs work. The research has sought to reveal the nuanced experiences of creative entrepreneurs, informed by the environment in which they work and the underpinning values which motivate them. The impact of COVID-19 has caused some challenges but in many ways, this did not come across as a significant factor for individual creative entrepreneurs, rather, its consolidated values and prior beliefs. As Banks and O'Connor (2020) state, the impact of the pandemic has highlighted the significance of arts and culture in everyday life 'as a spur to the reinvention, or rediscovery of the social, as shared relation in support of common life' (p. 15). Instead of a focus on growth, creative entrepreneurs can contribute to public value, yet during the pandemic they have been marginalised from funding and support structures (Banks & O'Connor, 2020; Comunian & England, 2020).

The limitation of this study is the small-scale nature of the research which offers an insight into possible ways of understanding creative entrepreneurship, but which cannot be generalised. However, I suggest that it can help us explore diverse factors in creative entrepreneurship which are evident in community spaces such as Make. As this chapter demonstrates, creative entrepreneurship is not 'slick' and is better characterised as negotiating different values and challenges which are informed in social spaces. The possible implications of this for policymakers and entrepreneurs are to embrace complexity, acknowledging that creative entrepreneurs are engaged in a process of 'becoming' and that this takes place in a messy social context. The creative entrepreneurs in this study invite us to consider values relating to environmental sustainability, community impact and social justice which jostle alongside the stability of their enterprise. Importantly for those supporting creative enterprises, there is a need to acknowledge that social environments will help to facilitate implicit and explicit motivations beyond the tensions between creative expression and entrepreneurial success. Future research could consider the relationship between creative entrepreneurship and environmental issues such as those identified by the United Nations Sustainability Development Goals (Embry et al., 2022). A further analysis of social spaces, community and creative entrepreneurship might contribute to how we re-imagine entrepreneurship and creative practices alongside the disruptions from climate change, social inequalities and the impact of the climate crisis.

REFERENCES

Bakare, L. (2020). *'Triple whammy' of funding cuts has left UK arts vulnerable – Report*. The Guardian. https://www.theguardian.com/culture/2020/jun/08/triple-whammy-of-funding-cuts-has-left-uk-arts-vulnerable-report

Banks, A., & O'Connor, J. (2020). A plague upon your howling: Art and culture in the viral emergency. *Cultural Trends, 30*(1), 3–18. https://doi.org/10.1080/09548963.2020.1827931

Banks, M. (2007). *The politics of cultural work*. Palgrave Macmillan.

Bandinelli, C., & Gandini, G. (2019). Hubs vs networks in the creative economy: Towards a 'Collaborative Individualism', In R. Gill, A. Pratt, & T.E. Virani (Eds.), *Creative hubs in question: Place, space and work in the creative economy* (pp. 89–110). Palgrave.

Beaven, Z. (2012, January 7–8). Complex entrepreneurial journeys: 'Pragmatic' and 'tactical' nascent musician-entrepreneurs. In *Institute for small business and entrepreneurship conference*, Dublin, Ireland.

Brook, O., O'Brien, D., & Taylor, M. (2018). *Panic! Social class, taste and inequalities in the creative industries*. Create London. https://createlondon.org/event/panic-paper/

Carter, O. (2018). *Making European cult cinema: Fan enterprise in an alternative economy*. Amsterdam University Press.

Chell, E., & Karataş-Özkan, M. (2010). *Nascent entrepreneurship and learning*. Edward Elgar Publishing Limited.

Comunian, R., & England, L. (2020). Creative and cultural work without filters: Covid-19 and exposed precarity in the creative economy. *Cultural Trends, 29*(2), 112–128.

Eikhof, R., & Haunschild, A. (2006). Lifestyle meets market: Bohemian entrepreneurs in creative industries. *Creativity and Innovation Management, 15*(3), 234–241.

Ellmeier, A. (2003). Cultural entrepreneurialism: On changing the relationship between the arts, culture and employment. *International Journal of Cultural Policy, 9*(1), 3–16.

Embry, E., York, J., & Edgar, S. (2022). Entrepreneurs as essential but missing actors in the sustainable development goals. In G. George, M. Haas, H. Joshi, A. McGahan, & P. Tracey (Eds.), *Handbook on the business of sustainability* (pp. 232–251). Edward Elgar.

Florida, R. (2002). *The rise of the creative class*. Basic Books.

Gill, R. (2002). Cool, creative and egalitarian? Exploring gender in project-based new media work in Euro. *Information, Communication & Society, 5*(1), 70–89. https://doi.org/10.1080/13691180110117668

Gill, R., & Pratt, A. (2008). In the social factory?: Immaterial labour, precariousness and cultural work. *Theory, Culture and Society, 25*(7–8), 1–30.

Gill, R., Pratt, A., & Virani, T. E. (Eds.). (2019). *Creative hubs in question: Place, space and work in the creative economy*. Palgrave.

Gray, A. (2002). *Research practice for cultural studies*. Sage.

Holland, D., Lachicotte, W., Jr, Skinner, D., & Cain, C. (2003). *Identity and agency in cultural worlds*. Harvard University Press.

Horvath, I., & Dechamp, G. (Eds.). (2021). *L'entrepreneuriat dans les secteurs de l'art et de la culture*. Editions EMS.

Johannisson, B. (2011). Towards a practice theory of entrepreneuring. *Small Business Economics, 36*(2), 135–150.

Jones, C., & Spicer, A. (2009). *Unmasking the entrepreneur*. Edward Elgar.

Leadbeater, C., & Oakley, K. (1999). *The independents*. Demos.

Lee, D. J. (2011). Networks, cultural capital and creative labour in the British independent television industry. *Media, Culture & Society, 33*(4), 549–566.

Long, P., & Naudin, A. (2019). Producing values: Impact hub Birmingham as co-working and social innovation space. In R. Gill, A. Pratt, & T. E. Virani (Eds.), *Creative hubs in question: Place, space and work in the creative economy* (pp. 211–227). Palgrave.

Luckman, S. (2012). *The politics and poetics of rural, regional and remote creativity*. Palgrave Mcmillian.

McKeever, E., Anderson, A., & Jack, S. (2014). Social embeddedness in entrepreneurship research: The importance of context and community. In E. Chell & M. Karatas-Ozkan (Eds.), *Handbook of research on small business and entrepreneurship*. Edward Elgar Publishing Limited.

McRobbie, A. (2002). From holloway to Hollywood: Happiness at work in the new cultural economy. In P. Du Gay & M. Pryke (Eds.), *Cultural economy* (pp. 97–115). Sage.

McRobbie, A. (2007). *The Los Angelisation of London: Three shirt-waves of young people's micro-economies of culture and creativity in the UK.* https://transversal.at/transversal/0207/mcrobbie/en

McRobbie, A. (2011). *Re-thinking creative economy as radical social enterprise.* Retrieved March 20, 2012, from http://www.variant.org.uk/

Morgan, G., & Woodriff, J. (2019). Herding Cats: Co-work, creativity and precarity in inner Sydney. In R. Gill, A. Pratt, & T.E. Virani (Eds.), *Creative hubs in question: Place, space and work in the creative economy* (pp. 29–50). Palgrave.

Naudin, A. (2018). *Cultural entrepreneurship: The cultural worker's experience of entrepreneurship.* Routledge.

Newth, J. (2018). "Hands-on" vs "arm's length" entrepreneurship research: Using ethnography to contextualize social innovation. *International Journal of Entrepreneurial Behaviour & Research, 24*(3), 683–696.

Oakley, K. (2014). Good work? Rethinking cultural entrepreneurship, In C. Bilton & S. Cummings, (Eds.), *Handbook of management and creativity* (pp. 145–159). Edward Elgar.

O'Brien, D. (2014). *Cultural policy: Management, value and modernity in the creative industries.* Routledge.

Patel, K. (2020). Diversity initiatives and addressing inequalities in craft. In S. Taylor & S. Luckman (Eds.). *Pathways into creative working lives.* Palgrave Macmillan.

de Peuter, G. & Cohen, N. (2015). Emerging labour politics in creative industries. In K. Oakley & J. O'Connor (Eds.). *The Routledge companion to the cultural industries* (pp. 305–318). Routledge.

Pickering, M. (2008). *Research methods for cultural studies.* Edinburgh University Press.

Pratt, A., Gill, R. & Virani, T. (2019). Introduction. In R. Gill, A. Pratt, & T. Virani (Eds.), *Creative hubs in question: place, space and work in the creative economy* (pp. 1–26). Cham, switzerland, Palgrave Mcmillan. ISBN 978-3-030-10652-2.

Ross, A. (2008). The new geography of work: Power to the precarious. *Theory, Culture and Society, 25*(7–8), 31–49.

Sandoval, M., & Littler, J. (2019). Creative hubs: A co-operative space? In R. Gill, A. C. Pratt, & T. Virani (Eds.), *Creative hubs in question: Place, space and work in the creative economy* (pp. 155–168). Palgrave Macmillan.

Scott, M. (2012). Cultural entrepreneurs, cultural entrepreneurship: Music producers mobilising and converting Bourdieu's alternative capitals. *Poetics, 40*(3), 237–255.

Shane, S. (Ed.). (2007). *Economic development through entrepreneurship*, Edward Elgar.

Taylor, S., & Littleton, K (2012). *Contemporary identities of creativity and creative work.* Ashgate.

Webb, J., Tihanyi, L., Ireland, D., & Sirmon, D. (2009). You say illegal, I say legitimate. Entrepreneurship in the informal economy. *Academy of Management Review, 34*(3), 492–510.

CHAPTER 14

CREATIVE PLACEMAKING IN THE SCOTTISH RURALITY: COMPARING TWO SMALL TOWNS

David Rae

De Montfort University, UK

ABSTRACT

This chapter explores two cases of small towns as creative places in the Galloway and Borders regions of Scotland. It considers and compares their cultural development, economic contributions, resilience and sustainability. The chapter uses prior works on policy, theory, and creative rural economies as conceptual framing.

The study is an empirical exploration, which used cultural observation as an interpretive method to undertake desk and field research in the two towns presented as cases, Wigtown (Scotland's National Book Town) and Coldstream. It offers findings related to the effects of the COVID-19 pandemic on the creative sector; cultural identity branding; the roles of anchor attractions and events; policy; digital economy; and cultural inclusion or exclusion. The conclusion is that creative placemaking is a medium-to-long term activity involving community and joint entrepreneurship between stakeholders to demonstrate sustainability and resilience. However, creative places need to be or become distinctive in some respects for the ingredients and enabling factors of placemaking to combine and sustain effectively as a destination.

Keywords: Creative places; Scotland; creative rural economies; creative placemaking; COVID-19 impact

INTRODUCTION

This chapter explores the cultural and economic contributions and sustainability of two small towns in the Borders and Galloway regions of Scotland as creative places. This extensive area is historic and scenic, but often neglected by visitors who drive through it on their way to better-known destinations. There are long-term challenges to economic and social sustainability in a region traditionally dependent mainly on agriculture, where farming incomes and related employment are in long-term decline. Set against this are the motivations of people for regeneration, cultural identity and enterprise, both indigenous and incoming, and their communities. The questions are why, and how, do small towns develop and survive as creative centres in the Scots rurality; how sustainable are they; and what may be learned from them? The chapter explores these cases within their cultural, geographic, political and economic contexts, and enhances understanding of the process of creative place-making in small rural towns affected by long-term economic decline. Such towns can be regionally significant in cultural terms, yet barely visible on national maps of the UK creative economy.

The Borders region, looking eastwards along the Tweed Valley, includes the small town of Coldstream, where a community of creative artists and artisans developed a cultural and creative micro-cluster. This is compared with Wigtown, Scotland's National Book Town in the Dumfries and Galloway region, located on the Southern coastal Whithorn peninsula in Galloway. This area includes other small towns with cultural attractions such as Kirkcudbright, enabling the promotion of the district as a cultural destination.

The cases were developed through an approach of cultural observation, including visits, conversations with artists and producers, and desk research. These data sources inform comparisons between the cases, with other examples of creative towns and villages, to support insights into the sustainability of small rural towns as creative places.

FRAMING THE STUDY USING THE PERSPECTIVES OF POLICY, THEORY, PRIOR WORK, AND CREATIVE RURAL ECONOMIES

The Policy Perspective

The Scottish Government published Scotland's National Strategy for Economic Transformation[1] in March 2022. This strategy proposed a commitment to national entrepreneurship development through learning, policy actions and targeted investments. At a regional level,

> The South of Scotland's first Regional Economic Strategy has a 10-year timeframe and targets a significant shift in the region's economic performance, its outward profile, and the way in which wealth is created by and shared amongst people. The strategy has been developed following an extensive period of engagement and will deliver against six themes including: Skilled and Ambitious People; Innovative and Enterprising; Rewarding and Fair Work; Cultural and Creative Excellence; Green and Sustainable Economy; and Thriving and Distinct Communities.

These commitments to entrepreneurship as an enabler for the thematic outcomes, including culture and creative excellence, provide a policy context for this chapter.

The Scottish government announced in 2021 an open competition aimed at creating a series of National Towns of Culture across the country as part of its manifesto. This initiative, aimed at enabling other towns to build on the success of Wigtown's status as a National Book Town, is discussed later.

There is continuing debate on the relationship between the cultural policies of the Scottish Nationalist-led government in Scotland towards Scots national identity and their creative and cultural policies, in which support for rural creative industries is modest in relation to the ambition for cultural identities:

> Cultural policy attempts to subject culture and cultural agents to the formation of the Scottish government's temporal regime, and in particular the relation between creative industries and the effects of economic temporality. (Valentine, 2020, p. 476)

There are both interactions and tensions between public policy directions and the needs and aspirations experienced by creative entrepreneurs seeking supportive interventions for their businesses and communities (Roberts & Townsend, 2016). This interplay is accentuated by the tendencies of both UK and Scottish governments towards using cultural policies as levers for their own national and sectional agendas.

Prior Literature and Theoretical Framing

There is extensive literature at an international level on creative enterprise and entrepreneurship, creative and cultural industries and economies, the role of placemaking and related topics such as tourism, heritage, conservation and education. The chapter draws from and contributes to the literature on cultural industries (Hesmondhalgh, 2002), entrepreneurship and the creative economy (Henry & De Bruin, 2011), value construction in the creative economy (Granger, 2020), micro-cultural entrepreneurship and creative placemaking (Rae, 2021); rural creative enterprise and placemaking (Hill et al., 2021).

There is an awareness of culture as a living resource and practice, being continually enacted or co-created and evolving between the writer, producer or performer(s) and the reader or audience. There are also expectations from visitors to creative places that they will be able to experience the ambience, distinctive character and some form of cultural participation within the symbolic interaction and exchange of their stay. Such expectations are not new (Dewey, 1938 is a source of the interaction between artist and audience) but they also form part of the 'design principles' of the influential movement of Creative Placemaking (as set out by Markusen & Gadwa, 2010) and expanded since; as by Courage et al. (2021).

The literature on creative placemaking in rural areas is limited, but a useful conceptualisation, developed by Hill et al. (2021, p. 634), draws on process theory and builds on prior work by Platt (2021) and Courage (2021). This article theorises 'place as socially constructed continuous organising processes of becoming', enacted by place co-creators, using assets and tools available, and recognising the multi-layered exchanges of building equitable thriving communities by interlinking the public space with personal interactions between entrepreneurs, community residents and visitors. This approach focusses on the social enaction of 'places' rather than static location, recognising dynamic interactions between stakeholders generate social and emergent creativity, and it provides a useful conceptual base for this chapter.

Creative Economies in the Border Rurality

The Scots cultural dimension is relevant to social and national identity, as well as economically. There have been insightful research studies on the potential and development of the rural creative economy for Scotland. For example, Munro (2016) explored creative entrepreneurs in rural and remote Scotland as market-builders for the rural creative economy. MacLeod (2010) explored identity development in Scottish theme towns. Roberts and Townsend (2016) considered the contributions of cultural and digital capital in the creative economy and resilience of rural communities. Seaton (1996) contributed extensively to the understanding of Scots cultural tourism, introducing the concept of the 'book town' for Scotland.

The Scottish Borders is a regional belt of rivers, pastoral and forested higher moorland with a network of small towns and villages. Its history includes sporadic conflicts with English armies in the period up to the Jacobite rebellion in 1745, but much deeper long-term agrarian development. The Border and Lowland cultures speak distinctive dialects (such as 'Lallans') which varied along the Border and melded with the English Northumbrian and Pennine dialects. Culturally, the people along both sides of the Border arguably enjoy more in common with each other than they do with their compatriots to the North in Scotland and South in England.

In this rural society, the role of small and market towns as economic, cultural and social centres is symbolically important, since rural depopulation and the declining agrarian economy has reduced the number of businesses and jobs. These towns decline unless they can stimulate their economies in new ways, such as through tourism, in which heritage, creativity and culture are important contributors. Their cultural identities can be essential ingredients in place marketing for visitor attraction as well as both competitive positioning with other destinations and regional promotion as part of a wider offer. Hence creative placemaking (Markusen & Gadwa, 2010) is a topical aspect of the identity and cultural production of towns seeking to distinguish themselves.

Considering the economic context, a detailed assessment of the contribution of the Arts and Creative Industries in Scotland (DC Research, 2012) for Creative Scotland was based on 2010 data and found total employment in the creative and cultural sectors of 84,400 jobs, 6,500 being self-employed proprietors, with further employment resulting in related sectors such as tourism and hospitality. Whilst the majority of jobs and businesses were located in the central belt and major cities, rural employment featured with the Scottish Borders showing 3.4% and Dumfries & Galloway 1.6% of employment in the sector, totalling 5% or some 4,220 jobs. The Borders and Galloway regions provide a small but recognisable southern belt in the Scottish creative economy, with the role of textiles in the Borders described as 'very important'. The study also showed the significant tourism attraction, benefits and economic impacts of rural creative businesses.

However, there is an interesting mismatch between observations of creative firms 'on the ground' in rural areas when compared with recent UK national research data, which reports that 5% of creative businesses are located in Scotland, compared with 13% in the North of England. In 2020, creative employment in Scotland was assessed at 87,000 jobs, with 14,515 registered enterprises operating in the Creative Industries sector in 2021 (Scottish Government, 2022).

However, the NESTA Creative Industries Policy and Evidence Centre (PEC) mapping tool of creative industry clusters for the UK showed creative clusters in Scotland as mostly proximal to the major cities of Edinburgh and Glasgow, with limited micro-clusters in other towns and some rural areas. In the entire Borders region, this shows just one cluster of 85 creative firms in the Galashiels and Peebles commuting area, with none in the Dumfries and Galloway region. For policy purposes, even long-established Scottish rural creative clusters, such as the Galloway towns, simply did not exist on the PEC map (Siepel et al., 2020), suggesting its deficiency for Scotland when compared with the 2012 study.

However, in 2022 the report 'Creative Industries in the South of Scotland' (EKOS, 2022), commissioned by South of Scotland Enterprise (SOSE), provided a detailed mapping and analysis of the health of the creative industries sector in the South of Scotland region. This demonstrated the economic, social and cultural significance of the creative sector across the region. It reviewed the creative placemaking projects in Dumfries & Galloway supported by The Stove Network (Wheeler, 2020). This evidenced a community-based approach to placemaking. It noted Creative placemaking as an area in which the South of Scotland is increasingly recognised nationally for its expertise.

METHODOLOGY

The questions explored in this chapter are why, and how, do the selected creative centres develop and survive in the rural Borders; how sustainable are their cultural economies, and what may be learned from them? The interpretive approach used in the study is described as cultural observation in the sense of the researcher's stance as a long-term observer of cultural places, communities and movements; and of creative producers and entrepreneurs. The aims of cultural observation are to appreciate, compare, make sense interpretively and reflexively; and to document chosen cultural questions, phenomena and situations. There are theoretically complex methods for cultural research and critique which are necessary and valuable, but at the level of the experiential case, the researcher needs to balance their subjective appreciative and critical lenses with openness to observing, sensemaking, conceptualising and comparing cultural places and phenomena.

Methodologically, cultural observation shares common threads and methods with sensemaking (Weick, 1995), appreciative inquiry (Cooperrider & Srivastva, 1987), participant observation (DeWalt & DeWalt, 2011), and situated embeddedness (Kloosterman, 2010). It is a collection of discursive, qualitative and interpretive approaches used by an observer, writer or researcher to develop generally sociological understandings, for use within further enquiry and writing. Cultural observation can include passive and intentional attendance, participation, conversations (as distinct from formal interviews), bricolage through gathering discursive information such as texts, images, incidents, performances, events, social media, and artefacts such as books, reports, online social media and recordings.

The approach in each case was to conduct focussed online desk research into extant documentary, policy, geographical, cultural and social media materials, prior to visiting the locations. This work provided initial contextual understanding and awareness of the situational issues in advance.

Within the settings, cultural observations, visits and conversations took place with gallery and bookshop proprietors, artists and producers. Field notes were taken together with photographs and short videos of events, scenes, performances and locations. Conversations were not recorded. The researcher's conduct was in effect that of a normal visitor, combined with a creative writer gathering material for a story or comparable artefact. The writer made several visits to each of the case locations over a period of several years between 2019, and subsequent to the COVID-19 pandemic lockdown periods, in 2020–2021. His work as a researcher was declared during conversations with business owners. These visits provided direct access to the businesses, networks and market environment.

The cases were developed using storyboards, selected frameworks and techniques from case-based research including Convergence of Multiple Sources of Evidence (Eisenhardt & Graebner, 2007; Yin, 2003). The draft cases were circulated for informal comments and then compared using inductive categories developed from the perspectives section, which were used to frame the conclusions.

THE CASES
Case 1: The Scottish Borders

In the small town of Coldstream, a cluster of creative artists and artisans developed around the Hirsel Gallery, the Arts and Craft Centre on the Hirsel estate, and the independent White Fox gallery. These hubs provide display and retail spaces which attract visitors and sustain a network of individual artists, sculptors, jewellers, fabric and other independent producers. This helped Coldstream to advance from a drive-through town to a cultural destination of the first (or last) town in Scotland, and to assert its cultural identity. (Observation, Sept 2021)

The Scottish Borders is a unitary local authority district including 13 towns and a population of around 115,000. The district has a distinct history and cultural legacy of big country estates, fortified castles becoming stately homes, abbeys, and small towns. The local authority provides statutory services only, Live Borders being the delivery agent for Creative Scotland, as the leisure, sport and cultural trust for the Scottish Borders.

Coldstream is one locus within the network of small towns and villages which form the Borders creative economy. A Border Gallery Guide was produced by the Hirsel Gallery, running to three editions (2020) and listing 28 producers and galleries. Sadly, the gallery itself closed at the end of 2021, demonstrating the challenges of creative producers balancing their own creative practices with staffing and supporting a gallery. The Gallery provided a retail showcase for over 20 local artists and craft producers, but continuing limitations on the visitor economy, with increasing cost, time and commercial pressures for the organisers, led to the decision to close the gallery. The other pottery, glass and craft studios and café in the Hirsel Arts and Crafts Centre continued as a cultural destination.

A positive indication of the health of the creative economy is that 72 artists and galleries exhibited at the Borders Art Fair 2022, held in Kelso in March 2022 after a two-year interruption. This provided demonstrations and talks as well as 68 display stands by artists and producers, organised by the Border Arts Development C.I.C., based in Jedburgh. A further Fair is planned for 2023, demonstrating the attraction of this signature cultural event. At least ten other galleries in the Borders area continued to trade. However, events and 'pop-up' markets in some of the country houses which had been held prior to the pandemic, could not resume until late Spring 2022.

Considering public support for the creative sector, the Creative Arts Business Network (CABN) aims 'to develop the professional creative sector in the Scottish Borders through a diverse programme of support, and to seek to strengthen the sector by working towards longer-term strategic goals' with promotion of microbusinesses being one of these. CABN was a Place Partnership project funded by Creative Scotland, with funded staff members and an activity and network programme supporting cultural business and activities in the visual arts; crafts; music; performing arts; literature; public and community art; and creative services sectors.

CABN managed a Visual Artist and Craft Maker Awards scheme (VACMA) offering grant and non-financial assistance to businesses across the Borders and Dumfries and Galloway regions. Bursaries were awarded to individual visual artists and craft makers, supporting research, innovation and skills development projects. The CABN online directory listed ten galleries, six venues and four workspaces, with an events programme and weekly news bulletin. It aimed to champion the cultural sector and cultural role in the economy, environment, education, health and quality of life in the Scottish Borders. It supported the local cultural sector by creating networking spaces, sharing ideas, and resources and finding solutions to common problems.

During 2022, evaluation and discussions took place by the Live Borders funding agency with the aim of CABN becoming an independent, self-sustaining organisation. CABN was valued by the creative community for the support, networks, connections and cohesion it offers the sector with its knowledge, expertise, and track record. However, public support is being withdrawn from the rural creative business sector, unless it can become self-funded.

None of the Border region towns are promoted as self-standing creative or cultural destinations, despite the importance of creative design in the textiles industry around Hawick. Creative placemaking is local and self-organised, not institutional. The creative economy functions more as a regional network of galleries and venues, artists, producers and event promoters, than as a place-based approach. However, weakening government support risks damaging this.

Tensions appeared between the Scottish National Party-led government, and the Westminster government with a strong Unionist policy. COVID-19 lockdown policies affected the Scottish creative economy more severely than England. Berwick-on-Tweed, a border town in England with a unique culture stemming from its history, was less curtailed than the Scots border towns. Yet creative and arts businesses and practitioners work between Northumberland and Scotland, the border being an artefact of administrative geography and cultural identity, which has not been 'closed' in any sense for hundreds of years.

Case 2: Wigtown and the Galloway Cultural Ecosystem

> Wigtown became 'Scotland's National Book Town following a competition in the early 1990's which aimed to enable a small-town experiencing decline as a 'depleted community' to follow the example of Hay-on-Wye and to attract second-hand bookshops as a means of regeneration. It has experienced almost 30 years of development and resurgence. Retail and residential properties in Wigtown are in continuing demand and the town has 16 bookshops and related businesses. It also hosts an annual Book Festival and other events run by the Festival company. (Observation, Sept 2021)

Dumfries and Galloway extend westwards from the Solway Firth along Scotland's southern coast. It spans the County town of Dumfries, a string of coastal and upland towns along the main road to Stranraer, a former ferry port for Northern Ireland on the Rhins peninsula. Long overlooked by visitors, its farming and fishing industries declined in importance whilst the historic charm of towns such as Kirkcudbright started to diversify the regional economy through tourism and leisure. But the western towns on the fertile Machars promontory lost out, including Wigtown and historic Whithorn, site of the earliest Christian community in Scotland, dating from around 450 AD.

There are many sites of historic and cultural interest in the region, but our focus is on Wigtown. The competition to have a Scottish National Book Town was inspired by the example of Hay-on-Wye in regenerating the local visitor economy. Academic Tony Seaton (1996) proposed a competition from towns experiencing economic disadvantage, surplus properties, and natural beauty and this was accepted as a project for European Union and Scottish Executive funding. The competition considered six applicants, three from Dumfries and Galloway, which Wigtown had discovered by seeing a letter in the 'Glasgow Herald', applied, and won.

At the time, Wigtown had been 'like tumbleweed' with local businesses such as the Bladnoch Distillery and Creamery closing, and people unable to sell their houses. The Book Town was announced and launched in 1998, so the project has a 25-year history of sustained development. A local committee including the solitary local bookseller acted to attract book dealers and to brand the town. This was successful in bringing local properties around the square into use as shops and cafes. There was no direct aid for booksellers, with incomers taking the risk to buy and improve their properties. 44 empty properties were sold between 1996 and 2002, whilst property values continue to increase, outstripping nearby towns. Townscape Heritage Initiative funding gained in 1999 supported building and public space refurbishment. Research by Laing (2020) and Macleod (2023) charted the success of independent bookshops as cultural place makers and of the three culturally themed towns in Galloway respectively.

The role of local community organisations has been a major force in its resilience. The original 'Booktown Company', set up as a regeneration initiative, was replaced in 2007 by the Wigtown Festival Company. This organises and promotes the annual Book Festival and other events, whilst the 16 bookshops formed the Association of Wigtown Booksellers. Their creative placemaking is strategic, juxtaposing the cultural identity in the open townscape with the serene historic coastal and rural surroundings.

The Book Town generates a £4.3 million economic impact on the local economy through sales and tourism. Property is in high demand, with few buildings including a large hotel awaiting new roles. It attracts businesses, jobs, investment through the visitor, and cultural economy. A significant proportion of entrepreneurship is through incomers buying properties and opening book-related businesses. These include not only traders, but also specialist and online publishers, newspaper archives, book, and graphic designers. This presents a demographic issue as proprietors look to retire and sell their businesses, with potentially high valuations. There is limited opportunity for new start-ups in the rather crowded marketplace, and the Book Town serves a maturing market in all senses.

MacLeod (2023) explored the contributions to cultural identity from the three themed towns in Galloway, of Wigtown Book Town (WBT), Kirkcudbright Artists Town (KAT) and Castle Douglas Food Town (CDFT) which are within 40 miles of one another, providing a joined-up cultural tourism offer. Interestingly, Kirkcudbright and Castle Douglas gained their themes on the basis of long-standing recognition for their cultural appeal and economic base in these industries, whilst Wigtown's was conferred externally by a competition. Hence KAT and CDFT had greater embedded authenticity resulting from their existing strengths, whilst WBT developed this over a 20-year period. Macleod (2010) noted that:

> It would be fair to say that the theme town branding initiatives have, to date, led to an enhancement of development in terms of the economy, the cultural life and the social fabric of the towns and region. Furthermore, the growth of social capital in terms of formal and informal networks has been an undervalued result. It remains a crucial component of the broad process and continues to be one of the fundamental structures underpinning the ongoing development experience.

Sadly, nearby small towns and villages including Whithorn and Creetown see only marginal benefits. Only one town can become a national book or indeed food town, and other challenged communities have to decide whether a themed identity is a realistic and authentic option which enables them to combine their sources of capital in order to create one.

Scotland, with a devolved government and intent for national independence, sees Scots national culture as a major distinctive resource in transforming both perceptions and also the economic prospects of rural areas, to address the effects of Brexit, COVID-19, high energy costs and the need for local enterprise, employment and prosperity.

In April 2021, the Scottish government revealed plans for an open competition to expand the National Towns of Culture across the country. Whether a competitive approach and a government-led expansion of culture towns would work, remains an open question (Ferguson, 2021). This was included in their Manifesto for Culture and Creativity, but the competition was never launched.

'We will extend the reach of the arts by launching an open competition for further National Towns of Culture, for example, Scotland's National Live Music Town, Folk and Trad Town, or Scotland's Visual Art Town.' The initiative aimed to build on the success of Wigtown's status as a National Book Town, referencing West Kilbride in Ayrshire as Scotland's Craft Town, and nearby Dumfries as home to a new National Centre for Children's Literature and Storytelling. Artistic, musical and performing arts towns were suggested.

SUMMARY OF FINDINGS FROM THE CASES

This section provides a comparison between the regions of Dumfries and Galloway with the Borders on the feasibility and effectiveness of creative placemaking in small rural towns, offering useful discussion points for rural creativity. It presents findings grouped in categories developed from the prior work perspectives and the case analysis and writing.

The Effects of the COVID-19 Pandemic and Lockdown on the Creative Sector

Fieldwork started in 2019 before the pandemic and continued until late 2021. The pandemic had very severe adverse effects on the visitor and cultural sectors during the 2020–2022 period with differential public health restrictions by the Scots and English administrations. It limited artists, producers and galleries' abilities to retail their work and to sustain their businesses and creative practices. Events were largely cancelled with shop and gallery openings restricted. But the balance between resilience and fragility is demonstrated by the choice of many creative producers to continue, whilst others closed from various causes including health, mortality, ageing, poor sales and non-viability. However, rather than seeing the pandemic as a unique event, it is more useful to see it as a recurrent ecosystemic challenge, being followed by a period of economic stringency, which leads to some individuals and less resilient businesses closing, whilst it may prompt others to consider creative self-employment.

Branding: Cultural Identity and Recognition

There is no doubt that some of the Dumfries and Galloway towns are better branded than the eastern Borders. In several cases, place marketing delivers an experience with a sense of destination. The prime focus of this chapter is on Wigtown, a 'place made' by the Book Town award in 1997, supported by sustained co-operative and community entrepreneurship, in which individual businesses and the town's overall prosperity and visitor attraction have flourished over a 25-year period. Places which have organically developed cultural and artistic traditions, such as Kirkcudbright and Gatehouse of Fleet, have also thrived. Yet there are also towns with rich cultural and other assets, such as Whithorn, and the former ferry port of Stranraer, which are becoming 'left behind' backwaters with flagging economies, needing to reinvent themselves or continue to decline.

Placemaking and marketing is much less evident, if at all, in the Borders area, despite its geography of historic and attractive towns; Coldstream is still a drive-through town like many others. The 'Visit Scotland' website promotes specific attractions and businesses rather than place-marketing for the towns. If a district government decides not to favour some towns over others, when all have needs and merits for promotion, it is ultimately an issue for the local businesses, property owners, residents and community councils to take the initiative, if they have the leadership and co-creative energy to do so.

The Role of Anchor Attractions

Businesses or institutions such as art and craft galleries, museums, visitor centres, bookstores and cafes have crucial roles in small communities as anchor attractions in animating visible and attractive visitor destinations. These organisations, often run by cultural entrepreneurs, need to mediate effectively between visitor and place marketing, the local community, individual producers, and other interests such as local authorities and landowners. Their viability and survival can be tenuous, depending on trade or public funding, and their closure, such as the Hirsel Gallery, can impair the visitor attraction of a place and the market potential of its exhibitors and suppliers. Yet creative towns such as Wigtown and Kirkcudbright have developed multiple attractions which generate a mutually supportive cultural ecosystem and a relatively high level of visitor attraction, which is less evident in the Eastern Border towns such as Coldstream.

The Role of Events

Events are of symbolic, cultural, social and economic importance in the rural creative ecosystem. These vary in scale and ambition from the intimate, such as exhibition openings at the White Fox Gallery, to longer events such as the Wigtown Festival and the year-round events programme. These provide occasions for visitors to spend time, to meet artists and writers, to promote creative works, and to enable social and community appreciation of culture and place.

The Eastern Borders creative economy functions as more of a set of network connections between creative producers, businesses, galleries and organisers which attract visitors as buyers. This cultural entrepreneurship can be seen in events such as the Borders Art Fair and gallery exhibitions, with the symbolic branding of 'event' having prominence over 'place', whilst the levels of visitor attraction and sales can be significant at these events.

Policy Towards Cultural and Creative Economy

There is a sense in the Borders of public agencies, local government and Borders Live being less proactive in supporting the creative economy. Whilst public cultural and economic development policy should ideally be supportive, the sustainability of the creative enterprises and communities is (ideally) largely self-sustaining. Yet the role of policymakers and related support in economic recovery is a critical factor. This is especially so in Scotland as a country with a Nationalist government, and where policies and political ambitions are not easily separated. Nevertheless, the strength of local creative communities and networks of artists and artisans is possibly more enduring, combined with their effective self-organisation, marketing and promotion, increasingly via online social media.

Digital Economy

The adoption of online media increased during the COVID-19 pandemic, complementing, but not replacing direct personal engagements in events. There has been quite extensive coverage in the academic literature on the digital economy and digital placemaking (e.g., Hill et al., 2021; Roberts & Townsend, 2016). Yet in these two cases, the role of digital technologies and media, whilst present, is far from dominant. Digital marketing, for example via websites and Facebook is present and used, but reinforces in-person contact, and to an extent displaces print marketing.

Cultural Inclusion or Exclusion?

Finally, there are issues of cultural inclusion, exclusion and marginality. It can be argued that these places are run by, and mainly for, middle-class incomers and retirees, rather than 'local people'. Whose work and participation is included, and who may be excluded, even unintentionally? How integrated are they with the local communities? How open and representative are they for minority and disadvantaged groups, which is especially important for diversity as a cultural strength? Diversity and inclusion are issues for public policy. Yet the lesson of these cases is that inward attraction of new people, ideas, skills and financial capital can renew an extant but declining culture by introducing novel ventures, experiences, and means of value creation. They can, and do, balance local people with incoming creators and entrepreneurs (Wilson, 2010).

CONCLUSION

In conclusion, these cases add to the cited studies of rural creative enterprise and placemaking, in particular Hill et al. (2021). They suggest that the process of 'creative placemaking' should be seen, temporally, as a medium-to-long term activity. This involves community and joint entrepreneurship between business owners, residents, civic and governmental agencies, and spans several decades to demonstrate continuity across generations and resilience against economic and other setbacks. Hence, it can demonstrate both sustainability, continuing contributions and impacts on the local town, economy, visitor attraction and wider cultural and value creation. The ability of new generations of owners and producers to succeed community founders indicates the sustainability and embeddedness of a creative place's identity.

But creative placemaking is not a panacea. It may not be desired, feasible or successful in every place; if they are to be attractive and sustainable, then creative places need to be or become distinctive qualities. In some towns, such as Wigtown, the ingredients and enabling factors of placemaking combine and sustain effectively as a destination. In others, such as Coldstream, for whatever reasons, those conditions have yet to enable the creative cluster to develop placemaking capability.

NOTE

1. https://www.gov.scot/publications/scotlands-national-strategy-economic-transformation/pages/6/

REFERENCES

Cooperrider, D. L., & Srivastva, S. (1987). Appreciative inquiry in organizational life. *Research in Organizational Change and Development*, *1*, 129–169.
Courage, C., Borrup, T., Jackson, M.R., Legge, K., Mckeown, A., Platt, L., & Schupbach, J. (Eds.). (2021). *The Routledge handbook of placemaking*. Routledge.
DC Research. (2012). *An economic assessment of the contribution of the Arts and Creative Industries in Scotland*. https://www.creativescotland.com/resources/professional-resources/research/creative-scotland-research/economic-contribution-study
DeWalt, K., & DeWalt, B. (2011). *Participant observation: A guide for fieldworkers*. AltaMira Press.
Dewey, J. (1938). *Art as experience*. Putnam.
Eisenhardt, K., & Graebner, M. (2007). Theory building from cases: Opportunities and challenges. *Academy of Management Journal*, *50*(1), 25–32.
EKOS Ltd. (2022). *Creative Industries in the South of Scotland*. Report for South of Scotland Enterprise. https://www.southofscotlandenterprise.com/media/tqhpqyfa/creative-industries-in-the-south-ofscotland-report.pdf
Ferguson, B. (2021, April 16). New contest proposed to crown Scottish culture towns. *The Scotsman*. https://www.scotsman.com/whats-on/arts-and-entertainment/new-contest-proposed-to-crown-scottish-culture-towns-3204172
Granger, R. (Ed.). (2020). *Value construction in the creative economy: Negotiating innovation and transformation*. Palgrave.
Henry, C., & de Bruin, A. (2011). *Entrepreneurship and the creative economy: Process, practice & policy*. Edward Elgar Press.
Hesmondhalgh, D. (2002). *The cultural industries*, Sage.
Hill, I., Manning, L., & Frost, R. (2021). Rural arts entrepreneurs' placemaking - how 'entrepreneurial placemaking' explains rural creative hub development during COVID-19 lockdown. *Local Economy*, *36*(7–8), 627–649.
Kloosterman, R. (2010) Matching opportunities with resources: A framework for analysing (migrant) entrepreneurship from a mixed embeddedness perspective. *Entrepreneurship & Regional Development*, *22*(1), 25–45.
Laing, A. (2020). Indies in Scotland: Exploring the unique role of independent bookshops in Scotland's towns and villages. *Publishing Research Quarterly*, *36*, 585–600.
Lounsbury, T., & Glynn, M. (2011). Legitimating nascent collective identities: Coordinating cultural entrepreneurship. *Organization Science*, *22*(2), 449–463.
MacLeod, D. (2023). Scottish theme towns: Have new identities enhanced development? *Journal of Tourism and Cultural Change*, *7*(2), 133–145.
Markusen, A., & Gadwa, A. (2010). *Creative placemaking*. Mayors' Institute on City Design and the National Endowment for the Arts. www.arts.gov/publications/creative-placemaking
Munro, E. (2016). *Developing the rural creative economy 'from below': Exploring practices of market-building amongst creative entrepreneurs in rural and remote Scotland*. University of Glasgow Centre for Cultural Policy Research.

Platt, L. (2021). Preface: The problem with placemaking. In C. Courage, T. Borrup, M. R. Jackson, K. Legge, A. Mckeown, L. Platt, & J. Schupbach (Eds.), *The Routledge handbook of placemaking* (pp. 143–147). Routledge.

Rae, D. (2021). Intercultural entrepreneurship in creative place-making. In R. Granger (Ed.), *Value construction in the creative economy: Negotiating innovation and transformation* (pp. 131–150). Palgrave.

Roberts, E., & Townsend, L. (2016). The contribution of the creative economy to the resilience of rural communities: Exploring cultural and digital capital. *Sociologia Ruralis, 56*(2).

Scottish Government. (2022, March 25). *Growth sector briefing – Creative industries*. Office of the Chief Economic Adviser. https://www.gov.scot/publications/growth-sector-statistics/

Seaton, A. V. (1996). *Book towns and rural tourism development*. The Scottish Tourism Research Unit, Strathclyde University.

Siepel, J., Camerani, R., Masucci, M., Ospina, J., Casadei, P., Bloom, M. (2020). *Creative industries radar: Mapping the UK's creative clusters and microclusters*. NESTA Creative Industries Policy and Evidence Centre (PEC).

Valentine, J. (2020). Ambition and temporal sovereignty in recent Scottish cultural policy. *International Journal of Cultural Policy, 26*(4), 476–489.

Weick, K. (1995). *Sensemaking in organizations*. Sage.

Wheeler, K. (2020). *Embers: Creative placemaking for the South of Scotland*. The Stove Network. https://d1ssu070pg2v9i.cloudfront.net/pex/pex_carnegie2021/2020/05/06132244/LResEMBERS_Spread.pdf

Wilson, N. (2010). Social creativity: Requalifying the creative economy. *International Journal of Cultural Policy, 16*(3), 367–381.

Yin, R. (2003). *Case study research: Design and methods* (3rd ed.). Sage.

CHAPTER 15

HERITAGE CRAFT ENTREPRENEURING IN 'THE WILD': THE ROLE OF ENTREPRENEURIAL PLACEMAKING FOR RURAL DEVELOPMENT

Birgit Helene Jevnaker[a] and Inge Hill[b]

[a]*BI Norwegian Business School, Norway*
[b]*The Open University, UK*

ABSTRACT

This chapter investigates heritage craft entrepreneurship 'in the wild', creative start-ups emerging within a rural context in Norway and the UK. The research asks how entrepreneurs accomplish heritage craft entrepreneuring. To answer this question, we apply relational ontology, conceptualising entrepreneurship as the ongoing accomplishment of entrepreneurial activities, labelled entrepreneuring. We compare two rural heritage craft businesses: Running a spinnery located on a farm in a valley in Norway and a tweed-based textile creating organisation, co-located with other artisan entrepreneurs positioning in a community-led craft heritage building in the United Kingdom. Both entrepreneuring settings employ heritage craft in their businesses and engage in various forms of collaborations and placemaking in their creative entrepreneuring. This chapter unpacks three facets of artisan entrepreneuring through the lens of placemaking – connecting, organising, and co-developing in

---

Creative (and Cultural) Industry Entrepreneurship in the 21st Century:
Policy Challenges for and by Policymakers
Contemporary Issues in Entrepreneurship Research, Volume 18B, 213–226
Copyright © 2025 by Birgit Helene Jevnaker and Inge Hill
Published under exclusive licence by Emerald Publishing Limited
ISSN: 2040-7246/doi:10.1108/S2040-72462024000018B015

rural settings. We contribute to the entrepreneurship-as-practice and creative entrepreneurship literature and highlight the implications of placemaking for rural development.

Keywords: Rural development; heritage craft; entrepreneuring; placemaking; entrepreneurial placemaking; remote rural; 'wild' rural

INTRODUCTION

In this chapter, we investigate heritage craft entrepreneurship in the rural 'wild', that is entrepreneuring emerging in a natural setting (rural) rather than in a 'laboratory' (Hutchins, 1995). Our focus is thus on craft entrepreneuring unfolding outside of any incubator protection (Pret & Cogan, 2019). We study two such heritage craft entrepreneuring settings, one in a rural district of Norway, with traditions of artists, agriculture, and guest houses, and one located in a UK village in a community-led craft heritage building, co-located with other craft and artisan entrepreneurs. While these settings are located in different countries, the entrepreneurial practices have common characteristics and behaviours: Both were led by a woman entrepreneur and used heritage craft in their businesses. This creative entrepreneuring was accomplished by both businesses through various forms of organising collaborations (Jevnaker, 2009) and related performative dynamics (Jevnaker & Olaisen, 2022b), and as part of these processes, they engaged in placemaking. Hence, this research asks: How do craft entrepreneurs accomplish heritage craft entrepreneuring? To answer this question, we apply relational ontology and the concept of entrepreneurial placemaking (Hill et al., 2021) to shed light on dynamic entrepreneuring in the rural.

Specifically, we explore how working creatively with others impacts the workings of rural businesses, employing entrepreneurial placemaking as a lens to further illuminate this process. Working creatively with others requires some alignment of interests, temporary shared activities and resource sharing, and is potentially value-creating (Jevnaker, 2009). However, these activities are still inadequately understood as a facet of collaborative relations (Stadtler & van Wassenhove, 2016), especially when enacted via creative industry entrepreneuring (Jevnaker, 2005, 2009). Exploring such examples seems more relevant than ever in a growing creative industry economy, with increasing distribution and fragmentation of labour linked to the future of work (Hill, 2021; Jevnaker & Olaisen, 2022b). Herein, we untangle situated entrepreneuring (Hill, 2021; Johannisson, 2018; Thompson et al., 2020) and focus on relational aspects of collaborations (Jevnaker, 1993, 2009) and placemaking (Hill et al., 2021) as a lens on rural heritage craft entrepreneurship in the wild.

The next section develops the theoretical framing for our analysis, followed by the case studies and the discussion of our contributions to creative entrepreneurship (theoretical) and rural development (managerial). While we clearly discuss two women entrepreneurial practices, we are not focussing on the gender aspects in their entrepreneuring.

PERSPECTIVES ON HERITAGE CRAFT ENTREPRENEURING

Our most important conceptualisation considers creative industry entrepreneuring as enacted processes of business creation, applied to the creation of heritage crafts. Our case studies focus on the settings of heritage craft entrepreneuring in the rural 'wild', as unfolding phenomena in rural areas, beyond any shielded 'laboratory' or incubator. Creative industry entrepreneuring in the rural 'wild' appears fascinating and demanding to capture, thus some sensitising aspects (Jevnaker & Olaisen, 2022a) are briefly elaborated below.

Rural Entrepreneurship

The literature differentiates between businesses located in rural areas, and 'rural businesses' (Bosworth & Turner, 2018; Hill & Mole, 2022). The latter denotes those businesses interlinked with the local/regional socio-economic context, drawing on local suppliers, staff, material resources and customers. Our heritage craft entrepreneuring case studies are the latter type of business. The context for doing business in 'the rural' is unique; population and business density, and variability are lower than in urban areas. Hence, different business development strategies are needed, for example, to address limited access to business-relevant infrastructure (Beckmann et al., 2021; Mole et al., 2022; Turner et al., 2021). Consequently, the firm characteristics of rural businesses are different to urban ones; businesses in rural areas are usually smaller than in urban ones (Phillips et al., 2019). What is often overlooked is that over 80% of the rural economy consists of non-food and non-agricultural businesses (for the UK, Scott, 2020).

Placemaking

Placemaking is a location-related process-related concept (e.g., Courage, 2021; Hill et al., 2021; Rae, 2020). Existing research typically embraces the social and material dimensions of placemaking processes, including their messiness (Massey, 2005). Recent literature also acknowledges that placemaking is embedded in constructing work both *in* and *with* space, by human and so-called 'nonhuman' agents (such as production and service facilities, transportation routes, as well as dwellings). For example, unstable digital infrastructure such as internet connectivity may both foster and hinder digital placemaking (Hill et al., 2021). Thus, we contend that places and placemaking unfold in dynamic socio-material practices by and for agents. These unfolding practices include the aesthetic and flexible uses of buildings and nature for craft experiments and co-development, varieties of fabrication, selling events, meetings and other gatherings in an evolving landscape. Within the rural, craft-making sites may attract and become habited by diversely talented agents: humans, but also animals, plants – natural and artificial elements constituting what we call a 'place'. Our encounters suggest that field agents co-create meaning and attachment to places (Cilliers & Timmermans, 2014), by emergent actions. We thus address how entrepreneuring could be realised outside of formal planning mechanisms.

Placemaking adds value by attracting or retaining residents, contributing to employment and self-employment, making or reorganising new discourses for groups and communities, and other active community participation (Courage, 2021). Yet, we know less about how placemaking is actually unfolding – and how creative industries perform it. The process of placemaking requires agents or 'placemakers' (Courage, 2021; Hill et al., 2021) who engage in relevant activities. How this placemaking unfolds is theorised from a process-relational perspective in this chapter.

Creative and Heritage Craft Entrepreneurship

Creative industry entrepreneurs have a role beyond urban habitats, yet, it is lesser known *how* their entrepreneuring is accomplished in the rural (see Hill et al., 2021, 2023). So, why are rural creative start-ups important? Ample evidence suggests that creative industries firms tend to be small (Hill, 2021) and highly fragmented (Bruce & Jevnaker, 1998), and skilled creative specialists are often concentrated in some city landscapes (Florida, 2002). Yet, would-be entrepreneurial agents, start-ups, also engage in creative industry and self-employed work in regional non-urban settings (Lagerqvist & Bornmal, 2015; Ratten & Ferreira, 2017). However, beyond organised creative hubs (Hill et al., 2021), creative industry entrepreneurship and artisan business practices in the rural landscape are rarely studied (but see Velez-Ospina et al., 2023).

Artisan entrepreneurs create a tangible small batch of unique 'crafted' products manually supported by tools (Arias & Cruz, 2019; Elias et al., 2018) and often suitable for everyday use. 'Craft' is related to handmade products but can also be performed in minor or greater parts with modern machinery (Arias & Cruz, 2019). Heritage crafting includes a variety of ancient skills and specialised materials such as textiles, paper, functional work, decorative work, and fashion craft, as well as aesthetic hybrids of these crafting forms (Lagerqvist & Bornmal, 2015). Heritage crafting is, paradoxically, regarded as a promising area of business for the future. The products, along with the creation processes and their meaningful outcomes, are in demand, while simultaneously the ancient craft-skilled practitioners are vanishing.

For the purposes of this research, heritage craft is defined as a practice, which employs knowledge, skills, and creative arts, and entails an understanding of traditional materials, design, and techniques, as well as familiarity with options that have been practised for two or more successive generations.

Entrepreneuring

Viewed as a subset of process-relational theories, the lens of practice theories (Gherardi, 2019; Schatzki, 2001) facilitates our focus on how human relations are actually enacted, via iterative dynamic interlinked sets of processes and activities (Langley & Tsoukas, 2017), which are by nature socio-material (Gherardi, 2019). Process-relational reasoning focusses on the dynamic aspect of social interactions, particularly between people, processes and institutions, ideas, and tangible objects, and hence, offers a greater understanding of how actions unfold and outcomes are accomplished (Jevnaker & Olaisen, 2022b; Langley & Tsoukas, 2017).

The term 'practice' acts as a heuristic device and focusses on interconnected and organising sets of activities, which are situated in and mediated by their socio-material contexts and social macrostructures (Gherardi, 2019). Practices, usually used in the plural, vary from simple sets – such as buying a cinema ticket – to the increasingly complex, like starting a business (Hill, 2018; Schatzki, 2001). Agents enact these practices within fields, conceptualised as arenas of power (Johannisson, 2018; Sklaveniti & Steyaert, 2020).

Theoretical Framing Summary

To answer our explorative research question, (how artisan entrepreneurs accomplish heritage craft entrepreneuring in the rural), we employ a process-relational lens (Langley & Tsoukas, 2017). This lens enables us to zoom in on actual activities among agents over time in the settings studied. We specifically explore how rural creative placemaking unfolds via analysing heritage craft entrepreneuring through the lens of entrepreneurial placemaking (Hill et al., 2021). Hence, we conceptualise entrepreneurial placemaking as the heuristic device needed to explain rural creative business creation.

METHODOLOGY

The study adopts a phenomenological inspired approach to reconstruct situated entrepreneurial activities (Pret et al., 2016) through a comparative case study strategy (Yin, 2018). As Eisenhardt and Graebner (2007) argue, unusual or extreme cases are instances of theoretical sampling that may be very useful for building new insights and theories. The process-relational lens (Hill, 2021; Jevnaker & Olaisen, 2022b) allowed us to explore creative industry collaboration (Jevnaker, 2009) unfolding in real-world entrepreneuring (Johannisson, 2018). Zooming in on everyday activities helped to reconstruct and openly reflect upon the specific efforts and challenges (Johannisson, 2018). As a point of departure, this chapter is based on the entrepreneurs' narratives of situated practices. Both entrepreneurial settings are regarded as extreme cases, as the socio-material context in which entrepreneuring is enacted are unique and yet typical of two types of rural contexts.

Case Selection and Researcher Positionality

The chapter investigates entrepreneurial practices in rural contexts, illuminated by two artisan entrepreneurs, Sheila and Elbjorg, who both started creative industry firms using heritage craft activities and resources: Elbjorg started a spinnery on a farm in a valley in Norway, while Sheila is using tweed in a UK village, in a community-led craft heritage building co-located with other artisan entrepreneurs. Both micro-businesses are led by a woman entrepreneur, apply heritage craft practices in their businesses and engage in various forms of collaborations in their creative entrepreneuring.

The cases were selected by each researcher with the aim to have comparable creative entrepreneurial settings. Each author researched a case study in their country of residence. This explicit positionality is important as it impacts the data gathering and interpretation (Johannisson, 2018). The Norwegian case is known to the Norwegian researcher informally through networks pre-dating the empirical research phase. The UK case is part of a larger study of a rural creative hub conducted by the UK researcher.

Data Collection and Data Analysis

The process-relational lens (Hill, 2018, 2021, 2022; Jevnaker & Olaisen, 2022b) allowed us to explore creative entrepreneurs' collaborations (Jevnaker, 2005, 2009) as they unfold in real-world entrepreneuring (Johannisson, 2018). Zooming in on everyday activities helped to reconstruct and openly reflect upon the specific efforts and challenges (Cunliffe & Scaratti, 2017).

Studying real-life entrepreneurial activities requires open ways to capture all possible details of daily entrepreneuring (Johannisson, 2018). Thus, the data collection instruments need to be able to capture as much rich and nuanced data as possible, including narratives. The data were collected from several sources: interviews, observations, websites, press clippings, informal documents, and social media. Interviews (semi-structured and probing explorative) and recurrent informal conversations were grounded in the informants' first-hand experiences. One long interview face-to-face and several site visits allowed recurrent conversations and observations in Norway. The research in the United Kingdom includes two interviews within 2021, one online during the COVID-19 related lockdown phase when the artist was at home and one face-to-face in the studio with associated visits to the whole building and the site, and event observation.

Recurrent site visits included walking around and having reflective conversations on site. Specifically, rich narratives helped identify and understand recurrent aspects of the ongoing placemaking (Hill et al., 2021) resulting from collaborative work with other place agents (Jevnaker, 2003, 2009). Interviews were recorded and transcribed verbatim. We applied inductive coding in line with our interpretative approach twice (see Table 15.1, following Brinkmann & Kvale, 2014, we identified meaningful themes going back and forth in thematic analysis) leading to the emergent themes and aggregated codes.

FINDINGS AND ANALYSIS

First, we delineate the two settings of rural heritage craft entrepreneuring. The two settings illuminate similar yet different solutions for rural heritage craft entrepreneuring to have a wider impact on rural socio-economic development.

Case Vignette 1: Sheila, Textile Artist, UK – 'Wildlife Inspired'

Sheila (a pseudonym) is a textile artist based in the United Kingdom, creating accessories, homeware and original artwork, mainly using original English and Scottish tweeds. Her products include brooches, hair clips, bags, lampshades, and scarves, which feature nature and imaginatively enhance animals and landscapes. Using tweed connects her to the family history of her two great uncles who manufactured

Heritage Craft Entrepreneuring in 'The Wild' 219

Table 15.1. Codes for Emerging Entrepreneurial Practices and Indicative Quotes.

Codes	First order categories	Aggregated codes / entrepreneurial practices	Indicative quotes from both research sites
People: Communicating with other artisan entrepreneurs and specialists Processes: communication processes, exchange processes, linking processes	Making connections with other artists and specialists via social media, phone, physical encounters	**Connecting people and processes**	(Elbjorg) 'We were 5 women who started this…Now there is a very young community in this valley.' 'Previously, I travelled around a lot. That was important in a building phase in order to create network.' 'It was a coincidence that I came in contact with NN, who is a specialist in small cattle.' (Sheila) 'So my results will benefit … my response would be that it's not about making place, it's about making connections and community (…) I think I just see there's been enormous benefits having a creative community particularly during COVID. You know, this, a lot of us makers work on our own'(…)
Working with others on projects / business marketing / running a centre / exhibiting craft offerings, committee work, social encounters in co-development	Co-creating an online market place / fair; co-creating a business / a local network; employment, developing and showing practical coping and knowing; building community in developing crafts	**Co-developing**	(Elbjorg) 'We're part of a research project to develop production from the ancient sheep species and mohair goats.' 'Social media, the other women are good with that.' (Sheila) 'So, you know, it feels like we've got a very supportive case of community here [in the creative hub]. And there was a group of the building.' (…) I've made friends through the Open Studios committee, you know, and lots of informal conversations happen where suddenly you realise that someone's inadvertently showing you how to create a mailing list, you know, just somebody to talk to and check in with about the realities of being you know, a single creative business.'
Sorting resources; prioritising resources and activities; planning resources; time planning, sequencing activities and the people carrying them out; developing or acquiring needed resources for activities.	Combining resources, combining people and resources	**Organising** - combining spatial / local resources to a craft / heritage entrepreneurial activity	(Elbjorg) 'I came into this landscape. The values exist in this landscape and wool is part of it. For me it became very important early on to connect it together with my production.' 'My project was to make yarn.' 'Keep goats.' 'But today, here now, we are focussing on the ancient Norwegian sheep breeds.' 'Wild sheep and Norwegian short tail landrace - most of the wool is thrown away. That is what we will work with, ahead.' 'We're now starting a three year-research project on uses of… overlooked wool'. (Sheila) 'Yeah, it was a group have of you know, as women artists, at X, that put on the Open Studios here in this building and we met up a few times and you know, we've through the process of doing it together (…) you know, we're going to have a meet up in the next few weeks and have dinner together and talk about maybe putting on a collaborative exhibition.'

Source: The authors.

fine wool tweeds. Most of the fabrics are natural and sustainably produced, a small amount is repurposed (bags) using recycled plastic bottles and cotton.

Her love of nature and fabrics keeps her going. Sheila cannot earn a full-time salary with her creative work as yet, and hence, works as an employee in part-time jobs. One day a week she works for an alternative agriculture organisation in the administration team, and another day, she packages vegetables for an organic food delivery company.

Sheila works from a studio in a rural creative hub, where she gains inspiration and inspires others. Locally, she is engaged in an online community that she co-created during the COVID-19 lockdowns during 2020-2021 to raise the profile of local artists and increase the local market size for handcrafted goods. She communicates with customers via Facebook, Instagram pages and her website. She sells via Etsy directly and regularly takes part in craft fairs, regional Open Studio events and Open Days at her creative hub. She also sells her products in six shops around the UK, some of which are hundreds of miles away.

The COVID-19 lockdown phases forced her to engage much more with social media, including livestreaming her work from temporary fairs. During 2021, Sheila co-created an online fair with over 50 local artisan entrepreneurs, advertised on social media, and took part in two other local online markets. In 2022, she is back at in-person events and fairs, but streams live from these events and publishes short videos showcasing her art.

Case Vignette 2: Elbjorg, Spinning Wool Entrepreneur, Norway – 'Co-creating in the Wild'

When selling their home in Norway's capital Oslo, Elbjorg (a pseudonym) and her husband bought a small farm in a rural valley in 1992. Growing up with craft traditions performed by her mother (a 'modiste', hat-maker) and grandmother (weaving and sewing), Elbjorg is very interested in what she calls 'forgotten' craft traditions, and the fact that 'women in textiles have been creating for hundreds of years'. With this background, educated as a nurse, and an idea-historian university graduate, Elbjorg has broad experience in exploration, knowledge-creation, and caring work for and with others, which she applies to business creation. She also became dedicated to 'beginning with mohair goats', inspired by a rural-narrative TV program.

In the early 2000s, Elbjorg had a passion and practised skills for heritage craft with wool resources. Establishing a weaving room with several manual looms in the barn attic preceded the formal business foundation. However, the industrially spun wool yarn available in Norway in the early 2000 was chemically treated and did not include wool from the ancient sheep breeds. Elbjorg eventually started to engage with several researchers and teachers at two higher education schools in the region, especially interested in the prospective use of wool from local sheep and goats including her own mohair goats.

When Elbjorg discovered that her mohair goats' wool that she first sent to Denmark, was further transported as far as South Africa to be washed and spun, she began searching for new solutions. 'It was not sustainable', she says in the interview. Another eye-opener was a research-based report from one of the local universities that pointed to the opportunity for handling the local wool from sheep and goats, from around 70 interested farmers.

At that time, she did not find any small-scale wool handling and spinning solutions in Norway or other European countries. After a while, she and her IT-educated son found small-scale suitable spinning machines in Canada and ordered several in 2008. The woman-led company was then afterwards formally established the same year as a limited company with several owners. The wool-handling and spinning started on her farm property.

This local spinning company is among the very few spinning wools from sheep and goats in Norway, washing and handling the wool locally in ecological ways. Elbjorg and her team also spin custom-based yarn from other animals (e.g., moxas and dogs). The company now mainly sells varieties of self-produced natural yarn, and a few finished knitted or woven products, for example, shawls, jumpers, cardigans, mittens, tablecloths, pillowcases, and carpets.

Below we delineate three recurrent practices we identified in both the United Kingdom village and in the valleys of Norway, which underpin rural entrepreneurial placemaking. The creation of heritage craft businesses has required skilfully organising specific resources and processes, including placemaking for creative industry business collaborations, which we turn to next.

How Entrepreneurial Placemaking Unfolds

The regional context, with its sources for materials, related skills and people, is key in heritage craft entrepreneurship. However, it is less understood how entrepreneurs can actually foster or cultivate this type of entrepreneuring to create dynamic rural entrepreneurial places (Hill et al., 2021). Taking the two cases as our point of departure uncovers both similarities and differences in the two rural artisan entrepreneurs' placemaking activities. Both were immersed in enacting heritage-skilled entrepreneurial activities, but differences prevailed in making places (for buying and selling heritage goods) accessible for and with others, physically and online.

We start by analysing the spinning case in Norway to illuminate some placemaking dynamics and especially how they serve as a vehicle for business development in the rural area. After some years (2008–2011) with spinning machines only located in the barn, a new, separately located factory building was built with a visiting exhibition room/shop and its own parking lot. Not only machinery but the whole building helps to connect, co-develop and organise craft production, presentations and sales, as well as receiving visiting groups well (often with homemade cakes). Gaining funding from public sources, while initially dependent on 'much persuasion', became easier, and then with the new spinnery crafts production was 'clearly no hobby', Elbjorg underlined. In 2022, around 50 farmers from several regions are delivering wool to this spinning enterprise. Elbjorg is co-creating jobs for local women in the spinnery including specialists recruited to the site (around 5), as well as for one or two visiting apprentices staying a period at the farm.

Experimentation in a 3-year-long funded research project, on the use of wool from ancient sheep breeds, unfolds in the spinnery since 2022. One of Elbjorg's family members is leading this wool project in partnership with external researchers in crafts and agriculture education. Another family member is the spinning company's chairperson and has contributed for several years to the enterprise (e.g., organising the company webpage with net-based shopping generating around one third of its current sales). Everyone in this spinning company enjoys a salary on the same level, as a 'flat organisation'. A network of co-engaged knitters also contributes to the co-development of creative patterns and samples of finished products, displayed online and in the shop. The numerous collective events before the pandemic included both temporary scheduled group visits and more spontaneous heritage craft presentations for other visitors to the spinnery.

The UK entrepreneurial placemaking activities occurred during and after UK COVID-19-induced lockdown phases, as temporary digital and physical entrepreneurial placemaking (Hill et al., 2021). Sheila is involved in creating dynamic marketplaces using a variety of tools and channels. Her placemaking activities establish temporary marketplaces where selling to end customers is possible. Co-developing is very important to her, she has worked with other local artisan entrepreneurs in all marketplaces. Placemaking is the academic term, and she thoroughly explains the key ingredients of a place that works: 'it's not about making place, it's about making connections and community (...), I think I just see there's been enormous benefits having a creative community particularly during COVID-19'. She highlights how the fragmented working conditions of many artisan entrepreneurs with portfolio careers (part-time employment and self-employment simultaneously) can be overcome through online communities (see Hill et al., 2021) that meet to organise markets and sell at these temporary markets. Connecting with others often leads to peer learning and support, while co-developing a community of artisan entrepreneurs and organising marketplaces for selling their goods (see Table 15.1).

Entrepreneuring for Sheila is a vehicle that allows her to connect with other artisan entrepreneurs, overcome the loneliness as a single entrepreneur, and create places for social connections while organising activities for the wider local (artisan) community. These organising practices often lead to economically relevant exchanges where artisan entrepreneurs can also support each other. This peer support is a side-effect of organising events, fairs and exhibitions, as the last quote in Table 15.1 demonstrates: Returning to the first quote by Sheila, entrepreneurial placemaking (see Hill et al., 2021) is the ongoing accomplishment of various sets of interconnected activities (Gherardi, 2019; Hill, 2018), which can be fragile and is less understood (Bruce & Jevnaker, 1998; Jevnaker & Olaisen, 2022b). Our research hones in on connecting, co-developing, and organising. Sheila outlines explicitly what she regards as essential for being able to do business, not only during lockdown phases – connecting with people, meeting up, exchanging ideas, communicating, which leads to practical outcomes of organising events and fairs, including online and physical events in the locality via Open Studio events and Open days in the creative hub.

Thus, the three practices of connecting, organising and co-developing are interconnected and underpin the entrepreneurial placemaking practices. Both entrepreneurs set up their creative industry venture to cultivate local wool traditions, such as weaving or woven fabrics, using local materials.

SO WHAT DOES THIS MEAN FOR CREATIVE INDUSTRY RESEARCH? CREATIVE INDUSTRIES IN 'THE WILD'

Our research offers two theoretical contributions to the creative industries and entrepreneurship-as-practice literature we discuss before we outline some management implications.

Co-creating Synergies in Craft Entrepreneuring in the Rural

Rather than any single success factor for rural heritage craft businesses, we were intrigued by how Sheila and Elbjorg were both engaging in multiple voluntary processes of placemaking as a vehicle for 'successful' rural entrepreneuring. In the settings studied, the heritage craft entrepreneurs were recurrently exploiting materials, means, and matters such as events, fairs, and webpages to showcase offerings, sell craft products, or raise money for something genuinely embedded in their heritage craft networks.

This finding resonates with the idea of entrepreneuring in the rural as quite complex enactive interweaving (Johannisson, 2018), and illustrates 'rural business' activities using local resources (materials, networks, and employing local staff) (Bosworth & Turner, 2018; Hill & Mole, 2022). Yet, 'enactment' does not fully capture what Sheila and Elbjorg are doing and saying. The creative industry practices that surprised us rather involved making synergy when co-creating with – and in part against – other contemporary industry practices (Jevnaker, 2005). This seems to be an important element in whether collectively improved entrepreneurial places for local crafts (Hill et al., 2021) can work – or not work. An important implication for future research is to further investigate the possible 'bottom-up' creation of synergy in developmental micro-activities generated and shared with others (Jevnaker, 2009) as essential practices of co-creation among creative entrepreneurs in rural locations.

Organising In and 'With' the Wild

Another contribution emanates from studying creative industry entrepreneuring in the remote rural. As we have addressed heritage craft entrepreneurship as creative venturing emerging in the business world, rather than shielded in a laboratory (a well serviced and resourced urban environment), we found it useful to borrow the 'wild' cognition metaphor of Hutchins (1995). Using this contextual metaphor allowed us to identify the more hidden activities and challenges of the heritage craft entrepreneuring as both real-life joyful action and strivings (Jevnaker & Olaisen, 2022b). In short, it helped to convey more of the everyday efforts of, for, and with, particular artisans. 'We are working for the crafts, not for money', but 'we need to cover the salaries', Elbjorg contended. Evidently, both entrepreneurs Elbjorg and Sheila, are making heritage craft not only 'in the wild' but also 'with the wild', which is a novel application of this concept.

Implications for Enacting Heritage Craft Entrepreneuring in the Rural

Hence, rather than looking at heritage crafts as fixed cultural objects or given resources, the two artisan entrepreneurs proactively exploited heritage materials in new developments. In their ongoing collaborative enactments with others (Jevnaker, 2005), creative agents actually co-create *entrepreneurial placemaking in the rural*. Implications for rural development address the need to engage with creative entrepreneurs and their invisible supply chains – associates they work with and the roles as self-employed associates to other businesses (see Jevnaker, 2009; Jones & Ratten, 2020). Associates who support the creation processes do not show up on employment records, and hence, the wider economic contribution is less visible (Jevnaker & Olaisen, 2022b). Local development officers in local authorities would benefit from organising regular gatherings, not only for creative entrepreneurs, but also for their supply chain businesses, to foster relationship building. These gatherings would help to keep creative entrepreneurs in their locations in the wild, and overcome distance and cost by bridging this distance through on- and off-line business working events. These events would then recurrently contribute to realising entrepreneurial placemaking.

CONCLUSION

This research asked how craft entrepreneurs accomplish heritage craft entrepreneuring in the rural. Adopting a process-relational view, we studied two rural heritage textiles micro-business settings, which allowed for the identification of some entrepreneurial craft practices. Specifically, we identified how their craft of entrepreneuring is developed by many temporary connecting, co-creating and developing, and organising activities, in the rural 'wild'. We used the lens 'entrepreneurial placemaking' (Hill et al., 2021) to capture the performance of these entrepreneurial practices.

A common theme of all practices was co-creating with the material, the social, and the symbolic aspects of heritage craft such as becoming visible in many of the internet-based presentations. Notably, the two rural artisan entrepreneurial settings in Norway and the UK were both engaging in placemaking via 'wildlife inspired' new resource combinations.

In conclusion, we specifically point to the essential roles of creative 'heritage craft placemakers' and their continued co-creative entrepreneurial placemaking – as embedded in recurrent connecting, creatively co-developing, and organising practices with others *in* and *with* the rural 'wild'.

REFERENCES

Arias, R. A. C., & Cruz, A. D. (2019). Rethinking artisan entrepreneurship in a small island. A tale of two chocolatiers in Roatan, Honduras. *International Journal of Entrepreneurial Behaviour and Research*, 25(4), 633–661.

Beckmann, M., Garkisch, M., & Zeyen, A. (2021). Together we are strong? A systematic literature review on how SMEs use relation-based collaboration to operate in rural areas. *Journal of Small Business & Entrepreneurship*, 35(4), 1–35.

Bosworth, G., & Turner, R. (2018). Interrogating the meaning of a rural business through a rural capitals framework. *Journal of Rural Studies,60*, 1–10.

Brinkmann, S., & Kvale, S. (2014). *InterViews: Learning the craft of qualitative research interviewing*. Sage Publications Ltd.

Bruce, M., & Jevnaker, B. H. (Eds.). (1998). *Management of design alliances: Sustaining competitive advantage*. J. Wiley & Sons.

Cilliers, E., & Timmermans, W. (2014). The importance of creative participatory planning in the public place-making process. *Environment and Planning B: Urban Analytics and City Science, 41*(3), 413–429.

Courage, C. (2021). Preface: The radical potential of placemaking. In Courage, C., Borrup, T., Jackson, M. R., Legge, K., Mckeown, A., Platt, L., J. Schupbach. (Eds.), *The Routledge Handbook of Placemaking* (pp. 217–223). Routledge.

Cunliffe, A. L., & Scaratti, G. (2017). Embedding impact in engaged research: Developing socially useful knowledge through dialogical sensemaking. *British Journal of Management, 28*, 29–44.

Eisenhardt, K. M., & Graebner, M. E. (2007). Theory building from cases: Opportunities and challenges. *Academy of Management Journal, 50*(1), 25–32.

Elias S. R. S. T. A., Chiles, T. H., Duncan C. M., & Vultee, D. M. (2018). The aesthetics of entrepreneurship: How arts entrepreneurs and their customers co-create aesthetic value. *Organisation Studies, 39*(2–3), 345–372.

Florida, R. (2002). *The rise of the creative class: And how it's transforming work, leisure, community and everyday life*. Perseus Book Group.

Gherardi, S. (2019). How to conduct a practice-based study. *Problems and methods* (2nd ed.). Edward Elgar Publishing.

Hill, I. (2018). How did you get up and running? Taking a Bourdieuan perspective towards a framework for negotiating strategic fit. *Entrepreneurship and Regional Development, 30*(5–6), 662–696.

Hill, I. (2021). Spotlight on UK artisan entrepreneurs' situated collaborations: Through the lens of entrepreneurial capitals and their conversion. *International Journal of Entrepreneurial Behavior & Research, 27*(1), 99–121.

Hill, I. (2022). Ethnographic methods for capturing the sociomateriality of entrepreneurial practices. In N. Thompson, O. Byrne, B. Teague, & A. Jenkins (Eds.), *Research handbook on entrepreneurship as practice. Research handbooks in business and management series* (pp. 266–280). Edward Elgar Publishing.

Hill, I., & Mole, K. (2022, July). *State of the art review - Supporting rural businesses*. National Innovation Centre for Rural Enterprise. Retrieved October 25, 2022, from https://nicre.co.uk/media/1wmhonux/nicre-sota-no-4-july-2022-supporting-rural-businesses.pdf

Hill, I., Elias, S., Dobson, S., & Jones, P. (Eds.). (2023). Creative (and cultural) industry entrepreneurship in the 21st century – state of the art. *Creative (and cultural) industry entrepreneurship in the 21st century* (Vol. 18A, pp. 1–14). Emerald Publishing Ltd.

Hill, I., Manning, L., & Frost, R. (2021). Rural arts entrepreneurs' placemaking - how 'entrepreneurial placemaking' explains rural creative hub evolution during COVID-19 lockdown. *Local Economy, 36*(7–8), 627–649.

Hutchins, E. (1995). *Cognition in the wild*. MIT Press.

Jevnaker, B. H. (1993). Creating an entrepreneurial management system in large corporations: The case of STK Innova. In H. Klandt (Ed.), *Entrepreneurship and business development, Fgf entrepreneurship research monographien* (Bd. 3, pp. 335–357). Avebury.

Jevnaker, B. H. (2003). Industrial designers as boundary workers. In N. Paulsen, & T. Hernes (Eds.), *Managing boundaries in organizations: multiple perspectives* (pp. 110–128). Palgrave Macmillan.

Jevnaker, B. H. (2005). Vita Activa: On Relationships between Design(ers) and Business. *Design Issues, 21*(3), 25–48.

Jevnaker, B. H. (2009). Mediating in-between: How industrial design advances business and user innovation. In S. Poggenpohl, & K. Sato (Eds.), *Design integrations: Research and collaboration* (pp. 87–118). Intellect, in the US distr. in collaboration with The University of Chicago Press.

Jevnaker, B. H., & Olaisen, J. (2022a). A comparative study of knowledge management research studies: Making research more relevant and creative. *Knowledge Management Research & Practice, 20*(2), 292–303.

Jevnaker, B. H., & Olaisen, J. (2022b). *Reimagining sustainable organization. Perspectives on arts, design, leadership, knowledge and project management*. Palgrave Macmillan, Springer Nature.

Johannisson, B. (2018). *Disclosing entrepreneurship as practice. The enactive approach*. Edward Elgar Publishing.

Jones, P., & Ratten, V. (2020). Knowledge spillovers and entrepreneurial ecosystems. *Knowledge Management Research & Practice*, *19*(1), 1–7.

Lagerqvist, B., & Bornmal, D. (2015). Development of new economies by merging heritage and entrepreneurship. The issue of preserving, using or developing – or all? *Ecocycles*, *1*(1), 16–21.

Langley, A., & Tsoukas, H. (Eds.). (2017). Introduction. *The SAGE handbook of process organisation studies* (pp. 1–26). Sage Publications Ltd.

Massey, D. (2005). *For space*. Sage Publications Ltd.

Mole, K., Hill, I., Nguyen, T., & Maioli, S. (2022). *Rural family businesses and exporting behaviour*. In NICRE research reports. National Innovation Centre for Rural Enterprise. https://oro.open.ac.uk/91288/

Phillips, J., Gorton, M. Tiwasing, P., Cowie, P., Maioli, S., & Newbery, R. (2019). *Progressing rural contributions to the UK Industrial Strategy. Rural economy and land use policy and practice note* (Vol. 8). Newcastle University.

Pret, T., & Cogan, A. (2019). Artisan entrepreneurship: A systematic literature review and research agenda. *International Journal of Entrepreneurial Behavior & Research*, *25*(4), 529–614.

Pret, T., Shaw, E., & Drakopoulou Dodd, S. (2016). Painting the full picture: The conversion of economic, cultural, social and symbolic capital. *International Small Business Journal*, *34*(8), 1004–1027.

Rae, D. (2020). Intercultural entrepreneurship in creative place-making. In R. Granger (Ed.), *Value construction in the creative economy: Negotiating innovation and transformation* (pp. 131–150). Palgrave MacMillan.

Ratten V., & Ferreira J. J. (2017). Future research direction for cultural entrepreneurship and regional innovation. *International Journal of Entrepreneurship and Innovation*, *21*(3), 163–169.

Schatzki, T. (2001). Introduction: Practice theory. In T. R. Schatzki, K. Knorr-Cetina, & E. von Savigny (Eds.), *The practice turn in contemporary theory* (pp. 1–15). Routledge.

Scott, E. (2020). *Rural economy and UK agriculture: Issues for the New Parliament*. House of Lords Library.

Sklaveniti, C., & Steyaert, C. (2020). Reflecting with Pierre Bourdieu: Towards a reflexive outlook for practice-based studies of entrepreneurship. *Entrepreneurship & Regional Development*, *32*(3–4), 313–333.

Stadtler, L., & van Wassenhove, L. N. (2016). Coopetition as a paradox: Integrative approaches in a multi-company, cross-sector partnership. *Organization Studies*, *37*(5), 655–685.

Thompson, N., Verduijn, K., & Gartner, W. (2020). Entrepreneurship-as-practice: Grounding contemporary theories of practice into entrepreneurship studies. *Entrepreneurship and Regional Development*, *32*(3–4), 247–256.

Turner, R., Phillipson, J., Gorton, M., Cowie, P., Dwyer, J., Goodwin-Hawkins, B., Hill, I., Mole, K., Nguyen, T., Roper, S., Thompson-Glen, M., Rowe, F., Tocco, B., & Wishart, M. (2021). What is the contribution of rural enterprise to Levelling up, and how can this be further enabled? *Briefing Paper No 1*. National Innovation Centre for Rural Enterprise (NICRE). https://nicre.co.uk/media/rgfbvgkc/what-is-the-contribution-of-rural-enterprise-to-levelling-up-and-how-can-this-be-further-enabled.pdf

Velez-Ospina, J., Siepel, J. , Hill, I., & Rowe, F. (2023). Determinants of rural creative microclustering: Evidence from web-scraped data for England. *Papers in Regional Science*, *102*(5), 903–943.

Yin, R. K. (2018). *Case study research and applications: Design and methods* (6th ed.). Sage Publications Ltd.

INDEX

Aardklop festivals, 36
Academic research process, 117
Access, 149–150
Accessibility, 132
Action research approach, 125, 129
Active listening, 130
Affordability, 132
Africa's creative and cultural industries, policy context of, 139–140
Africa's creative industries, 138
African CCIs, 151
   challenges of, 145
African countries CCIS, challenges and potential of, 140–142
African music business, 141
African Union (AU), 139
Afropop genre, 140
AmberScript, 98
Analytic process of IPA, 71
Anchor attractions, 207
Anecdotal evidence, 68, 87
Art entrepreneurs, 51, 57
Art entrepreneurship, 51
   in public realm, 51–52
Art spaces, 24, 29
Artisans, 89
   creating products, 85
   entrepreneurs, 214
Artistes, 147, 149
   and consumer education, 146–147
Artistic logics, 95
Artistic merit and societal impact, 85
Artists, 56, 112, 190
   spaces, 24–25
   studio, 25
Arts enterprises, 83
Arts festivals, 36
Authenticity, 149
Average variance explained (AVE), 160

Bonding concept, 126–127
Book Town, The, 205
Borders Art Fair (2022), 203, 207
Branding, 206–207
Bridging concept, 126–127
Building in-person, comparison between online communities and, 131
Businesses, 207

Castle Douglas Food Town (CDFT), 205
Castlefield Gallery, 30
Charter for African Cultural Renaissance, 139
Chief Executive Officer (CEO), 188
Chinese entrepreneurship education performance, 157
Chinese government, 157
City centre Vinyls, 56–57
Closed space, 27–30
Cluster sampling, 158
Clustering, 110
Clustering of enterprises, 187
Co-creating synergies in craft entrepreneuring in rural, 221
Co-working, 112
Coaching, 126
Cognition, 172
Cognitive mental models
   concept map for potential themes of underlying cognitive mental models of CCI managers, 75
   findings from triangulation, 76
   master table of themes for CCI managers, 74
   potential themes of underlying, 74
Cognitive neuroscience techniques, 173

Cognitive science, 66
Cold cognition, 171
Coldstream, 202, 207
Collaboration, 66, 77, 111–112, 186–187
Collaborative individualism, 189
Collaborative propinquity, 111
Commercial performance, 85
Commercial success, 85–86
Commercial thinking, 99
Communication tools, 130
Community/communities, 43, 112, 133, 186–187
 building, 126–127
 collaboration, community, and creative entrepreneurship, 186–187
 community-based workspace, 184
 context and framing, 185–186
 creative entrepreneurship, 186
 developing enterprise, 191–193
 findings, 188
 methodology, 187–188
 motivation and shared values, 190–191
 and significance of place, 188–190
 structured approach to, 130–131
Competition
 in CCI, 86
 in selection and reviewing of performance criteria for cultural entrepreneur, 89
Composite reliability (CR), 160
Computed tomography (CT), 172
Concept map, 77
Connectivity, 150
Constructivism, 66
Consumer education, artiste and, 146–147
Coping strategies, 94, 96–97, 100, 102–103
Coronavirus (COVID-19), 51–52, 58, 124, 192
 art opportunities in public realm during, 50–51
 effects of COVID pandemic on creative sector, 206
 epidemic, 164
 lockdowns, 218
 pandemic, 10, 124, 127, 138, 156, 208
Craft entrepreneuring in rural, co-creating synergies in, 221
Creative and cultural entrepreneurship, 51
Creative and Cultural Industries (CCI), 82, 140
 collaboration between CCI and nonCCI, 71–74
 collaboration with nonCCI, 67
 competition and performance measurement in CCI, 86
 competition role in selection and reviewing of performance criteria for cultural entrepreneur, 89
 context and theoretical framing, 67–68
 contribution, 74–77
 cultural entrepreneurship in Zimbabwe, 86–87
 data analysis, 69–71
 data collection, 69
 enterprises, 66–67
 entrepreneurs, 12
 entrepreneurship, 15–16
 expert interviews, 74
 experts, 71
 findings, 71
 limitations, 90
 lived experience, 87
 managers, 66–69, 74
 measuring performance in, 83–84
 mental models, 68
 methods, 68
 performance criteria selected, reviewed, 88
 performance criteria used by cultural entrepreneurs to guide day-to-day business, 87–88

Index

policies, 185
potential themes of underlying cognitive mental models, 74
research design and strategy, 68–69
selecting criteria for measuring performance in CCI, 84
Creative and heritage craft entrepreneurship, 214
Creative Arts Business Network (CABN), 203
Creative Canada policy framework, 4
Creative cities strategies, 13
Creative economy, 110
    in border rurality, 200–201
Creative enterprises, 66, 110
Creative entrepreneurial process, 50
Creative entrepreneurs, 94–97, 100–101, 103, 186, 190–191
    coping strategies, 100
    data collection, 98
    dual goals, 94–95
    dual logics, 95–96
    entrepreneurial identity, 96–97
    identity, 99–100
    literature review, 94
    logics, 98–99
    method, 97
    mitigation strategies, 100–101
    reconciliation strategies, 101–103
    research design, 97
    results, 98
Creative entrepreneurship, 94–95, 185–186
    collaboration, community, and, 186–187
Creative industries, 24, 74
    in 'the Wild', 221–222
    co-creating synergies in craft entrepreneuring in rural, 221
    collaboration and creativity, 111–112
    entrepreneurs, 214
    entrepreneurship, 67
    flux state or state of uncertainty, 118–119
    implications for enacting heritage craft entrepreneuring in rural, 222
    interviewee, 113–118
    methodology, 113
    organising in and 'with' the wild, 221
    propinquity *vs.* proximity, 111
    research, 221
    sector, 4
    self-discovery state, 120
    synergy state, 119
Creative Industries Council, 3
Creative Labs, 113–116
    cohort, 117
    programme, 111, 113, 118
Creative or cultural organisations (CCO), 83
Creative placemaking, 56
    anchor attractions, 207
    branding, 206–207
    cases, 202
    creative economies in border rurality, 200–201
    cultural inclusion or exclusion, 208
    digital economy, 208
    effects of COVID pandemic and lockdown on creative sector, 206
    events, 207
    findings from cases, 206
    framing study using perspectives of policy, theory, prior work, and creative rural economies, 198
    prior literature and theoretical framing, 199
    methodology, 3, 201–202
    policy perspective, 198–199
    policy towards cultural and creative economy, 207–208
    process, 12, 198–199
    in Scottish Rurality, 198
    The Scottish Borders, 202–204
    Wigtown and Galloway cultural ecosystem, 204–206

Creative places, 199
Creative process, 100
Creative production process, 84, 88–89
Creative professional, 101
Creative rural economies, framing study using perspectives of policy, theory, prior work, and, 198
Creative Village, The (APP), 11
  access, 149–150
  artiste and consumer education, 146–147
  authenticity, 149
  challenges and potential of African countries CCIS, 140–142
  challenges of African CCIs, 145
  concept, 142
  connectivity, 150
  contributions, 150–151
  creative village experience, 147
  data collection and analysis, 144
  education, 149
  experience, 147
  findings, 144
  inclusion, 147–149
  methodology, 142
  policy context of Africa's creative and cultural industries, 139–140
  research design, 143
  solution, 142
  underdevelopment of music industry value chain, 147
  weak structures and infrastructure, 145–146
Creatives in Zimbabwe, 88
Creativity, 111–112, 173–176
Cultural and creative economy, policy towards, 207–208
Cultural and creative industries (CCIs), 2, 66
  contributing to meeting SDGs, 7–8
  contribution of creative and cultural industries to sustainability, 5–9
  directions for future research, 13
  entrepreneurs, 66
  micro-entrepreneurs, 184
  policy and practice implications of research, 13
  value of creative industries and policy challenges, 2–5
Cultural entrepreneurs, 37, 43–44, 82
  performance criteria used by cultural entrepreneurs to guide day-to-day business, 87–88
  profile of, 40
  role of competition in selection and reviewing of performance criteria for, 89
Cultural entrepreneurship, 37 (see also Neuro–entrepreneurship)
  community and shared identity, 43
  EE, 37–39
  findings, 39–41
  interactions and networks, 42
  motivation for participation, 41
  in Zimbabwe, 86–87
Cultural identity and recognition, 206–207
Cultural inclusion or exclusion, 208
Cultural industries, 82
Cultural observation, 201
Cultural policy, 199
Cultural value, 95
Culture, 36
Culture Hack movement, 112
Curriculum System Construction (CSC), 159

Data coding, 113
Decision–making, 172
  contexts, 68
  in entrepreneurs, 173
  process, 170
Department for Culture Media and Sport (DCMS), 3
Department of Canadian Heritage, 4
Detection method, 159
Developing country context, 82
Devolved nation, 3

Index

Digital economy, 208
Digital illustrations, 55
Digital platform prototype, 143
Digital technology, 127
Dopamine receptors, 172
Dual goals, 94–95
Dual identity, 99
Dual logics, 95–96
Dual spaces, 30
Dutch Chamber of Commerce, 97

East Street Arts (ESA), 28, 30
Eastern Borders creative economy functions, 207
Economic context, 200
Economic environment, 3
Economic logics, 95, 99
Economic value, 95
Ecosystem, 150, 164
Ecosystem Insights Approach (EIA), 143
Education, 146, 149
Electro-dermal activity (EDA), 171
Electroencephalogram (EEG), 12, 172
Emergence of labs, 111–112
Emotion, 172
End-user focus groups, 144
Engineered serendipity, 113
Enterprise, 191–193
Entertainment and Media market (E&M market), 140
Entrepreneurial capabilities, 51
Entrepreneurial ecosystems (EE), 37, 110
  literature review, 157
  methodology, 38–39
  perspective, 43
  programme, 11
Entrepreneurial identity, 96
  coping strategy, 96–97
Entrepreneurial placemaking, 219–220
Entrepreneurial process, 50, 52
Entrepreneuring, 214–215
Entrepreneurs, 42, 44, 60, 67, 94, 172
  reflections of, 59–60

Entrepreneurship, 12, 36, 41, 94, 158, 170, 185, 191
  domains, 170
  ecosystem, 157
  necessary combined capabilities for, 51
  research, 111
Entrepreneurship education (EE), 156
  Chinese entrepreneurship education performance, 157
  context and literature review, 157
  development of instruments, 159
  findings, 161
  and innovation capability among undergraduates, 158
  measurement model, 159–161
  methodology, 158
  moderator effect model, 163
  and other contributing factors, 157–158
  population and sampling technique, 158–159
  results of moderator effect model, 163
  structural model, 161
Entrepreneurship education programme (EEP), 159
Environment, 41
Events, role of, 207
Explorative abductive approach, 66, 68
External capabilities, 61
External expectations, 84

Federation House, 31–32
Festivalgoers, 39
Festivals, 36, 38–39
Financial performance, 88
Financial thinking, 99
Flux state, 118–119
Focus groups, 144
Freedom, 98
Freedom logics, 104
Frontal cortex, 176
Frontal polar cortex (FPC), 175
Functional distance, 111

Functional imaging techniques, 171
Functional magnetic resonance imaging (fMRI), 12, 171–172, 174–175

Galloway Cultural Ecosystem, Wigtown and, 204–206
Geographic proximity, 110–111
Global economic networks, 138
Gross Value Added (GVA), 110
Group diversity, 132–133
GROW coaching questions model, 130

Henley Business School, 149
Heritage craft, 214
   in 'the Wild', 213
   case selection and researcher positionality, 215–216
   codes for emerging entrepreneurial practices and indicative quotes, 218
   creative and heritage craft entrepreneurship, 214
   creative industry research, 221–222
   data collection and data analysis, 216
   Elbjorg, 218
   entrepreneurial placemaking unfolds, 219–220
   entrepreneuring, 214–215
   entrepreneurship, 212
   findings and analysis, 216
   implications for enacting, 222
   methodology, 215
   perspectives on, 213
   placemaking, 213–214
   rural entrepreneurship, 213
   Sheila, 216–218
   theoretical framing, 215
Higher Education Institutions, 10, 111
Higher education sector, 156
Hot cognition, 171

Identity, 99–100
In-depth semi-structured interviews, 69
In-depth stakeholder interviews, 144
Inclusion, 147–149
Individual circumstance, 88
Inductive approach, 130
Innovation
   capability interaction theory, 158
   process, 118
Innovative Capability Assessment (ICA), 159
Innovative talent training model in China, 157
Institutional Environmental Assessment (IEA), 159
Institutions, 207
Intellectual Property (IP), 110
Interactions and networks, 42
Internal capabilities, 59, 61
   intent, 59
   reflexivity and learning, 60
   taking action, 59
Interpretative phenomenological analysis (IPA), 69–70
Interpretive approach, 201
Interpretive phenomenological approach, 38
Interviews, 98, 113
Intrapreneurs, 170
Intrapreneurship, 170

Kirkcudbright Artists Town (KAT), 205

Leeds Creative Labs, 113
Local community organizations, 204
Lockdown on creative sector, effects of, 206
Logics, 98–99

Magnetoencephalography (MEG), 171
Make (Workspaces), 188, 190, 193
Management science, 170
Market concentration, 86
Mass entrepreneurship, 157
Mass innovation, 157
Mass media genres, 86

Massachusetts Institute of
    Technology, 112
Measurement model, 159–161
Media box murals, 50, 53
Media box project, 53
Mental models, role of, 68
Micro-enterprises, 40
Micro-entrepreneurs, 184
Microclustering, 111
Microclusters, 110
Microcreative enterprises, 111
Mitigation strategies, 100–101
Moderator effect model, 163
Monetisation, 141
MTN Yello Star Music Reality
    Show, 143
Multicultural community, 188
Multicultural society of South
    Africa, 44
Multistakeholder research approach,
    143
Multivariate linear regression, 161
Murals, 50
Music, 140
    education, 146
    underdevelopment of music
        industry value chain, 147
Mutual support, 186
    models of, 187

National Bureau of Statistics of
    China, 156
National identity, 200
National policies, 2
Navigation, 101–102
Necessary combined capabilities
    application of, 57
    for entrepreneurship, 51
    possibility of capturing value,
        58–59
    possibility of recombining
        resources, 57–58
    possibility of transaction, 58
NESTA Creative Industries
    Policy and Evidence
    Centre, 201

Networking, 103
Networks, interactions and, 42
Neuro–entrepreneurship, 171
    context and theoretical framing,
        171–172
    creativity and neuroscience
        techniques, 173–176
    rationale in organisational
        settings, 172–173
Neuroscience techniques, 171–176
New Art Spaces, 30
New Art Spaces Leigh, 32
New Art Spaces Warrington, 30
New economy, 157
NewBridge Project, The, 31
NewBridge Project's Cariol House,
    The, 29
Nigeria, reflections on, 140–142
Nigerian music industry, 141, 147
Non-entrepreneurs, 172
NonCCI
    collaboration between CCI and,
        67, 71–74
    managers, 66, 68
Nonhuman agents, 213
Norham House (NewBridge Project),
    31–32

Office for National Statistics,
    The, 124
One-on-one approach, 98
Online communities
    accessibility and affordability, 132
    coaching and peer-coaching, 126
    community building and social
        capital, 126–127
    comparison between building
        in-person and, 131
    data analysis, 130
    findings, 130
    group diversity, 132–133
    literature review, 125
    methodology, 128
    online learning and, 127–128
    research philosophy, design, and
        data collection, 129

structured approach to community building, 130–131
women creative entrepreneurs, 125–126
Online learning and online communities, 127–128
Online media, 208
Online peer coaching, 132
Open community, 130
Open Public Experimental Residential Activity (OPERA), 26
Open space, 27–30
Open temporary art space, 28
Openness, 27, 29
Orbitofrontal cortex (OFC), 173
Organisational settings, rationale in, 172–173
Out of the studio and into the street, 53
  city centre vinyls, 56–57
  suburban media boxes, 53–54
  52 window installations, 54–56

Pan-African policy, 139
Paradox literature, 96
Paradox theory, 94
Parallel processing strategy, 102
Peer input (PI), 158
Peer Input Assessment (PIA), 159
Peer-coaching, 126, 132–133
  benefits of, 128
  perspectives, 127
  sessions, 133
  techniques, 124–125
Performance criteria, 84
  competition in selection and reviewing of performance criteria for cultural entrepreneur, 89
  used by cultural entrepreneurs to guide day-to-day business, 87–88
Performance management in CCI, 83
Performance measurement in CCI, 83–84

artistic merit and societal impact, 85
commercial performance, 85
competition and, 86
creative production process, 84
selecting criteria for, 84
Physical spaces, 24
Place, 3
Placemaking, 50, 57, 213–214, 220
Places, 24–26
Play, 117
Policy and Evidence Centre (PEC), 201
Policy context of Africa's creative and cultural industries, 139–140
Policy towards cultural and creative economy, 207–208
Policymakers, 5
Policymakers and encouraging impactful research, 13–16
Policymaking, 6, 16
Population and sampling technique, 158–159
Position emission tomography (PET), 172
Post-COVID-19, 41
Primary data, 88
Private spaces, 28
Proactive approach, 128
Probabilistic sampling, 158
Process-relational lens, 12, 215–216
Process-relational theories, 214
Professional coaching, 126
Propinquity, 111
Proximity, 110, 111
Public art, 50

Qualified Faculty Assessment (QFA), 159
Qualitative empirical data, 188
Qualitative mixed-method approach, 188
Qualitative textual analysis, 188

Real-life entrepreneurial activities, 216
Reconciliation strategies, 101–103
Regional context, 219

Regional Economic Communities (RECs), 139
Remote rural, 221
Research design, 113
 and strategy, 68–69
Resources, possibility of recombining, 57–58
Respondents, 100
Rural, implications for enacting heritage craft entrepreneuring in, 222
Rural development, 212
Rural entrepreneurship, 213
Rural society, 200

Sampling technique, 158–159
Scotland, 198–201, 203, 205
Scotland's National Strategy for Economic Transformation, 198
Scottish Borders, The, 200, 202–204
Scottish creative economy, 201
Scottish Government, The, 198–199, 205
Scottish National Party-led government, 203
Secondary data, 88
Secondary research, 87
Self-discovery state, 120
Self-employed artists, 24, 111
Serial entrepreneurs, 171
Shared identity, 43
Social capital, 42, 126–127, 132, 163–164
Social identity, 200
3Space Manchester, 32
Spaces, 25
Street art, 50, 58
 application of necessary combined capabilities, 57–59
 art entrepreneurship in public realm, 51–52
 art opportunities in public realm during Covid-19, 50–51
 case study, 53–57
 internal capabilities, 59–60
 limitations and future research, 61
 methodology, 52
 necessary combined capabilities for entrepreneurship, 51
Structural equation model (SEM), 159
Structural identity theory, 96
Structured approach to community building, 130–131
Structured interviews, 69
 with CCI experts, 71
Subnational policies, 2
Suburban media boxes, 53–54
Superior cognitive processes, 172
Supply chain management, 15
Supporting infrastructure (SI), 158
Supporting Infrastructure Assessment (SIA), 159
Sustainability, contribution of creative and cultural industries to, 5–9
Sustainability Development Goals, 193
Sustainable Development Goals (SDGs), 5
Synergy state, 119
Systematic approach to triangulation, 74

Temporary Art Spaces, 25–26
 artist spaces, 24–25
 conceptual framework, 27
 limitations of, 26–27
 open and closed space, 27–30
 time in operation, 30–32
The Empty Shop Think Tank (TESTT), 26
Thematic Analysis (TA), 144
Thematic coding, 98
Thematic qualitative analysis, 113
Theoretical sampling, 69
Townscape Heritage Initiative, 204
Transaction, possibility of, 58
Translation, 51
Trial-and-error approach, 191
Triple Helix Model of Innovation, 157

UK entrepreneurial placemaking activities, 220
UK lockdown, 124
UK Sector Vision strategy, 3
Uncertainty, state of, 118–119
Undergraduates, EE and innovation capability among, 158
Unit of analysis, 69
United Kingdom (UK), 2
United Nations, 5
University of Leeds Creative Labs Programme, 112

Values, 184, 190–191
 possibility of capturing value, 58–59
Visual Artist and Craft Maker Awards scheme (VACMA), 203

Welsh government, The, 3
Westminster government, 203
Wigtown and Galloway Cultural Ecosystem, 204–206
Wigtown Book Town (WBT), 205
Wigtown Festival, 207
Women creative entrepreneurs, 125–126
Women entrepreneurs, 126
Workspaces, 188

Young creatives, 149

Zimbabwe, cultural entrepreneurship in, 86–87